Substance Use Disorders in Lesbian, Gay, Bisexual,
and Transgender Clients

FOUNDATIONS OF SOCIAL WORK KNOWLEDGE

Foundations of Social Work Knowledge
Frederic G. Reamer, Series Editor

Social work has a unique history, purpose, perspective, and method. The primary purpose of this series is to articulate these distinct qualities and to define and explore the ideas, concepts, and skills that together constitute social work's intellectual foundations and boundaries and its emerging issues and concerns.

To accomplish this goal, the series will publish a cohesive collection of books that address both the core knowledge of the profession and its newly emerging topics. The core is defined by the evolving consensus, as primarily reflected in the Council of Social Work Education's Curriculum Policy Statement, concerning what courses accredited social work education programs must include in their curricula. The series will be characterized by an emphasis on the widely embraced ecological perspective; attention to issues concerning direct and indirect practice; and emphasis on cultural diversity and multiculturalism, social justice, oppression, populations at risk, and social work values and ethics. The series will have a dual focus on practice traditions and emerging issues and concepts.

David G. Gil, *Confronting Injustice and Oppression: Concepts and Strategies for Social Workers*

George Alan Appleby and Jeane W. Anastas, *Not Just a Passing Phase: Social Work with Gay, Lesbian, and Bisexual People*

Frederic G. Reamer, *Social Work Research and Evaluation Skills*

Pallassana R. Balgopal, *Social Work Practice with Immigrants and Refugees*

Dennis Saleeby, *Human Behavior and Social Environments: A Biopsychosocial Approach*

Frederic G. Reamer, *Tangled Relationships: Managing Boundary Issues in the Human Services*

Roger A. Lohmann and Nancy L. Lohmann, *Social Administration*

David M. Austin, *Human Services Management: Organizational Leadership in Social Work Practice*

Roger A. Lohmann and Nancy L. Lohmann, *Social Administration*

Toba Schwaber Kerson, *Boundary Spanning: An Ecological Reinterpretation of Social Work Practice in Health and Mental Health Systems*

David M. Austin, *Human Services Management: Organizational Leadership in Social Work Practice*

Anthony M. Maluccio, Barbara A. Pike, and Elizabeth M. Tracy, *Social Work Practice with Families and Children*

Joan Shireman, *Critical Issues in Child Welfare*

Robert G. Madden, *Essential Law for Social Workers*

Jerrold R. Brandell, *Psychodynamic Social Work*

Frederic G. Reamer, *Social Work Malpractice and Liability: Strategies for Prevention,* Second Edition

Stuart A. Kirk, *Mental Disorders in the Social Environment*

Sheila H. Akabas and Paul A. Kurzman, *Work and the Workplace*

Frederic G. Reamer, *Social Work Values and Ethics*, Third Edition

Nancy R. Hooyman and Betty J. Kramer, *Living Through Loss: Interventions Across the Life Span*

Thomas P. Holland and Roger A. Ritvo, *Nonprofit Organizations: Principles and Practices*

Substance Use Disorders in Lesbian, Gay, Bisexual, and Transgender Clients

Assessment and Treatment

SANDRA C. ANDERSON

Columbia University Press   *New York*

Columbia University Press
Publishers Since 1893
New York   Chichester, West Sussex
Copyright © 2009 Columbia University Press
All rights reserved

Library of Congress Cataloging-in-Publication Data
Anderson, Sandra Caughran, 1942–
Substance use disorders in lesbian, gay, bisexual, and transgender clients :
assessment and treatment / Sandra C. Anderson.
p.   cm. — (Foundations of social work knowledge series)
Includes bibliographical references and index.
ISBN 978-0-231-14274-8 (cloth) — ISBN 978-0-231-14275-5 (pbk.)
— ISBN 978-0-231-51269-5 (ebook)
1. Sexual minorities—Substance use.   2. Substance abuse—Treatment.
I. Title.   II. Series
HV4999.S49A53 2009
616.860086'6—dc22
2009007999

This book is dedicated to

Nancy, Christopher, Jennifer, Jason, Sophie, and Evan

Contents

Contents

Acknowledgments

A number of people have been instrumental in the writing of this book. A post–tenure review award from Portland State University allowed me to have a graduate research assistant, Gúy Holady, who was of enormous help in locating and reviewing existing literature on substance use disorders in LGBT populations. Relevant clinical case examples were provided by Michele Pearce and Tia Plympton. I am particularly indebted to Tia, who also contributed a valuable critique of the first draft of the book, and to Outside In, the Portland social service agency where she is an HIV-prevention specialist. Outside In provides healthcare, syringe exchange, housing, and mental health and substance abuse services for homeless and low-income youth and young adults. These services are critical to helping Oregon youth, many of whom are LGBT, successfully transition off the streets.

In addition, I am grateful to the other readers of the first draft of this book. Maria Talbott provided excellent suggestions, as did Ann Fields, whose expertise in motivational interviewing was particularly helpful. I thank them both for their thoughtful critical feedback as well as their friendship. My thanks also to Rick Reamer, editor of the Foundations of Social Work Knowledge Series, and Lauren Dockett, editor at Columbia University Press, who have provided support and helpful ideas since the initiation of this project.

It is impossible to adequately thank my partner, Nancy E. Wilder, who mastered relevant databases, searched diligently for obscure articles, and read and word-processed numerous drafts. Her attention to detail and wise counsel throughout the entire process were invaluable to me. Throughout late nights, weekends, and holidays spent writing, her patience and encouragement were unwavering.

My final thanks go to the most important contributors of all—the clients who have trusted me with their stories for the past forty-four years.

Substance Use Disorders in Lesbian, Gay, Bisexual, and Transgender Clients

[1]

Introduction

Goals of the Book

Treatment of substance use disorders in lesbian, gay, bisexual, and trans-gender (LGBT) clients is critically important, yet underexamined, in the professional research and clinical literature. Human service professionals who work with these clients must have access to the latest research on the treatment of substance use disorders as well as current knowledge of the unique challenges of working with LGBT clients. This book aims to bring together the most up-to-date knowledge bases in both of these areas, to provide the reader with state of the art information in treating substance use disorders in LGBT clients. Substance use disorders and sexual orientation and gender identity are defined, and heterosexism, relevant diversity issues, ethical challenges, and assessment and work with LGBT clients are examined. Practice with individuals, couples, families, and small groups, as well as practice at the program level, is discussed. Case materials are derived from the independent practice of the author and from social service agencies that treat LGBT clients with substance use disorders.

Particular attention is given to evidence-based treatment models. To date, there are insufficient numbers of controlled trials demonstrating superior differential outcomes of specific interventions for LGBT clients with

substance use disorders. Given this, it is reasonable to first become familiar with treatment models that have proven effectiveness with substance
use disorders in heterosexual clients and then apply, adapt, and evaluate
these models in respect to LGBT clients. Effective models include motivational enhancement therapy, contingency management, the matrix model,
and community reinforcement. It will be made clear throughout the book
which treatment approaches have been evaluated with LGBT clients, which
have shown some degree of efficacy with these clients, and which remain
to be tested with them. Although this book focuses on *problems,* it should
be recognized that the majority of LGBT individuals are well adjusted and
do not suffer from substance use disorders.

Connection Between LGBT Issues and Substance Use Disorders

People who are LGBT and those with a substance use disorder often share
a history of social oppression and neglect. Although there is no agreement
about the exact incidence and prevalence of substance use disorders in
LGBT individuals, most studies conclude that these disorders are more
prevalent in this population. Gay men report more cigarette smoking than
men in general and are at high risk for abuse of specific substances. A high
percentage of aging LGBT people suffer from alcoholism, and lesbian and
bisexual women report higher incidences of cigarette smoking and heavy
drinking than their heterosexual peers. LGBT youth have higher rates of
cigarette smoking and alcohol and other drug use than their heterosexual
peers. Few studies currently focus on substance use disorders in bisexual
or transgender individuals, but the latter group appear to have a high rate
of substance abuse, including injection drug use. Specific prevalence rates
will be discussed in chapter 2.

The connection between sexual orientation and substance use disorders
is often mediated by internalized homo/bi/transphobia, which can result
in profound feelings of shame, depression, and self-hatred. Substances
can then become part of a person's coping system. Stress resulting from
lack of validation and victimization puts many LGBT individuals at risk for
substance use disorders.

In addition, gay bars and dance clubs continue to be an important part
of life for many, and "club drug" use is popular among many gay and bisexual men. Because of the emphasis on body image and sexual prowess

in gay male socialization, many use alcohol and other drugs to elevate their self-esteem when searching for sexual partners.

Among youth, alcohol abuse is a "gateway" to other drugs, since it can lead the user into social environments where other drugs are abused, and experimentation with alcohol and other drugs is beginning at earlier ages. LGBT youth may develop substance use problems, homelessness, and prostitution. Homeless LGBT adolescents involved in prostitution are at very high risk for substance use disorders, hepatitis C, HIV disease, and suicide.

Consequences of Substance Use Disorders

LGBT individuals experience the general consequences of substance abuse and dependence. Substance use disorders are implicated in premature deaths, health problems, employment disruptions, child abuse and neglect, domestic violence, crime, and prenatal development problems, and as a co-occurring feature of many psychiatric disorders. Causes of alcohol-related deaths include liver and pancreatic disease, cardiovascular disease, and various cancers. Gay men and lesbian and bisexual women, with their high rates of cigarette smoking, are at increased risk for cancers, lung disease, and heart disease. In addition, people who smoke are much more likely to drink, and those who are dependent on tobacco are four times more likely than the general population to be dependent on alcohol (Grant, Hasin, Chou, Stinson, and Dawson 2004). Tobacco and alcohol are particularly dangerous when used together, dramatically increasing the risk for certain cancers (Pelucchi, Gallus, Garavello, Bosetti, and La Vecchia 2006).

HIV disease is also highly prevalent among those with substance use disorders. Anal sex is the main transmission route of the HIV virus in gay and bisexual men and, since substance abuse lowers inhibitions, the risk of unsafe sex (unprotected anal intercourse) increases with use (Cabaj 1997; CDC 2007). Unsafe sex practices also increase when HIV positive gay and bisexual men use alcohol, amyl nitrate, crack cocaine, or "club drugs" (Clatts, Goldsamt, and Yi 2005; Robins, Dew, Kingsley, and Becker 1997).

Sharing drug-injection equipment is another major route of HIV transmission, also putting at risk both LGBT and "straight" individuals who have sex with injection drug users. In addition to HIV disease, the use of shared injection equipment can result in tuberculosis, cardiovascular disease, pneumonia, and hepatitis. Turning to prostitution to support a substance use disorder results in a high incidence of sexually transmitted diseases when unsafe sex occurs (O'Connor, Esherick, and Vieten 2002).

History of Mental Illness Diagnosis of Homosexuality

Prior to the 1950s there was an entrenched view of homosexuality as a pathology, resulting in its inclusion as a sociopathic personality disturbance in the first edition of the *American Psychiatric Association's Diagnostic and Statistical Manual of Mental Disorders* (DSM-I; American Psychiatric Association 1952). During the 1950s research findings began to emerge indicating that homosexuality per se did not constitute a psychiatric disorder. For example, Evelyn Hooker (1957) found no difference between nonclinical samples of heterosexual and homosexual men on projective test responses. The 1968 edition of the DSM reclassified homosexuality as an "other nonpsychotic mental disorder." On July 17, 1969, bar patrons resisted a police raid of the Stonewall Inn in Greenwich Village in New York City, resulting in the beginning of the gay and lesbian liberation movement. A reflection of this movement was the 1973 removal of homosexuality as a diagnostic category from the DSM (DSM-III; American Psychiatric Association 1980). A diagnosis of "ego-dystonic homosexuality" was added, addressing individuals who were distressed about their homosexual orientation, but this diagnosis was dropped from the revision of the third edition (DSM-III-R; American Psychiatric Association 1987). Subsequent studies, which will be reviewed in relation to assessment issues, have attributed differences between heterosexual, homosexual, and bisexual people on a wide range of psychological variables to the effects of stress from stigmatization and victimization. All major American mental health associations have taken the position that homosexuality and bisexuality are not mental disorders.

The diagnosis of gender identity disorder (GID) remains in the current edition of the DSM (DSM-IV-TR; American Psychiatric Association 2000). This disorder has been used to pathologize children and adults whose experience of their gender is opposite to that assigned to them at birth. Bartlett, Vasey, and Bukowski (2000) argue that this diagnostic category in children as currently conceptualized should be removed from the DSM. They note that very few children continue to have GID as adolescents or adults, and that the most likely outcome is homosexuality. In adults, this diagnosis is also controversial, but it is currently the only diagnosis that allows transgender individuals to obtain insurance reimbursement for hormone therapy or surgery. Given this rationale for the diagnosis, it is interesting that few are ever actually reimbursed for hormones or sexual reassignment surgery.

History of Diagnostic Criteria for Substance Use Disorders

When addictive behaviors began to be scientifically studied in the 1930s, people addicted to drugs were described as immoral or criminal, which resulted in judgmental and punitive interventions. Currently drug addiction is defined as "a chronic, relapsing brain disease that is characterized by compulsive drug seeking and use, despite harmful consequences" (National Institute on Drug Abuse 2007:5). The most commonly used diagnostic criteria of substance use disorders, the DSM-IV-TR, uses the term *dependence* instead of *addiction*, and separates substance dependence and substance abuse. The diagnosis of substance dependence disorder requires the presence of a maladaptive pattern of substance use, resulting in distress or clinically significant impairment and involving at least three of an additional seven symptoms (all of which must occur within the same twelve-month period). The diagnosis of substance abuse is made in the absence of physical and psychological habituation. Both substance dependence and substance abuse will be discussed in detail in the chapter addressing assessment issues.

It should be noted that the DSM criteria have been criticized by those who do not adhere to the disease model of addiction for dichotomizing dependence and abuse (when they view addiction as actually occurring along a continuum), not recognizing that many problem drinkers move in and out of dependent drinking, and using substance *abuse* instead of the more accurate *use* and *misuse* of substances (van Wormer and Davis 2003).

Conclusions

LGBT people have high incidence and prevalence rates of substance use disorders. Stress resulting from the internalization of homo/bi/transphobia and victimization significantly increases their risk for these disorders. Drugs can provide relief and escape from stress, eventually leading to an addictive cycle. Dependence and abuse of particular substances may put LGBT individuals at risk for serious health problems, including HIV disease resulting from unsafe sex and the sharing of dirty drug-injection equipment.

Although homosexuality has been removed from the DSM as a diagnostic category, the controversial diagnosis of gender identity disorder remains. Substance dependence is no longer viewed by most as a sin or crime, but as a chronic brain disease characterized by tolerance, withdrawal, and a pattern of compulsive use.

Beginning in 1991, the Council on Social Work Education (CSWE), the accrediting body of social work education programs, required content on sexual orientation in social work programs. The National Association of Social Workers' (NASW) *Code of Ethics* (1996) clearly states that practitioners cannot discriminate against clients or refuse to provide services because of a client's sexual orientation. In spite of this and similar statements in the ethical codes of other professions, clinical education and supervision related to LGBT issues is quite substandard in social work, psychology, and medicine (Hellman 1996; Makadon 2006; Tesar and Rovi 1998). Corliss, Shankle, and Moyer (2007) found that curricula on LGBT issues extending beyond HIV/AIDS are uncommon in most public health school programs. Social work education related to substance use disorders is also very limited or nonexistent, even though social workers encounter substance use disorders in nearly all settings. While the market demand for professionals trained in substance use disorders is increasing, this continues to be a neglected component of MSW education (McNeece 2003).

Currently CSWE has no standard on substance abuse content for MSW programs (McNeece 2003), and substance abuse education is marginal to core courses. In 2001 a NASW survey found that only 38 percent of social workers reported any formal training in substance use disorders. A 2005 study examined substance abuse content in forty of the fifty MSW programs that were top-ranked by *U.S. News and World Report* in 2000. It was found that 60 percent offered just one course, 36 percent offered two or more courses, and two programs did not offer any substance abuse courses (Saarela 2005). Forty-five percent mentioned LGBT populations in their substance abuse courses, and 43 percent contained content on HIV disease. No program *required* a course in substance abuse disorders for MSW students.

Thus, in spite of calls by many experts to increase exposure to content on LGBT issues and substance use disorders, content in these areas continues to be limited. Sexual and gender identity and substance use disorders are interrelated in complex ways. LGBT clients have unique needs, and the professionals who treat those with a substance use disorder need to have solid, empirically based knowledge in both chemical dependency and the specific issues faced by being LGBT.

[2]
Definitions, Prevalence, and Etiology

In this chapter definitions and the prevalence of substance use disorders in the LGBT population are addressed. The etiology of sexual orientation and gender identity as well as the etiology of substance use disorders in the LGBT population is also discussed.

Definitions

The lack of standard definitions is a serious obstacle to understanding the research on substance use disorders, sexual orientation, and gender identity. In some clients it can be difficult to distinguish the boundary between substance abuse and substance dependence. And a person can be labeled lesbian, gay, or bisexual on the basis of attraction, behavior, and/or self-identity. While sexual attraction, behavior, and identity may coincide for some people, they do not for all (Patterson 2000). For example, men who have sex with men (MSM) do not necessarily self-identify as gay. The term *MSM* is frequently used in the literature and will be used here to include all men who have sex with men, whether they identify as gay, bisexual, or heterosexual. In addition, sexual identities can shift over time. Although some people have a consistent lifelong sexual orientation, others do not.

Stein (1998) notes the great variability of patterns of developing sexual orientation, not always following a linear pathway. This variability allows for the fluidity in sexual orientation that is frequently described by women (Baumeister 2000; Bem 1998; Golden 1987).

In the past twenty years there has been a gradual shift away from a dichotomous view of gender and sexual orientation, and bisexuality is now viewed by most as a distinct sexual orientation. *Bisexual* people have some degree of attraction and/or sexual experience with persons of the same sex and the other sex. Some are self-identified as bisexual, some are attracted to and may be considering sexual experiences with men and women (bicurious), and some have sexual experiences with men and women and do not identify as bisexual.

It is important to distinguish *sexual orientation* from *gender identity.* Gender identity is a person's internal sense of being male or female, regardless of his or her genitals. The term *transgender* is an umbrella concept that includes people who believe that the gender they were given at birth, based on their genitals, is at odds with the gender they feel themselves to be. The term may also be used to include all people who are gender variant, such as cross-dressers, drag performers, transsexuals, and those who identify as androgynous (Ellis and Eriksen 2002). Lev (2004) defines *gender variant* people as those who diverge from what is most common, without the assumption that what is normative is necessarily more functional. Transgender, gender variant people may self-identify as asexual, heterosexual, lesbian, gay, or bisexual.

Cross-dressers (formerly called *transvestites*) dress in other-gender clothing but do *not* experience a dissonance between their gender identity and their biologic body and do *not* wish to change their sex or gender. Most cross-dressers are heterosexual men who cross-dress for stress relief or erotic pleasure (Ellis and Eriksen 2002). Biologic women are not called cross-dressers when they wear men's clothes because this is much more culturally acceptable. Cross-dressers differ from *drag performers* (kings and queens), who cross-dress for entertainment or sex-industry purposes (Israel and Tarver 1997; Kirk and Kulkarni 2006).

Transgenderists (more currently referred to as nonoperative transsexuals) live and work in the other gender continuously. They may take hormones and have cosmetic surgery, but do not wish to have sex reassignment surgery (SRS) (Israel and Tarver 1997). Unlike transgenderists, *transsexuals* experience a profound dissonance between their gender identity and their biologic body. They are the most interested in cross-living and receiving hormones and SRS. Preoperative male-to-female (MTF) transsexuals (or transwomen) are born male, but self-identify as female. Preoperative female-to-male (FTM) transsexuals (or transmen) are born female, but self-identify as male. Many postoperative transsexuals do not continue to call themselves *transsexual*, preferring to identify instead as simply a man or a woman. Some transgender activists argue that sex reassignment surgery should be abandoned altogether because it does not challenge the binary gender system that limits all of us to the choice of being either male or female.

Finally, *androgynous* persons may prefer gender neutral pronouns, such as *ze* or *hir*. They may wear gender-neutral clothing, may identify as both male and female, or may prefer to not be identified as either male or female (Israel and Tarver 1997). *Intersex* individuals, born with ambiguous genitals or sexual anatomy or with genitals of both sexes, may also report feeling neither entirely male nor entirely female. Many of these babies are surgically altered at birth, removing the penis when it is determined to be too small for a boy or doing a clitoral reduction when the clitoris is determined to be too big for a girl. This is done to keep intersex individuals within a two-sex gender system and to make parents feel comfortable. The assumption is that a child can be raised successfully in either gender as long as the parents believe in the one assigned by the physicians (Fausto-Sterling 2000). As adults, intersex individuals may identify as transgender and/or have a LGB sexual orientation. Many suffer enormously as a result of being incorrectly assigned to a sex/gender at birth (Chase 2005). The Intersex Society of North America (ISNA) argues that sex reassignment surgery at birth should be stopped and that intersex individuals should have the right to make their own informed decision about surgery (http://www.isna.org). There has been relatively little research on psychiatric or substance use disorders in adult intersex people. For this reason there is as yet no solid knowledge base to guide assessment and intervention with this population.

Prevalence

Lesbian, Gay, Bisexual, and Transgender Populations

The lack of standard definitions complicates efforts to determine the incidence and prevalence of LGBT people in the overall population. It has been estimated that between 1.4 percent and 4.3 percent of women and 2.8 percent and 9.1 percent of men in the United States are lesbian, gay, or bisexual (Laumann, Gagnon, Michael, and Michael 1994). Michaels (1996) reviewed the literature and found that 2.8 percent of males and 1.8 percent of females report a gay, lesbian, or bisexual identity, 9.8 percent of males and 5 percent of females report same-sex sexual behavior since puberty, and 7.7 percent of males and 7.5 percent of females report same-sex sexual desire. More recently, the 2000 U.S. Census found that 1.2 million individuals identified as living with a same-sex partner (Simmons and O'Connell 2003). The 2002 National Survey of Family Growth found that 4.1 percent of the U.S. population aged 18 to 44 years (more than 4.5 million individuals) identified as homosexual or bisexual. Among women in this survey, 1.3 percent self-identified as homosexual and 2.8 percent as bisexual. Among men in this survey, 2.3 percent identified as homosexual and 1.8 percent as bisexual (Mosher, Chandra, and Jones 2005).

Prevalence appears to vary greatly among populations. For example, women and men of color are more likely to identify as bisexual than as gay or lesbian (Chu, Peterman, Doll, Buehler, and Curran 1992; Patheia, Hajat, Schillinger, Blank, Sell, and Mostashari 2006; Ross, Essien, Williams, and Fernandez-Esquer 2003). In fact, most studies likely underestimate the incidence of bisexuality. Hoburg, Konik, Williams, and Crawford (2004) studied 202 undergraduate and graduate students and found that 32 percent of women and 19 percent of men who self-identify as heterosexual also have sexual feelings for persons of the same sex.

Definitions of transgender populations are even more confusing, and prevalence data vary widely among studies. Conway (2002) estimates the prevalence of MTF transsexualism to be 1 in 500, a figure consistent with prevalence in recent studies in other countries. Conway estimates that at least 1 in every 2,500 adult males in the U.S. has had sexual reassignment surgery and become a postop woman. Approximately 800–1,000 MTF operations are performed in the U.S. each year, and another 500–1,000 are performed on U.S. citizens abroad.

Substance Use Disorders in the LGBT Population

There is significant disagreement about the exact incidence and prevalence of substance use disorders in the LGBT population (Anderson 1996).

Relatively few studies focus on lesbians and gay men, and even fewer on bisexual or transgender individuals. Given this, there is still substantial agreement that large numbers of this population suffer from substance use disorders.

Most earlier studies, in the 1970s, reported extremely high rates of substance abuse among lesbians and gay men. These studies, although often still quoted, had serious methodological problems. They tended to use small homogeneous samples, often recruited in gay bars, without appropriate control or comparison groups. Measures of substance use were not standardized and sexual orientation was inconsistently defined. Bisexuals were typically grouped with lesbians or gay men or excluded from data analysis because of their small number. Transgender populations were biased toward those who were receiving hormone or surgical treatment (Hughes and Eliason 2002).

More recent studies report high rates of substance use disorders in lesbians and gay men, but these rates are substantially lower than in the earlier studies. Cochran, Ackerman, Mays, and Ross (2004), analyzing data from the 1996 National Household Survey on Drug Abuse, found a moderate elevation of drug, particularly marijuana, use and dependence in gay and bisexual men and women when compared to heterosexual men and women. It was also determined that lesbians reported higher frequency and amounts of alcohol use and greater alcohol-related morbidity than heterosexual women (Cochran, Keenan, Schober, and Mays 2000). Gruskin and Gordon (2006) and Roberts, Grindle, Patsdaughter, and Demarco (2005) also found that lesbians were significantly more likely than heterosexual women to be heavy drinkers. Drabble and Trocki (2005), analyzing data from the 2000 National Alcohol Survey, found that lesbians and bisexual women had lower rates of abstention from alcohol and other drugs and higher rates of alcohol dependence, alcohol-related problems, and history of substance abuse treatment. Ridner, Frost, and LaJoie (2006) studied college students at a southeastern university and found that lesbian/bisexual women were 4.9 times more likely to smoke, 10.7 times more likely to drink, and 4.9 times more likely to use marijuana than heterosexual women.

As discussed by Hughes and Eliason (2002), bisexual men are included in studies of gay men in much greater numbers than bisexual women are in studies of lesbians. This is because of the importance of *behavior* rather than *identity* in understanding risk factors associated with HIV/AIDS in men who have sex with men. As with early studies of lesbians, early studies of gay men found high rates of substance use disorders. In more recent comparisons of gay/bisexual men with heterosexual men, however, there were few significant differences in alcohol use (Drabble, Midanik, and Trocki 2005). Stall, Paul, Greenwood, Pollack, Bein, Crosby et al. (2001), in a study of urban gay and bisexual men, also found alcohol use rates comparable to men in the general population. Other drug use, however, was much higher than the use of men in a national sample. Meyer, Dietrich, and Schwartz (2008) found that bisexual persons had more substance use disorders than did gay men and lesbians. In some parts of the U.S., methamphetamine and certain "club drugs" have replaced alcohol as the drugs of choice of gay and bisexual men. These drugs will be discussed in depth in a later chapter.

There are little empirical data on the prevalence of substance use disorders in the transgender population. Most existing studies are HIV-related and focus on MTF sex workers. Reback and Lombardi (1999) found methamphetamine and crack cocaine to be most prevalent among this subgroup. Clements, Marx, Guzman, Ikeda, and Katz (1998) studied transgender persons in San Francisco, and found that 34 percent of MTF and 18 percent of FTM reported lifetime intravenous drug use. It is clear that rates of substance use disorders are high in some subpopulations of the transgender community, but these rates may not be generalizable to the entire transgender population.

Although data on smoking in the LGBT population are limited, the majority of studies report higher rates than in the general population. Gruskin, Hart, Gordon, and Ackerson (2001) found that lesbians and bisexual women (25.4 percent) were significantly more likely than heterosexual women (12.6 percent) to be current smokers. Burgard, Cochran, and Mays (2005) and Ridner, Frost, and LaJoie (2006) also found that lesbians and bisexual women were more likely to currently smoke as well as to consume higher levels of alcohol.

Numerous studies have found that gay and bisexual men smoke at higher rates than do men in the general population (Greenwood, Paul, Pollack, Binson, Catania, Chang et al. 2005; Ryan, Wortley, Easton, Pederson, and Greenwood 2001; Stall, Greenwood, Acree, Paul, and Coates 1999). Greenwood et al. found that 31.4 percent of their sample of MSM were current smokers and 27 percent were former smokers. Tang, Greenwood, Cowling, Lloyd, Roeseler, and Bal (2004) found that gay men have a smoking prevalence of

33.2 percent, which is 55.9 percent higher than that of heterosexual men. Younger MSM (ages 18–24) show very high rates of smoking (McKirnan, Tolou-Shams, Turner, Dyslin, and Hope 2006). To date, there are no empirical data on smoking among transgender persons. Because smoking has historically been the cultural norm for many social venues frequented by LGBT individuals, it is possible that in the past they were at a disproportionately high risk for exposure to secondhand smoke and its associated negative health effects (GLMA 2001). More recently, many LGBT bars and dance clubs have become smoke-free, so smoking is no longer the norm in many frequented venues.

Although it is well known that patterns of substance use vary widely among minority groups, few studies of substance use disorders in LGBT populations include adequate numbers of racial/ethnic minority persons to yield significant findings. In the general population, smoking prevalence rates are as follows: 39.7 percent of American Indian or Alaska Natives, 22.7 percent of whites, 21.5 percent of African Americans, 16.4 percent of Latinos, and 11.7 percent of Asian Americans (Doolan and Froelicher 2006). Almost no data exist on smoking among LGBT people of color. One exception is a study by Hughes, Hass, Razzano, Cassidy, and Matthews (2000) suggesting that racial/ethnic minority lesbians may be at greater risk for smoking than their white counterparts.

Etiology

Sexual Orientation and Gender Identity

Although there continues to be great interest in discovering the origin of homosexuality in individuals, heterosexuality is assumed and apparently requires no explanation. That said, it has been known for more than fifty years that sexual orientation floats along a continuum ranging from exclusively heterosexual to exclusively homosexual (Kinsey, Pomeroy, and Martin 1948). Theories of etiology range from the biological and the psychological to the social and the interactional. *Biological* theories assume that there is a genetic predisposition to sexual orientation, and a number of studies reflect this theory. LeVay (1991, 1994), for example, studied autopsied brain tissue and found that one section of the hypothalamus was more than twice as large in the heterosexual men (attracted to women) as in the gay men and heterosexual women (attracted to men). There is evidence that at least one form of male homosexuality is genetically linked to a specific chromosomal region and transmitted through the maternal side of families (Hamer, Hu, Magnuson, Hu, and Pattatuci 1993; Bocklandt, Horvach, Vilain, and Hamer 2006). It has been hypothesized that sexual orientation is laid down in neural circuitry during early fetal development (Rahman 2005).

Studies of twins can be very informative in determining genetic causality because identical twins have identical genes and fraternal twins share only half of their genes. Because of this difference, a condition with a highly genetic basis should be concordant more often in identical than in fraternal twins. Bailey and Pillard (1991) and Bailey and Benishay (1993) found that gay male monozygotic (identical) twin concordance was 52 percent and dizygotic (fraternal) twin concordance was 22 percent. Lesbian monozygotic twin concordance was 48 percent and dizygotic twin concordance was 16 percent. Bailey and Benishay found greatly increased numbers of lesbian or bisexual sisters of a group of lesbians compared to a matched sample of heterosexual women. Thus it can be concluded that heredity appears to be a factor in sexual orientation, but it remains unclear what exactly is inherited. According to Mustanski, Chivers, and Bailey (2002), there is "consistent evidence that genes influence sexual orientation, but molecular research has not yet produced compelling evidence for specific genes" (89).

Psychological theories focus primarily on deficits in development and assume that normal psychosocial development always results in heterosexual adults. Theories based on histories of dysfunctional families with enmeshing mothers and distant fathers have not garnered empirical support. *Social* theories of etiology are undoubtedly relevant, but very difficult to study. An *interactional* perspective could explain how genetic predisposition might be reinforced or extinguished by environmental influences.

The etiological relationship between bisexuality and either heterosexuality or homosexuality has not been determined empirically. Clearly, bisexuality challenges the rigid homosexual/heterosexual dichotomy, which assumes mutually-exclusive categories of sexual orientation (Shuster 1987). In spite of Kinsey's delineation of seven points along a continuum of sexual orientation, the predominance of a dichotomous view has constrained the development of theoretical and research literature on bisexuality.

Finally, although there is great interest in searching for the etiology of gender-variant behavior, an integrated theory has yet to emerge. Many believe that a *biological* base will eventually be found. For example, Hofman,

Gooren, Swaab, and Zhou (1997) found a difference between transsexuals and the general population in the brain mass of the bed nucleus of the *stria terminalis*, which regulates sexual behavior and reproductive functioning. If a biological base is found, it will still be unclear how this vulnerability interacts with the environment. *Psychological* theories have been based, in general, on faulty early parenting, particularly mothering. The mothers of gender-variant boys have been described as overprotective and controlling, and the fathers as ineffective (Stoller 1968). The mothers of female-to-male transsexuals have been described as depressed and withdrawn and the fathers as passive, with the daughter serving as a surrogate husband (Stoller 1972). The family dynamics of many transsexuals, however, do not support Stoller's theory. As is the case in understanding the etiology of sexual orientation, social theories of causation are difficult to study and the interaction between biology and social forces is undoubtedly quite complex. Current research on the etiology of gender-variant behavior is limited because of sample selection, size, and lack of control groups. Much more research is needed before definitive conclusions can be drawn.

Substance Use Disorders

Theories of the etiology of substance use disorders can also be categorized as biological, psychological, and social. These theories will be reviewed first, followed by a discussion of their specific relevance to LGBT individuals.

Substance dependence is a complex multifactorial phenomenon, and *biological* theories are increasingly considered as a way to refine certain kinds of treatment. Multiple sources of evidence point to a genetic basis for alcohol and other drug dependence. A parental history of substance dependence, particularly paternal dependence, substantially increases the risk for developing substance abuse problems in both male and female offspring. Family pedigree studies and twin adoption studies provide significant evidence that genetic factors account for 50 to 60 percent of risk (Hesselbrock and Hesselbrock 2006). All recent twin studies have found significantly higher rates of alcohol or other drug dependence among twins than among siblings and among monozygotic than dizygotic twin pairs (McLellan 2002). Brain data suggest great variation in the ability to manage impulses and weigh future consequences, explaining why some are able to stop drug use with little or no treatment and others struggle desperately to achieve abstinence.

There are brain differences, likely the result of heredity, in addicted individuals in two critical systems: (1) one underlies the motivation for natural rewards, and (2) one decides when the pursuit of a reward would be dangerous in the long term. All psychoactive drugs, including drugs of abuse, act through the brain's system for natural rewards, increasing the level of dopamine in these regions. Chronic cocaine users have a blunted response to reward compared to controls and have defects in the brain's frontal regions that could explain their struggle to manage the pull of rewarding cues (Childress 2006). The prefrontal cortex is the first part of the brain affected by alcohol and other drugs, and excessive use first impacts inhibition and judgment. The longer a person abuses substances, the longer it takes to catch up developmentally. An understanding of the genetic base of substance use disorders could help identify those at risk and tailor treatment to the unique physiology of each client.

Psychological factors, many highly heritable, have also been implicated in the etiology of substance use disorders. Emotionality, distrust, cynicism, impulsivity, a tendency to be easily bored, negative affectivity, and behavioral problems in childhood have all been associated in varying degrees with later substance use problems (Hesselbrock and Hesselbrock 2006).

Personal and *social* factors are critical in determining whether or not a genetic vulnerability is expressed. Environmental influences include, for example, early parenting, family violence, peer influences, school, social support, neighborhood, and traumatic events. Larger social effects include local drug policies (availability and enforcement laws) and cultural and religious variables (Hasin, Hatzenbuehler, and Waxman 2006; Hesselbrock and Hesselbrock 2006). Although these factors are associated with substance use and dependence, causality cannot be determined.

Substance Use Disorders in the LGBT Population

To date, no evidence exists suggesting biological differences that would inordinately predispose LGBT individuals to develop dependence on alcohol or psychoactive drugs. If they are equally predisposed, however, the added oppression and/or unresolved "coming out" issues could produce higher rates of substance abuse or dependency among them. There can be considerable stress connected to having a stigmatized social status and dealing constantly with discrimination. Some LGBT individuals are targets of verbal, physical, and sexual assault, and may have lost friends and partners to the AIDS epidemic. Many have been alienated from family and friends since "coming out," and use substances to cope with loss and depression. For some, substances reduce the anxiety of needing at times to "pass" (to either publicly identify as heterosexual or appear as the gender they do not feel themselves to be); substance use can also help to deal with internalized homo/bi/transphobia. In the LGBT community, drug use norms are more permissive and bars are a primary social resource for many. Each of these factors could play a role in higher rates of substance abuse in this population.

[3]
Heterosexism

The effects of stigma and internalized homo/bi/transphobia and the correlates of heterosexist attitudes in practice are covered in this chapter. Countertransference issues and conversion (reparative) therapy are also discussed.

Effects of Stigma and Internalized Homo/Bi/Transphobia

In addressing this topic, it is useful to begin by differentiating between homophobia and heterosexism. *Homophobia*, coined by Weinberg (1972), is an unsatisfactory term for several reasons. First, it is not a real phobia in the clinical sense, and second, it implies that personal rather than political solutions are needed to eradicate negative attitudes. In essence, as noted by Kitzinger (1996), the term depoliticizes oppression "by suggesting that the oppression of lesbians comes from the personal inadequacy of particular individuals suffering from a diagnosable phobia" (p. 36). Herek (1996) views the phenomenon as a social one, "rooted in cultural ideologies and inter group relations" (p. 102). He also sees homophobia as resulting from heterosexism.

Heterosexism is defined as a belief system in which heterosexuality is seen as superior to and/or more "natural" than homosexuality (Morin 1997). It is an ideological system that denigrates any nonheterosexual form of behavior or relationship (Herek 1996). Both homophobia and heterosexism exist in passive (internal) and active (external) forms, and operate on the individual, institutional, and societal levels (Gruskin 1999). As heterosexuality is seen as normative, so are traditional gender roles. Gender refers to socially constructed characteristics that express femininity (associated with females) and masculinity (associated with males). *Gender expression* refers to how a person outwardly manifests gender. Homophobia reinforces traditional gender roles, and intolerance for gender nonconformity is an integral part of heterosexism. Because of this, those who are nonconforming in behavior or appearance are stigmatized. The term *homophobia* was used more often in the 1970s and 1980s, whereas *heterosexism* has been more widely used in the past fifteen years.

Negative attitudes toward their own sexual orientation and/or gender identity is experienced in varying degrees by almost all LGBT individuals raised in a heterosexist society. Cabaj (2000) describes how this sense of shame becomes unconscious as children disconnect from their true selves and present a false self, utilizing dissociation and denial as their major defenses. This sense of shame becomes a significant factor in the development of the self, which can result in substance abuse, depression, or suicide (Gair 1995). Weber (2008) found that gay males and lesbians reported experiencing more heterosexism than bisexuals, and gay males and bisexuals reported experiencing more internalized homophobia than lesbians. Those who had a substance use disorder were significantly more likely to have experienced heterosexism and internalized homophobia than those who did not have a substance use disorder. Amadio (2006) found that the number of days being very high or drunk over the past year was related to internalized heterosexism in lesbians. Internalized homophobia can be even more painful than external forms of oppression.

There is a relatively robust association between discrimination and indicators of psychiatric morbidity (Mays and Cochran 2001). A number of studies confirm an elevated risk for mood, anxiety, and substance use disorders among LGBT individuals. The greater lifetime risk for major depression and suicide attempts is particularly consistent across surveys (Clements-Nolle, Marx, and Katz 2006; Cochran 2001; Cochran, Sullivan, and Mays 2003; Fitzpatrick, Euton, Jones, and Schmidt 2005; Newfield,

Hart, Dibble, and Kohler 2006; Xavier, Bobbin, Singer, and Budd 2005). LGBT adolescents may experience familial abuse on disclosing their sexual orientation or gender identity, sometimes leading to homelessness and all of the risks of living on the streets. In their study of sexual minority youth 14 to 24 years of age, Walls, Freedenthal, and Wisneski (2008) found that over 45 percent stated that they had been victimized by their family. For many this is a time of excessive risk for suicide attempts (Mays and Cochran 2001). LGBT people with HIV infection are further subjected to discrimination and hostility, and develop complex coping strategies to manage the stigma (Siegel, Lune, and Meyer 1998; Vanable, Carey, Blair, and Littlewood 2006). They are frequently subjected to bias in medical encounters, resulting in the dispensing of substandard care (Bockting, Robinson, and Rosser 1998; Schuster, Collins, Cunningham, Morton, Zierler, Wong et al. 2005). Schuster and colleagues found that 26 percent of HIV-infected adults in their nationally representative probability sample reported discrimination by a health care provider, including 8 percent who had been refused service. Those whose first positive HIV test was longer ago were more likely to report discrimination. Discrimination was attributed to physicians (54 percent), nurses (39 percent), dentists (32 percent), hospital staff (31 percent), and social workers (8 percent).

It is not unusual for LBGT individuals to also be verbally, physically, or sexually abused by peers or coworkers. Males are more likely to be victimized than females, probably a result of lower tolerance of gender nonconforming behavior in males (McDaniel, Purcell, and D'Augelli 2001). There is a stronger link between workplace harassment and alcohol abuse for lesbian and bisexual women than for heterosexual women. Although gay and bisexual men experience significantly more sexual harassment than heterosexual men, they do not report a corresponding increase in alcohol abuse (Nawyn, Richman, Rospenda, and Hughes 2000). Bernhard (2000) found that significantly more lesbians (51 percent) than heterosexual women (33 percent) had experienced nonsexual physical violence, but there was no difference in prevalence between lesbians (54 percent) and heterosexuals (44 percent) in sexual violence. The principal responses to violence were avoidance, talking to someone, and doing nothing—all "passive strategies with limited value for women's physical and mental health" (p. 78).

Heterosexist society is even less supportive of bisexual identity than it is of gay and lesbian identification, and bisexual women are even more discriminated against than bisexual men (Dworkin 2001, 2006). Many lesbians continue to question whether bisexuals actually exist, and even view bisexuality as a personal and political threat, and heterosexual men often view bisexual women as swingers open to sexual threesomes (Israel and Mohr 2004). There are many negative myths about bisexuals, resulting in *biphobia*, which is the fear or dislike of people who do not identify as either heterosexual or gay/lesbian (Hutchins and Kaahumanu 1991). When these negative stereotypes are accepted by those who are bisexual, internalized biphobia comes into existence. It is possible that there is now less biphobia among youth and young adults than among older individuals.

Research on the effects of stigma and gender bias on transgender individuals is fairly limited. It is probable, however, that the effects are even more problematic on them than on LGB people since transgender populations are marginalized by the LGB as well as heterosexual populations (Crosby and Pitts 2007). *Transphobia* is the irrational fear, hatred, or discriminatory treatment of people who transgress the boundaries of the binary sex/gender model established by society (Kirk and Kulkarni 2006). The majority of transgender individuals experience some form of harassment or violence, and lack of education and job opportunities and low self-esteem contribute to their poverty, substance abuse, depression, and high rates of HIV infection (Clements-Nolle, Marx, Guzman, and Katz 2001). Transgender youth are often forced to leave their homes and are subject to extreme discrimination and abuse. They are at very high risk for developing substance use disorders and HIV infection, and both suicide attempts and completed suicides are common (Bockting, Huang, Ding, Robinson, and Rosser 2005; Clements-Nolle, Marx, Guzman, and Katz 2001; Cochran and Cauce 2006; Lombardi and van Servellen 2000; Van Kesteren, Asscheman, Megens, and Gooren 1997).

Heterosexist Attitudes in Practice

Heterosexist bias—reflections of a belief system in which heterosexuality is seen as superior to and/or more "natural" than homosexuality—is common among mental health providers (Anderson and Holliday 2007; Liddle 1999; Mohr, Israel, and Sedlacek 2001) and substance abuse counselors (Eliason 2000). A study of urban and rural treatment counselors by Eliason and Hughes (2004) found that both groups lacked formal education regarding the needs of LGBT clients, and nearly half reported negative or ambivalent attitudes. Many lacked knowledge about relevant legal issues, internalized homophobia, and issues related to family of origin and current family. Cochran, Peavy, and Cauce (2007) found that substance abuse practitioners' negative biases regarding LGBT individuals were stronger for heterosexual counselors and for those with few LGBT friends. Internalized homophobia, when unexamined, can render the counselor unable to effectively deal with this issue in clients' lives. Buloff and Osterman (1995) note that the therapist's *unexamined* heterosexism is potentially more damaging to clients than overt prejudice.

Whatever the sexual orientation of the practitioner, she/he must learn to deal with her/his own homophobia and heterosexist bias. During the 1970s and 80s, a number of articles focused on how heterosexism can impede client change. For example, it was noted that therapists might assume that all presenting problems were created by the client's sexual orientation, with little recognition of the role of societal homophobia, heterosexism, or sexism. They may encourage gay or lesbian clients to move toward heterosexuality or may perceive sexual orientation as a symptom of an underlying psychiatric problem. They may be preoccupied with the causes of homosexuality (Riddle and Sang 1978). Clients' self-denigrating comments about gays or lesbians may go unchallenged. The therapist may collude with the client to "make the best of it," accept certain limitations without question, and treat relationships as if they could never be as valid or healthy as heterosexual ones (Cabaj 1988). Therapists who are uncomfortable with a lesbian couple's closeness may label it as immature and pathological (McCandlish 1982). Therapists needing to establish themselves as liberal may divert attention from clients' treatment needs by assuring them repeatedly of their positive views about homosexuality. Others may point out all of the supposed lost opportunities being gay or lesbian carries, emphasize the positive aspects of clients' heterosexual relationships and the negative aspects of their gay or lesbian relationships, and discourage coming out to family and friends (DeCrescenzo 1984). Finally, Tievsky (1988) noted that the attitude that sexual orientation makes no difference ignores the significance of a rejecting society, and being too accepting may lead to missing important issues and romanticizing a couple's out relationship.

During the 1990s several articles added significantly to the literature on heterosexist bias. Sanders (1993) noted that heterosexist beliefs are reflected in framing same-sex love as a "phase" that the client will "grow out of," assuming that lesbians have no interest (sexual or emotional) in men, and assuming that lesbians are not really sexually interested in one another. McHenry and Johnson (1993) noted that the biases of homophobia and heterosexism are present in all practitioners in varying degrees and, when denied, interfere with empathy and objectivity. Important transference and countertransference issues are ignored, and therapist and client collude with each other to avoid the issues that arouse the most anxiety and pain. "This mutual collusion prevents the knowing and accepting of the real self, and instead fosters the continuation of numerous aspects of self-hate" (p. 143). Therapists may collude with client ambivalence, homophobic statements, and emotional isolation. They may also ignore gay and lesbian co-parents and devalue positive gay and lesbian experiences.

Since 2000 the literature on heterosexist bias has continued to grow, and more attention has been given to biphobia and transphobia. Kasl (2002) has discussed how therapists reveal homophobia while working with lesbians, noting specific dynamics and concerns that need to be addressed with this population. These include basic knowledge of issues lesbians face in their daily lives, internalized oppression, the lack of cultural support for lesbian relationships, homophobia, common sexual difficulties in lesbian relationships, and the coming out process. Eliason (2000) found that substance abuse counselors lacked critical information about lesbian and gay men's experiences and that although many were accepting, a large percentage were ambivalent or negative. Matthews and Selvidge (2005) found that "at best, addiction counselors engage in affirmative behavior with LGB clients only some of the time" (p. 87). While all of these heterosexist attitudes could impede client change, the actual prevalence of heterosexist behavior in therapists is not known.

Therapists may also internalize the myths about bisexuals that are believed by many in the bisexual and general populations. Some of these myths, reviewed by Dworkin (2001), are that bisexuals cannot commit to relationships, are only content when in simultaneous relationships with both genders, and are just avoiding a gay or lesbian identity by identifying as bisexual. As noted by Page (2004), the invalidation of bisexuals can result in inaccurate assessments and unhelpful treatment. Bisexuals may themselves in fact experience dual prejudices, against both homosexuality and bisexuality, resulting in their encountering more stressors than what are experienced by gay and lesbian clients. Jorm, Korten, Rodgers, Jacomb, and Christensen (2002) found that, compared to lesbian, gay, and heterosexual individuals in their study, bisexuals experienced more "current adverse life events, greater childhood adversity, less positive support from family, [and] more negative support from friends" (p. 423).

Finally, there are many examples of *transphobia* in the professional literature. Eliason (2000) found that substance abuse counselors expressed the greatest negativity about transgender clients, and also knew the least about this group. Raj (2002) has reviewed a number of articles reflecting clinical transphobia. Some of the forms include pathologizing gender-variant clients by assuming they are mentally ill, recommending psychoanalytic psychotherapies or conversion therapies contrary to the client's stated needs and goals, and withholding recommendations for desired gender reassignment procedures.

Many service providers do not want to work with transgender clients, and this impacts whether these clients can have access to and stay in treatment. There is evidence of discrimination against transgender men and women in HIV/AIDS programs (Clements, Wilkinson, Kitano, and Marx 1999), and there are reports of general dissatisfaction among transgender clients with the quality of health and social services provided to them (Nemoto, Operario, and Keatley 2005). Because of the high prevalence of unemployment and poverty in the transgender community, commercial sex work often becomes an economic necessity. To cope with continuing discrimination and stress, many then turn to substance use (Bockting, Robinson, and Rosser 1998). For example, transgender clients in residential settings or shelters have experienced verbal and physical abuse by other clients and staff, have been required to wear only those clothes judged appropriate for their biological gender, and have been required to shower and sleep in areas appropriate for their biological gender (Transgender Substance Abuse Treatment Policy Group of the San Francisco Lesbian, Gay, Bisexual, and Transgender Substance Abuse Task Force 1995). For agency strategies for implementing training related to appropriately serving LGBT clients, the reader is referred to CSAT 2001a.

Correlates of Heterosexist Attitudes

Messinger (2006b) has noted that all social workers "have internalized to different degrees the homophobia, heterosexism, biphobia, and transphobia that shape current society" (p. 463). The correlates of negative attitudes and behavior toward lesbians and gay men have remained fairly consistent over time. As summarized by Herek (1996), those with negative attitudes are less likely to have had personal contact with lesbians or gay men and more likely to report being strongly religious and to subscribe to a conservative religious ideology. They are also more likely to support traditional gender roles, to be older and less well educated, to be more authoritarian, and to have resided in rural areas of the midwestern or southern United States. In addition, heterosexual males tend to manifest higher levels of prejudice than do heterosexual females, especially toward gay men. A recent study of U.S. public opinion polls between 1977 and 2003 (Hicks and Lee 2006) showed that public opinion of homosexuals has become more positive over time. Those who believed that sexual orientation was innate were more likely to hold a positive view, as were women, people who were younger, strong supporters of the Democratic party, people who were more educated, people who were less religious, and those who supported gender equality, abortion rights, and providing aid to racial minorities.

A study of undergraduate and graduate social work students (Black, Oles, and Moore 1998) found a significant relationship between homophobia and sexism, with male students more homophobic and sexist than female students. This is supportive of other findings wherein negative attitudes toward lesbians and gay men have been consistently linked to negative attitudes toward women and racial and ethnic minorities, suggesting that the dynamics of prejudice are similar across categories (Kite 1994). In a more recent study of graduate students in psychology, Korfhage (2006) did not find a gender difference, but did find that those who held more traditional gender role attitudes tended to hold more negative attitudes toward lesbians and gay men. There is high congruence between parental and child attitudes toward gay men and lesbians (Kulik 2004), and people tend to be more homophobic when they think homosexuality is a purely voluntary choice (Wills and Crawford 2000). Van Wormer (2004) argues that:

> Of all the forms of oppression, the oppression of gender non-conformity is perhaps the most virulent. Unlike other victims of acts of prejudice and discrimination, sexual minorities are taunted on the basis of behavioral characteristics and inclinations that are thought to be freely chosen. . . . Lesbians suffer a double whammy from homophobia because of its line with sexism.   (pp. 66–67)

Countertransference Issues

In addition to dealing with their own homo/bi/transphobia, therapists must recognize and work through countertransference reactions that could negatively affect their clients. Cohler (1999) discusses his reactions to a gay client who is practicing unsafe sex (anal intercourse without using condoms) in a setting where there is a high possibility of hepatitis C and HIV infection. The concern, anger, and disgust regarding the client's potential for infecting himself and others are further intensified when the therapist has lost a friend or partner to AIDS. These powerful countertransference feelings may lead to a negative view of the therapy and even to premature termination.

Gainor (2000), discussing countertransference issues with transgender clients, notes that these clients can trigger extreme discomfort, and that "therapists may discover in themselves an unexpected gut-level disgust for people who do not conform to traditional expectations of gender expression" (p. 155). Kirk and Kulkarni (2006) ask, "How do we maintain a nonjudgmental posture when dealing, for example, with a transwoman who dresses in the sometimes outrageous 'femme' style that so many biologic women, informed by the feminist movement, see as regressive or abhorrent?" (p. 169).

Lev (2004) discusses how the transgender liberation movement has been met with resistance, even hostility, by the feminist movement. She notes that some feminists see transsexualism as "a perpetuation of the binary system through technological enhancement" (p. 128). Jeffreys (1997) views sex-reassignment surgery as self-mutilation that should be made illegal. She also views cross-dressing and drag behavior as disrespectful of women. It is not known how prevalent these views are today.

For the past twenty-five years, authors have taken the position that LGBT therapists are just as susceptible as straight therapists to countertransference issues and homo/bi/transphobia. McHenry and Johnson (1993) point out that sexual orientation indicates little or nothing about the skill level or self-awareness of the therapist, and some LGB therapists are more homophobic and thus more harmful to LGB clients than heterosexual therapists. Certainly practice with LGBT clients presents a number of challenges to LGB therapists. Mutual blindspots can lead to collusion to avoid shared areas of conflict, impeding the therapeutic process (Schwartz 1989). Internalized homo/biphobia can be either under- or overemphasized by the therapist. The LGB therapist may also attribute all problems to societal and internalized homophobia, losing sight of important family of origin and relational issues.

McCandlish (1982) points out that lesbian therapists are particularly prone to idealizing the relationship of lesbian couples, overinvesting in the treatment outcome, and overidentifying with the couple. Cadwell (1994) also points to overidentification and anger as countertransference issues of particular relevance to lesbian and gay therapists. Overidentification with the clients' issues can lead to the avoidance of certain feelings or content areas for fear of causing discomfort in the client. According to Fickey and Grimm (1998), "this over-identification can trigger the therapist's own anger concerning feelings of victimization and societal marginalization and result in the therapist's impotence as an agent of change for the client" (p. 83). Sarah Pearlman, a lesbian therapist, has written about her "overwhelming inclinations to rush in, to protect, overprotect, and rescue in order to make their feelings (and my own) disappear" (1996:78). Lesbian and gay therapists should be very clear about the guidelines for the appropriate use of self-disclosure (Anderson and Mandell 1989; Gabriel and Monaco 1995).

Cohler (1999) points out that the LG therapist is not necessarily better able to empathize with the situations of LGB clients, and may be even more critical of the client's lifestyle and sexual practices than the straight therapist. Cohler states, "Indeed, the gay therapist's feelings about his own sexuality and sexual identity may be a more significant source of countertransference response than might be experienced by a straight therapist" (p. 168). Therapy with gay men who continue to engage in unsafe sex can stimulate the gay therapist's own self-criticism, making it harder to fully understand the reasons for the behavior.

Gainor (2000), discussing countertransference with transgender clients, notes the importance of therapists' understanding their own bigender and other gender-related biases. She points out that transgender therapists need to be careful not to overidentify with transgender clients. If they do, they will expect the client to have feelings and experiences identical to their own.

More recently, it has been noted that homoerotic countertransference has been mostly ignored in the literature (Sherman 2002). Homoerotic countertransference refers to any sexual feelings between therapist and client of the same gender, regardless of their sexual orientation. Sherman states that gay male therapists who are struggling with their own internalized homophobia "may be more vulnerable to feeling shame and guilt about their own sexuality and erotic countertransferences than heterosexuals are; they may be particularly afraid of being out of control and leading their patients on" (p. 654). Even so, these feelings are more likely to be identified than heterosexual same-sex feelings, which may be so frightening that they are easier to dissociate and deny. Maroda (2000) points out that the erotic countertransference often hinders treatment due to the therapist's discomfort over having sexual feelings toward the client.

In their qualitative study of therapists and clients, Milton, Coyle, and Legg (2005) concluded that some countertransference issues might have a greater effect on lesbian and gay therapists than on heterosexual therapists. For example, lesbian and gay therapists may be in more danger of colluding with unhealthy subculture issues or overidentifying with their lesbian and gay clients. Alessi (2008) notes that unidentified countertransference reactions when working with gay men married to straight women can result in hurried judgments and recommendations that are unhelpful to clients.

Horowitz (2000) notes that there are very few articles addressing how therapists process their countertransference experiences with lesbian and gay clients. Sherman (2002) concludes that professionals need to talk more openly about countertransference feelings with these clients. "Growing up in a heterosexual society, we all have biases about sex and intimacy between two men or two women, as well as about specific sexual activities" (p. 665).

Similar countertransference issues arise when any therapist treats members of groups to which the therapist belongs. Therapists who are in recovery from substance dependence must also be concerned about overidentifying with clients with substance use disorders (Anderson and Wiemer 1992). This can lead to inflexibility, mutual blindspots, and an overinvestment in outcome. There is no evidence that recovering counselors produce any better (or worse) outcomes when compared with counselors not in personal recovery (McLellan, Woody, Luborsky, and Goehl 1988). Level of empathic skill and nonconfrontational style are, however, powerful predictors of therapeutic success (Miller and Baca 1983; Miller, Benefield, and Tonigan 1993).

For a discussion of additional countertransference issues and the attributes of effective therapists, the reader is referred to Kasl 2002. For recommendations on affirmative counselor behaviors with lesbian and gay clients struggling with addiction, see Matthews, Lorah, and Fenton 2005.

Conversion (Reparative) Therapy

In opposition to affirmative behaviors of counselors with LGB clients, conversion (reparative) therapy attempts to change a person's sexual orientation from lesbian, gay, or bisexual to heterosexual. These therapies often occur in a conservative Christian context, and may include prayer, exorcism, or punitive forms of behavior modification (Tozer and McClanahan 1999). According to Murphy (1992), conversion therapy first appeared in the 1800s and has included such techniques as visits to prostitutes, substance use, electroshock, inhalation of toxic substances, induction of convulsions, lobotomies, and castration.

In spite of the fact that homosexuality was removed from the DSM more than thirty-five years ago, conversion therapy is still in use today. The "sexual reorientation therapy" movement consists of hundreds of programs attached to religious organizations that are dedicated to proving that sexual orientation is not an immutable characteristic but a choice. Discussing these "ex-gay" ministries, Sanchez (2007) states, "in the hands of the anti-gay Christian Right, they have become full-fledged propaganda machines depicting gays as sex-addicted, mentally ill, and stunted heterosexuals" (p. 49). LGB individuals are believed to be "sexually broken" as a result of a domineering mother, a distant father, or sexual abuse. It is thought that sexual orientation can be changed by making gay men more masculine and lesbians more feminine. Of course this therapy ignores clear evidence that homosexuality is not an illness and sexual orientation is unlikely to change (Haldeman 1994). Yet many LGB individuals have received harmful treatment because their sexual orientation has been pathologized.

In fact there is no credible empirical support that conversion therapies are successful in changing sexual orientation (American Psychological Association 2008; Haldeman 1994; Tozer and McClanahan 1999). Changing overt sexual behaviors does not equate to changing one's sexual orientation. These therapies can, however, cause harm by reinforcing internalized homophobia and—when they fail—by causing depression, low self-esteem, and sexual dysfunction (Haldeman 2001). According to some anecdotal case reports, they may also increase suicide risk (Stein 1996). According to Scott Harrison (2007), who tried desperately to change his sexual orientation in various "ex-gay" ministries for eight years:

There's psychological damage when change doesn't occur, when sexual orientation remains homosexual. I certainly heard stories and knew people who committed suicide. I've seen what I believe is a higher incidence of risky behavior and alcohol and drug use among a lot of people who go through an ex-gay ministry. A lot of it is because of spiritual conflict that emerges going through that, feeling betrayed by God, feeling betrayed by the church.   (p. 57)

Tozer and McClanahan (1999) discuss the ethical problems facing psychologists who provide conversion therapies. They point out that this practice violates the general principle of competence since there is no empirical evidence to support conversion therapy. In addition, these clinicians are not respecting the client's sexual orientation and, because the practice reflects homophobia and heterosexism, they are being discriminatory and oppressive. Tozer and McClanahan suggest that, if clients request reorientation therapy, clinicians should acknowledge that it does not work and, even if it did, it would raise serious ethical dilemmas for them.

Consistent with this position, reparative therapies are explicitly condemned by NASW, the American Psychological Association, the American Counseling Association, and the American Psychiatric Association. Clinicians are encouraged to develop expertise in gay affirmative practice, which encourages clients to think in new ways about their LGB identity. According to Crisp (2006):

An absence of homophobia is not sufficient to practice affirmatively. Rather, affirmative practice requires that practitioners celebrate and validate the identities of gay men and lesbians and actively work with these clients to confront their internalized homophobia to develop positive identities as gay and lesbian individuals.   (p. 116)

Like the strengths perspective, affirmative practice can be used with any treatment model or modality. For further discussion of gay affirmative practice, the reader is referred to Appleby and Anastas 1998 and Hunter and Hickerson 2003.

[4]
Assessment

In this chapter the relevant risk and protective factors to be assessed in LGBT clients presenting with a substance use issue are addressed. The client's motivational readiness to change and the appropriate level of care are also discussed. The assessment outline in this chapter builds upon the National Institute on Alcohol Abuse and Alcoholism Social Work Education Module on Sexual Orientation and Alcohol Use Disorders (NIAAA 2002). In this document *risk factors* are defined as those variables positively associated with substance abuse and thought to have etiological significance in the development of substance use disorders. *Protective factors* are those variables negatively associated with substance abuse and thought to have significance in the prevention of substance use disorders.

Table 4.1 lists the risk, protective, and other relevant factors to be assessed in the LGBT client presenting with a substance use issue.

Lifestyle Variables

Impact of Societal Heterosexism

Heterosexism is a powerful force in the lives of many LBGT individuals, who are systematically discriminated against by most social institutions.

TABLE 4.1

Assessment

1. LIFESTYLE VARIABLES
   a. Impact of societal heterosexism
   b. Role of bars, bathhouses, and circuit parties
   c. Coming out and identity formation and effect on substance use disorders

2. DEMOGRAPHIC VARIABLES
   a. Age, gender, race/ethnicity, and geography
   b. Social roles and responsibilities
   c. Spirituality/religion

3. PSYCHOSOCIAL FACTORS
   a. Co-occurring mental health disorders
   b. Internalized homo/bi/transphobia
   c. Defense mechanisms

4. INTERPERSONAL FACTORS
   a. Patterns of conducting intimate relationships
   b. Partner violence and substance abuse
   c. Sexual compulsivity

5. FAMILY OF ORIGIN FACTORS
   a. History and patterns of substance use disorders in extended family
   b. Sexual, emotional, and physical abuse
   c. Current relationship with family

6. HEALTH-RELATED FACTORS
   a. Psychiatric/medical history and current condition
   b. HIV-infection status

7. PATTERNS OF ABUSIVE AND DEPENDENT BEHAVIOR
   a. Treatment history
   b. DSM-IV-TR criteria
   c. Screening and assessment instruments

8. ASSESSMENT OF SPECIFIC DRUGS
   a. Central nervous system depressants
   b. Central nervous system stimulants
   c. Narcotics or opiates
   d. Hallucinogens
   e. Club drugs
   f. Other drugs and polydrug use

9. MOTIVATIONAL READINESS TO CHANGE

10. AMERICAN SOCIETY OF ADDICTION MEDICINE LEVELS OF CARE

These individuals may endure rejection by family and friends, victimization in hate crimes, and denial of equal protection under the law. Those who are bisexual or transgender may endure additional antagonism from the gay and lesbian communities. Hostility toward gender-variant behavior is an integral part of heterosexism, and transgender clients report ridicule, abuse, and denial of essential medical care (Lawrence, Shaffer, Snow, Chase, and Headlam 1996). It is critical that the practitioner assess the impact of heterosexism on the client and the client's substance use.

Role of Bars, Bathhouses, and Circuit Parties

Much of what is known about these factors is based on research with gay men. But for many LGBT individuals, the gay or lesbian bar continues to be central to their social life. The most recent research on drinking context made use of a large, national, probability population survey, the 2000 National Alcohol Survey. Trocki, Drabble, and Midanik (2005) found that exclusively heterosexual women spent less time at bars and parties than lesbians and bisexual women, and gay men spent much more time at bars than other groups of men. Bisexual women drank more alcohol at both bars and parties than heterosexual women, but greater bar attendance among lesbians was not associated with heavier drinking. For men, there were no significant differences in consumption in either bars or parties. When controlling for symptoms of alcohol problems, Fergus, Lewis, Darbes, and Butterfield (2005) found that going to gay bars and clubs independently predicted more HIV risk for gay male couples.

Gruskin, Byrne, Kools, and Altschuler (2006) found both positive and negative outcomes from attendance at urban lesbian bars. Many lesbians go to bars to feel safe, find an extended community, and relieve stress. On the negative side, there are sometimes health, legal, and work consequences of bar attendance.

Halkitis and Parsons (2002) studied gay and bisexual men frequenting gay social venues (bars, dance clubs, and bathhouses) and found that their participation was associated with more substance use. The use of alcohol and of inhalant nitrates were the two factors that best predicted unprotected oral and anal sexual behaviors in these venues. A number of studies report that bathhouses are high-risk zones for unsafe sex, multiple partners, and HIV transmission (Binson, Woods, Pollack, Paul, Stall, and Catania

2001; Breban, McGowan, Topaz, Schwartz, Anton, and Blower 2006; Van Beneden, O'Brien, Modesitt, Yusem, Ross, and Fleming 2002).

Circuit parties are large weekend dance events that last for several days and attract primarily upper-middle-class white gay and bisexual men in their thirties. There is a high prevalence of drug use during these weekends, and unprotected anal intercourse is relatively common (Mansergh, Colfax, Marks, Rader, Guzman, and Buchbinder 2001). These drugs, known as "party drugs," result in sexual disinhibition, and risky sex occurs with partners of unknown or opposite HIV serostatus, greatly increasing the risk of HIV transmission (Colfax, Mansergh, Guzman, Vittinghoff, Marks, and Rader 2001). Ross, Mattison, and Franklin (2003) found that gay circuit party patrons attend these events either to be with friends and dance or to have sex and take drugs. Unsafe sex was associated only with the latter reason for attendance.

It is important that the practitioner assess the role of bars, bathhouses, and circuit parties in clients' substance use and risky sexual behavior. It is also important to know the extent and reliability of the clients' support systems. It is possible that, with the growing influence of the Internet and the increase in LGBT organizations, the role of the bar will decrease in the lives of gay and lesbian individuals.

Coming Out, Identity Formation, and Substance Use Disorders

"Coming out" is the process in which LGBT individuals self-identify and disclose to others their sexual orientation or gender identity. A number of models for the coming out process have been proposed, and these will be described and critiqued in the chapter addressing coming out as a therapeutic issue. These processes are not necessarily linear, and can begin anytime between preadolescence and late middle-age. During the assessment, the practitioner attempts to ascertain the client's degree of self-acceptance and location in the coming out process. The process can generate significant confusion, stress, and anxiety, which are then alleviated by substance use and abuse. Sexual identity development may provide a partial explanation for the higher rates of alcohol-related problems experienced by lesbians (Parks and Hughes 2007). It is important to understand the relationship between coming out issues and substance use, both historically and currently. *

* Harry is an eighteen-year-old gay male who receives services from a community agency's needle-exchange and medical programs. When he was fifteen he came out to his parents, who immediately kicked him out of the home and changed the door locks because of his "sinful life." In the past three years, Harry has gone from hospital to hospital, looking for treatment of his "deep stomach pain." Although no organic abnormalities have been found, he has been able to get schedule II drugs from some of his emergency room visits. He has also, on one occasion, been kept in a psychiatry unit for a short time. Harry is convinced that he has one of the "gay diseases," and he continues to search for pain relief. Currently, he moves from IV heroin to alcohol and/or marijuana and then back to heroin. Because he has needle tracks on his arms and permanent vein collapse, he gets little attention from the various emergency departments he continues to frequent. His current heroin use is just enough to avoid withdrawal, and does not include feelings of euphoria.

Demographic Variables

Age, Gender, Race/Ethnicity, and Geography

Data are routinely gathered on a client's age, race/ethnicity, education, employment, and economic status. Age is an excellent predictor of both alcohol and illicit drug use in the general population, where both quantity and frequency of use decrease with age. Comparable data are not available for bisexual and transgender populations, but it appears that rates of drinking in lesbians and gay men decrease less with age compared with those of heterosexual women and men, and that fewer older lesbians are abstainers (Skinner 1994; Valanis, Bowen, Bassford, Whitlock, Charney, and Carter 2000). Given this, older age seems to be less of a protective factor for substance use disorders in lesbians and gay men than in the heterosexual population.

Gender differences are relevant in assessing substance use disorders, as women's drinking is more variable than men's and their drinking and related problems fluctuate more over time (Wilsnack, Wilsnack, and Hiller-Sturmhofel 1994). In spite of this, men are more likely to report current use of illicit drugs, alcohol, and tobacco than females. Males aged twelve or older in 2005 were twice as likely to be classified with substance abuse or dependence as females (Office of Applied Studies 2006). Being female, however, is less protective against substance abuse for lesbians than for heterosexual women. Lesbians are significantly more likely than heterosexual women to be heavy drinkers (Gruskin and Gordon 2006; Roberts, Grindle, Patsdaughter, and De Marco 2005), and lesbian/bisexual college students are more likely to drink, smoke, and use marijuana than heterosexual women students (Ridner, Frost, and LaJoie 2006).

Women of all racial/ethnic groups report fewer substance-related problems than men. In 2006 it was found that 55.8 percent of whites, 41.8 percent of Latinos, and 40 percent of African Americans reported alcohol use. Almost 10 percent of African Americans, 8.5 percent of whites, and 6.9 percent of Latinos reported use of illicit substances (Office of Applied Studies 2006). Over the past decade, rates of self-reported drinking problems have declined among whites, remained unchanged among African Americans, and increased among Latinos. The illicit drug most frequently used by whites is marijuana, followed by cocaine and amphetamines, and the drug most frequently used by African Americans and Latinos is cocaine, followed by marijuana (Holder 2006).

In 2006 it was also found that 37.2 percent of Native Americans reported alcohol use and 13.7 percent reported use of illicit substances. Native Americans begin using substances at a younger age and at higher rates than any other group. Alcohol dependence, often multigenerational, is a very serious problem, and accounts for three-quarters of all Native American hospital admissions for substance use. Finally, it was found that 35.4 percent of Asians and 36.7 percent of Native Hawaiians or Other Pacific Islanders reported alcohol use and 3.6 percent of Asians and 7.5 percent of Other Pacific Islanders reported use of illicit substances (Office of Applied Studies 2006).

There are relatively little data on race/ethnicity in LGBT clients with substance use disorders. Hughes, Wilsnack, Szalacha, Johnson, Bostwick, Seymour et al. (2006), in a large, diverse sample, found that black lesbians were more likely than white and Hispanic/Latina lesbians to report heavy drinking and potential alcohol dependence. Nemoto, Sausa, Operario, and Keatley (2006) found that MTFs of color have alarming rates of substance use and unprotected sex under the influence of alcohol and other drugs.

Men of color who have sex with men are less likely to identify as gay, and bisexual activity appears to be more common among African American and Latino men (Chu, Peterman, Doll, Buehler, and Curran 1992). It has not been shown, however, that black men who engage in same-sex sexual behavior engage in greater rates of substance use (Millett, Peterson, Wolitski, and Stall 2006). In summary, according to Hughes and Eliason (2002), "it appears that patterns of substance use among lesbians and gay men of color may be more like those of white lesbians and gay men than their racial/ethnic heterosexual counterparts" (p. 279).

In regard to geography, it is known that residence in urban areas is associated with being more open about sexual orientation and gender identity. Many rural LGBT people enjoy close relationships and an excellent quality of life, but live within a homophobic social climate with weak LGBT resources (Oswald and Culton 2003). The rate of adult alcohol use is lower in rural areas, but rates of heavy alcohol use among youth twelve to seventeen years of age in rural areas are almost double those in urban areas. Women in rural areas also have higher rates of alcohol use and alcoholism (Office of Applied Studies 2006). Residents of rural communities are more likely to resist seeking help, have concerns about privacy and confidentiality, and be suspicious of substance abuse treatment. Because of these factors and the relative unavailability of treatment, few controlled trials have been conducted with rural populations. It is not known how the Internet has influenced rural LGBT persons. Many of the evidence-supported treatments discussed in later chapters, particularly brief motivational interventions, could be easily incorporated into primary healthcare in rural settings.

In summary, practitioners need to assess carefully the demographic variables of age, gender, race/ethnicity, and geography and their association with presenting symptoms of a substance use disorder.

Social Roles and Responsibilities

Employment and other responsibilities are thought to protect against substance abuse in heterosexual men and women. This may not be operative with LGBT individuals, however, since they do not have federal sanctions for marriage or workplace protection from discrimination and are less likely to bear and raise children. When education is controlled, lesbians earn about the same amount as heterosexual women, but gay men earn about 26 percent less than comparable heterosexual men (Badgett 1998). Substandard salaries and managing self-disclosure in the workplace can lead to financial and psychological stress. Transgender individuals who are transitioning in the workplace may face substantial harassment and even termination (Brown and Rounsley 1996; Transgender Law and Policy Institute 2006). It is important that practitioners assess the client's social roles and responsibilities, the stress associated with them, and the potential connection to substance use as a coping strategy.

Spirituality/Religion

Many religious institutions perpetuate heterosexism toward LGBT individuals, labeling them as sinful or immoral. Religious groups with strong anti-LGBT positions include the Roman Catholic Church, the Southern Baptist Convention, the Church of Jesus Christ of Latter-Day Saints, and Orthodox Judaism. More accepting groups include the United Church of Christ, the Episcopal Church, Quaker Friends Meetings, and Unitarian Universalists. The Universal Fellowship of Metropolitan Community Churches and the Unity Fellowship Church Movement are major LGBT-positive Christian denominations. Religion plays a large role in the lives of many ethnic/racial minority communities, and LGBT members of these communities are most reluctant to disclose their sexual orientation or gender identity (Kennamer, Honnold, Bradford, and Hendricks 2000). For example, the African American community devalues gay and lesbian relationships and nontraditional gender roles (Greene 1994), and conservative Catholic Latino communities highly value heterosexuality and traditional gender roles. For an in-depth examination of sexism and heterosexism in religion, the reader is referred to Morrow 2003.

It has been demonstrated that membership in a conservative religion is related to homophobic attitudes and behaviors (Schope and Eliason 2000). It is understandable that a majority of LGB individuals who have religious belief systems experience conflict between these beliefs and their sexual orientation. Schuck and Liddle (2001) found that nearly two-thirds of their LGB sample experienced shame, depression, and suicidal ideation as a result of this conflict. Their resolution strategies included changing religious affiliations, maintaining their beliefs but no longer attending services, or abandoning organized religion altogether. The practitioner needs to assess the extent of religious trauma experienced by the LGBT client, conflict resolution strategies utilized, and the potential relationship between shame, isolation, and depression and substance use disorders. *

* Betty is a forty-five-year-old attorney who has self-identified as a lesbian since high school. She comes from a large Evangelical family, and describes her parents as violent with each other, abusive, and emotionally neglectful. They did not allow any discussion of feelings and were blatantly sexist and homophobic. She married, as she was expected to do, and stayed in this marriage for twenty years. They were years filled with depression, anxiety attacks, guilt, shame, and increasingly out-of-control drinking. She never felt good enough, gave up all sense of self, and was convinced that she would never be happy. When she fell in love with her best friend, she decided to leave the marriage and address her alcoholism. In therapy she talks about how hard it is to unlearn all those "lessons of evil." She wonders if she will eventually be punished for being who she is and if it is possible to be both lesbian and Christian.

Psychosocial Factors

Co-occurring Mental Health Disorders

Compared to heterosexual persons, LGB individuals have a higher risk of mental health problems (Cochran, Sullivan, and Mays 2003), even though the groups do not differ significantly on general psychological adjustment (Gonsiorek 1991). Cochran et al. found a higher prevalence of depression and panic attacks in gay and bisexual men compared to heterosexual men and a higher prevalence of generalized anxiety disorder in lesbian and bisexual women compared to heterosexual women. Mravcak (2006) concluded that the risks of suicidal ideation, self-harm, and depression in lesbians and bisexual women may be especially high in those who are not open about their sexual orientation, are not in satisfying relationships, or lack social support. Cochran, Mays, Alegria, Ortega, and Takeuchi (2007) found that compared to heterosexuals, Latino and Asian American MSM were more likely to report a suicide attempt, and Latina and Asian American lesbian/bisexual women were more likely to have a history of depressive disorders. As mentioned previously, a number of studies have found higher rates of substance use disorders in LGB clients (Gilman, Cochran, Mays, Hughes, Ostrow, and Kessler 2001).

In the general population the co-occurrence of alcohol abuse and depression is much more common in women than in men, and depression can be both a cause and a consequence of substance abuse (Hesselbrock and Hesselbrock 1997). Although there appears to be an association between alcohol dependence and depression in lesbians (Bostwick, Hughes, and Johnson 2005), it is not possible to determine causality. These associations are usually understood as resulting from stigma and stress attached to heterosexism and internalized homophobia. It is clear that LGB individuals, particularly lesbians, have high rates of mental health service utilization, often with depression as the presenting problem (Razzano, Cook, Hamilton, Hughes, and Matthews 2006; Roberts, Grindel, Patsdaughter, Reardon, and Tarmina 2004b).

The actual incidence of mental health disorders in transgender persons is unknown, but Bockting, Huang, Ding, Robinson, and Rosser (2005) found MTFs to be at higher risk for depression and suicide than gay or bisexual men. Lev (2004) notes that mental health symptoms of gender-variant people can be etiologically related or independent of gender issues. Most transgender individuals do not have difficulties with substance use or suicidality, but in comparison to heterosexual, lesbian, and gay respondents, Mathy (2002) found that significantly more transgender people reported suicide ideation and attempts than any group except lesbians. Attempters and ideators were more likely to report difficulties with both alcohol and other drugs.

Perdue, Hagan, Thiede, and Valleroy (2003) found high rates of depression in injection drug users and MSM. Respondents who were depressed were more likely to report recent syringe sharing, putting them at high risk for HIV transmission. Estimates of co-ocurring psychiatric and substance use disorders among HIV-positive people are not available. It has been found, however, that the prevalence of co-occurring disorders is higher among male and white HIV-positive individuals as compared to females and African Americans (Watkins, Burman, Kung, and Paddock 2001).

It is important for practitioners to screen for a co-occurring disorder in clients presenting with a substance-related disorder as well as in clients who are HIV-positive. In particular, one needs to assess depression and suicide ideation/attempts and their relationship to substance use disorders. It is important to ascertain client and family history of mental health issues and treatment. A full psychiatric evaluation should be done only after withdrawal and its effects have passed. Instruments for determining substance-related and psychiatric diagnoses can be found in chapter 5 of *Substance Abuse: Clinical Issues in Intensive Outpatient Treatment* (CSAT 2006b).*

* Patricia is a forty-two-year-old lesbian who came out after fifteen years of marriage. She describes her parents as physically and emotionally abusive, and viewed herself as a lonely child who never fit in with her peers. As an adult she has had difficulty asking for help and looks for reasons to leave lesbian relationships. Her initial concerns were her depression and heavy drinking. With considerable support, she was able to maintain abstinence for a month, and her depression persisted. At that point she was started on anti-depressant medication, to which she had a very positive response. She has been able to successfully control her drinking for the past three years.

Internalized Homo/Bi/Transphobia

Most LGBT people internalize to some degree the negative messages perpetuated by society, resulting in feelings of shame regarding their sexual orientation or gender identity. Finnegan and McNally (2002) note numerous ways of dealing with internalized homo/bi/transphobia. Individuals may have same-sex experiences while in heterosexual relationships or live unhappily in the "wrong" gender. They may become depressed or highly anxious, turning to alcohol or other drugs to self-soothe and medicate their pain. Cabaj (2000) discusses how alcohol and other drugs aid dissociation from this anxiety and allow the individual to act on long-denied or suppressed feelings. Although substances may temporarily relieve feelings of shame and worthlessness, these negative feelings are again reinforced during the drug withdrawal period. Cabaj points out that the internal states accompanying internalized homophobia and substance abuse are very similar:

The following traits can be seen in both: denial; fear, anxiety, and paranoia; anger and rage; guilt; self-pity; depression, with helplessness, hopelessness, and powerlessness; self-deception and development of a false self; passivity and the feeling of being a victim; inferiority and low self-esteem; self-loathing; isolation, alienation, and feeling alone, misunderstood, or unique; and fragmentation and confusion. These close similarities make it very difficult for gay men or lesbians who cannot accept their sexual orientation to recognize or successfully treat their substance abuse.   (pp. 12–13)

The practitioner needs to carefully assess the degree and impact of the client's internalized homo/bi/transphobia. It is important to understand how it has been internalized and whether substances are used to cope with related depression and anxiety. †

It is also important to remember that *not* coming out does not necessarily signify internalized homo/bi/transphobia (Anderson 2001). In some cultures and under certain circumstances, not coming out is the most rational decision (Smith 1997). Anderson and Holliday (2004), in a study of "passing" as heterosexual among lesbians, found that an overwhelming majority chose to pass in situations involving their jobs or careers. Some also chose to pass in confrontational situations with authority (police, judges, physicians), for their families, and for safety purposes. Most felt that passing was perfectly understandable in certain circumstances, and not necessarily a reflection of internalized homophobia.

---

† Deeann is a sixty-five-year-old graphic designer who has "always" known she is a lesbian. In her family of origin, women were unable to take care of themselves emotionally, and were devalued and dominated by strong men. She describes her father as arrogant, abusive, and sexist. Deeann felt invisible in her family, had few friends, and is aware of her internalized homophobia. She has felt shame and self-hatred about being lesbian since elementary school. Her mother completely rejected her when she came out in her twenties, and while she longs for acceptance, she feels unlovable and judged by everyone she meets. She views her attraction to straight women as a reflection of her internalized homophobia. Deeann has been a very heavy drinker for more than forty years, and is beginning to evidence serious physical problems as a result.

Defense Mechanisms

In discussing the development of major defense mechanisms, Cabaj (2000) points out that pre–lesbian/gay/bisexual children may deal with feeling different by disconnecting from their true selves and presenting a false self to the world. In this way they attempt to adapt to their parents' expectations and cope with criticism and rejection. And it follows that denial and dissociation may become their major defense mechanisms as adults. Finnegan and McNally (2002) discuss the practitioner's need to discriminate among the varying reasons LGBT substance abusers use different defenses at different times. For example, are they utilizing denial to protect their substance abuse or their sexual orientation/gender identity? Or to protect themselves against the effects of both? If defenses are highly developed before the onset of substance abuse, they become even stronger, often complicating treatment and recovery. Other defenses used by LGB substance abusers include reaction formation, rationalization, and hostility. It is critical that practitioners assess and understand the major defense mechanisms utilized by LGBT clients, so that the defense structure can be appropriately managed in treatment.

Interpersonal Factors

Patterns of Conducting Intimate Relationships

It is important to assess sexual risk, the client's history of intimate relationships, and the role of substances in these relationships. Blank (2006) points out that sexual risk assessments are often inadequate, and notes that clinicians should never make the following assumptions:

- "Sex" means only anal or vaginal intercourse.
- Oral sex is "safe."
- Well-dressed patients have no drug or domestic violence problems.
- Married people are monogamous.
- Pregnant women have only one sex partner, or the same partner throughout a pregnancy.
- Persons who self-identify as heterosexual have no same-sex partners.

- Persons identifying as gay or lesbian have no opposite sex partners.
- Older people don't have sex. (p. 76)

Presence at gay social venues (bars, dance clubs, and bathhouses), poly-drug use, and HIV status are associated with risky sexual behaviors (Hal-kitis and Parsons 2002). And it is unclear whether engaging in sexual risk behaviors with casual partners is related to being in a regular partnership (Elford, Bolding, Maguire, and Sherr 1999; Kuyper, Lampinen, Chan, Mill-er, Schilder, and Hogg 2005). It was found by Appleby, Miller, and Roths-pan (1999) that risky sex may symbolize trust and commitment between primary partners, while safer sex can be viewed as a sign of infidelity. There is also some evidence that HIV-positive men engage in unprotected sex to affirm their own health (Halkitis 2004).*

Common stereotypes of bisexual men and women are that they are pro-miscuous, unable to commit, and must have simultaneous relationships with men and women to be satisfied. In fact, many bisexual individuals are in committed intimate relationships that are often, but not always, mo-nogamous (McLean 2004).

Patterns of conducting intimate relationships can be even more complex with transgender clients. Transgender adolescents often drop out of school, leave home, and end up on the streets using alcohol and other drugs. Trans-phobia and employment discrimination frequently lead to their turning to prostitution to earn a living. MTF sex workers tend to attract customers who prefer a mix of sexual characteristics or need to deny having sex with a biological male (Oggins and Eichenbaum 2002). Safer-sex intentions

---

* Jerry and Thomas are twenty-one-year-old gay injection drug users seeking services at a community needle-exchange program. Thomas was HIV-nega-tive when tested a year ago, and Jerry has not been tested. Both men engage in survival sex for cash or drugs. This is often oral sex, the most frequently requested sex act, which both men view as safe. In their first counseling ses-sion, Jerry stated that he was feeling pressured by Thomas to have anal sex without condoms. Thomas argued that he is HIV-negative and "condoms point out you are dirty."

with these customers are often undermined by financial needs, and drugs are used to cope with the stresses of relationships, sex work, and poverty (Nemoto, Operario, Keatley, and Villegas 2004). Because of drug use and unprotected anal intercourse, MTF transgenders are highly vulnerable to HIV infection. Many use intravenous drugs, share syringes, have multiple sexual partners, use condoms inconsistently, exchange sex for drugs, and have steady partners who use drugs and are HIV positive (Nemoto, Luke, Mamo, Ching, and Patria 1999).

Although MTF transgenders of color are at highest risk for HIV infection, they have been marginalized by many treatment programs (Clements-Nolle, Marx, Guzman, and Katz 2001). These individuals engage in unprotected sex with primary partners because they love and trust them and need affirmation of their gender identity. Primary partners, however, are frequently abusive, unfaithful, substance abusers who share needles and transmit HIV infection to their trusting trans partners (Nemoto, Operario, Keatley, and Villegas 2004).

In summary, practitioners need to understand the meaning attached to the client's risky sexual behaviors, the characteristics of their steady partners, and their contracts around monogamy. They then need to assess the relationship between these factors and the use and abuse of substances.

Partner Violence and Substance Abuse

There have been relatively few studies acknowledging that LGBT individuals are at risk of violence at the hands of their partners. There continues to be a perception that intimate partner violence is a solely heterosexual phenomenon, even though it is quite prevalent in LGBT relationships. It is estimated that lesbians experience a 41–68 percent lifetime prevalence of intimate partner violence (National Coalition of Anti-Violence Programs 2007). Nieves-Rosa, Carballo-Diéguez, and Dolezal (2000) found that 33–50 percent of the MSM in their study had been victims of psychological violence by their partners, and 25 percent had participated in unprotected anal sex under some type of coercion. Toro-Alfonso and Rodriguez-Madera (2004) studied domestic violence in well-educated Puerto Rican gay men, and found a high level of emotional violence (48 percent) in their relationships. Participants also reported high levels of violence in their families of origin. A recent study of MSM in the Chicago area (Houston and McKirnan 2007) found that 21 percent reported verbal abuse, 19 percent physical violence, and 19 percent unwanted sexual activity. Depression and substance abuse were among the strongest correlates of intimate partner abuse. Most of this violence is unreported, but even when it is reported, LGBT individuals are not afforded the same legal protections as their heterosexual counterparts.

In summary, it is clear that intimate-partner violence is a significant problem in lesbian and gay relationships. Fortunata and Kohn (2003) found that lesbians who batter their partners were more likely than nonbatterers to report childhood physical and sexual abuse and substance use disorders. Less is currently known about the prevalence or correlates of violence in bisexual and transgender relationships. Practitioners need to ask openly about the existence of domestic violence and, because of the associations between violence and substance abuse, be aware of this possibility when conducting an assessment (Schilit, Lie, and Montagne 1990).*

* Jen is a thirty-year-old woman who identifies as lesbian. She says that she drinks alcohol and uses oxycontin to escape her feelings. She reports that she loves her partner, but they are always fighting. Jen says sometimes when they are drunk they hit each other and throw things. Jen says she is concerned because recently there have been times when she did not take her six-year-old daughter to school because she was too hung over.

It is important to assess the substance use of partners even in the absence of violence. Women's drinking patterns tend to parallel those of significant others (Wilsnack 1996), so it is possible that lesbians, with higher rates of alcoholism than women in the general population, may have a partner who abuses alcohol (Hughes and Eliason 2002). Both partners and peers influence gay men's drinking (Weinberg 1994), and partners and peers may also influence the substance use of lesbian, bisexual, and transgender clients.

Sexual Compulsivity

Studies in the last fifteen years have consistently documented an association between sexual compulsivity and unsafe sexual practices in HIV-negative

MSM and HIV-positive gay and bisexual men and women. Sexual compulsivity is also associated with greater frequency of unprotected anal and oral sex and a larger number of HIV-negative partners (Semple, Zians, Grant, and Patterson 2006b). There are, in addition, significant positive relationships between sexual compulsivity, problem drinking, and use of other substances (Benotsch, Kalichman, and Kelly 1999). A substantial body of research links methamphetamine (meth) use and high-risk sex among gay and bisexual men (Koblin, Murrill, Comacho, Xu, Liu, Raj-Singh et al. 2007). Clearly, if the meth user is HIV-positive and sexually compulsive, the risk of HIV transmission is greatly increased (Reece 2003). In support of earlier studies, Semple et al. (2006b) found sexual compulsivity in HIV-positive meth-using gay and bisexual men to be positively associated with high-risk sexual behaviors, more HIV-negative or unknown serostatus partners, meth use before or during sex, lower levels of self-esteem, and visits to sex clubs and street corners to find sex partners. Parsons and Halkitis (2002) compared HIV-positive MSM who frequented bathhouses and sex clubs to those who cruised outdoor areas, and found that the former were more likely to use stimulant drugs and perceive less responsibility for protecting their sexual partners from HIV infection.

In addition to pursuing sexual partners in commercial or public areas, many LGBT individuals engage in online sexual activities. Access to the Internet allows for information, support, and making connections with others. There are numerous Web sites dedicated to all kinds of sexuality, with thousands of visitors each month. These resources are particularly important for transgender individuals, who often feel isolated and alone. The Internet is also used to arrange meetings for offline sexual encounters, and frequent chat room visitors are more likely to engage in unprotected anal intercourse with casual partners (Tikkanen and Ross 2000). Mettey, Crosby, DiClemente, and Holtgrave (2003) found that men using the Internet to meet sex partners were more likely to report fisting, group sex, and using poppers and ecstasy during sex. Benotsch, Kalichman, and Cage (2002) found that these men reported substantially higher rates of unprotected sex and use of methamphetamine and Viagra.

The Internet has become the most common meeting place for MSM diagnosed with sexually transmitted infections (Rietmeijer, Bull, Sheana, McFarlane, Patnick, and Douglas 2003), and the Internet was associated with a syphilis epidemic in San Francisco in 2002 (Morbidity and Mortality Weekly Report 2003). There are limited empirical data on the use of the Internet by lesbian, bisexual, and transgender individuals, and the link between the Internet, sex, and substance use disorders is not fully understood at present.

Guss (2000) discusses the assessment and treatment implications of the link between sex and substance use disorders in gay men. He notes that stimulant drugs, particularly cocaine and methamphetamine ("crystal"), are very appealing to men in a highly sexualized gay subculture. When they are high, they feel sexier and more attractive and self-confident. They believe that other men are more attracted to them, and when sex is combined with their drug use, their preexisting sexual anxieties and fears of rejection are further diminished. According to Guss:

> Users frequently report that crack and "crystal" facilitate participation in uninhibited, "over the top" sex, sometimes including sadomasochism, the use of dildoes or fistfucking in ways that seem wholly inaccessible without drugs. Some are able to enjoy anal sex only when using these stimulant drugs. Orgasm may be delayed, or even impossible to achieve. While these drugs may cause impotence ("crystal dick"), sildenafil (Viagra) is sometimes utilized to facilitate maintenance of an erection.   (p. 109)

In sum, it is important to explore sexual compulsivity and other compulsive behaviors in LGBT clients and understand their relationship to unsafe sexual practices and substance use disorders. An understanding of the individual's HIV status and his or her thinking about disclosure of that status to sexual partners is also critical.

Family of Origin Factors

History and Patterns of Substance Use Disorders

Assessment of the family of origin includes the client's relationship with parents, stepparents, siblings, grandparents, aunts, uncles, and cousins. An understanding of family dynamics, adaptive patterns, strengths, and major themes in the family is facilitated by the use of a genogram (Weinstein 1992). The genogram allows the practitioner to organize a large amount of complex data in such a way that major themes and patterns are immediately visible. The data collected on the genogram include multigenerational naming patterns, dates of entry and exit from the family, sibling positions, places of birth and residence, occupations, health and illness patterns, major losses, cutoffs, and family themes. For more information on the construction of the multigenerational family genogram, the reader is referred to McGoldrick, Gerson, and Shellenberger 1999.

It is also important to understand the client's role in the family and any history of parental or extended family substance abuse. Of great significance is the client's experience of growing up LGBT in the family of origin. Early experiences of dissociating and/or adapting to parental expectations should be noted, as well as experiences of discrimination, rejection, and abuse by family or peers. There is also interest in the experience of coming out to the family and their reactions to this disclosure. Parents often experience denial, grief, and shame as they confront their own homo/bi/transphobia, but families vary greatly in their emotional responses. The best predictor of the family's response is the quality of the parent-child relationship prior to the disclosure (Patterson 2000), so it is important to inquire about how things changed in the family after the disclosure. *

* Nick is a twenty-one-year-old gay male whose family, from Puerto Rico, kicked him out of his home two years ago upon learning he is gay. He is not allowed to have contact with any family members. On the street with other young gay males, he became quite dependent on alcohol and was arrested for fighting and public nuisance. Mandated to substance abuse treatment, he became very involved in a number of LGBT programs and groups. He developed friendships that did not revolve around substances, and although he continued to enjoy the gay male party scene, he attained better control over his use of alcohol.

The adjustment process for families of transgender children is often more difficult, and can result in painful rejection and abuse. This is probably why many transgender people wait until they are well into transition to come out to their families. Lev (2004) notes that, in families with a long history of addictions and abuse, the client rarely expects support. Quite often, however, the family is aware of the gender issues but has coped through denial, and their reactions can range from hostile to accepting.

In summary, assessment of the client's family of origin includes the quality of the client's relationship with parents, the experience of coming out in the family, and the adaptive patterns of the family. It also addresses the major multigenerational themes of the family, strengths, and history of substance use disorders.

Sexual, Emotional, and Physical Abuse

It is important to ascertain from all clients whether they have ever been emotionally, physically, or sexually abused. Pilkington and D'Augelli (1995) found that 33 percent of the LGBT youth in their study had been verbally abused and 10 percent physically assaulted by a family member. In a large national sample, Balsam, Beauchaine, and Rothblum (2005) found that lesbians, gay men, and bisexual men and women reported higher levels of emotional, physical, and sexual violence in both childhood and adulthood than their heterosexual counterparts. These findings are supportive of earlier ones by Hughes, Hass, Razzano, Cassidy, and Matthews (2000) and Hughes, Johnson, and Wilsnack (2001). Balsam et al. (2005) also found that LGB siblings are at greater risk for victimization than their heterosexual siblings and that bisexuals, particularly men, are at very high risk. Little is known about the prevalence of childhood abuse in transgender individuals. There is also relatively little research on racial/ethnic differences in childhood abuse in LGBT individuals. It has been found that lesbians of color have higher rates of lifetime victimization than European American lesbians (Morris and Balsam 2003) and significantly more Latino MSM report childhood sexual abuse than non-Latino MSM (Arreola, Neilands, Pollack, Paul, and Catania 2005).

MSM with high rates of childhood sexual abuse (involving penetrative sex and physical force) are more likely than never-coerced MSM to engage in high-risk sex (Paul, Catania, Pollack, and Stall 2001). These researchers hypothesize that victimized individuals may use substances during sex as a coping tool to manage unresolved feelings from these early experiences. In a sample of gay and bisexual men, Brennan, Hellerstedt, Ross, and Welles (2007) found that more than one in seven (15.5 percent) reported a history of childhood sexual abuse. Those who had been abused regularly were more likely to be HIV-positive, to have exchanged sex for payment, and to be a current user of sex-related drugs. These men are also more likely to experience nonsexual relationship violence (Kalichman, Gore-Felton, Benotsch, Cage, and Rompa 2004).

A number of studies support the association between childhood sexual abuse and alcohol abuse among women, and recent studies confirm the association among lesbians (Descamps, Rothblum, Bradford, and Ryan 2000; Hughes, Johnson, and Wilsnack 2001; Roberts, Grindel, Patsdaughter, DeMarco, and Tarmina 2004a). Hughes, Johnson, Wilsnack, and Szalacha (2007) found that childhood sexual abuse directly predicted lifetime alcohol abuse in adult lesbians. In their study of lesbian and bisexual women, Rankow, Cambre, and Cooper (1998) found that women with a history of childhood sexual abuse were twice as likely to report heavy drinking and three times as likely to report injection drug use as those without abuse histories. It also appears that there is an association between childhood sexual abuse and substance abuse in gay men and MSM (Bartholow, Doll, Joy, Douglas, Bolan, Harrison et al. 1994). It is not known if this association exists for transgender individuals.

In summary, the practitioner needs to do a thorough assessment of the client's victimization history and its association with high-risk sexual behaviors and substance use disorders. As pointed out by Hughes and Eliason (2002), these links are not always clear, since substance abuse could be directly related to childhood abuse or a coping mechanism to deal with depression or other consequences of childhood abuse.

Current Relationship with Family

The practitioner will need to inquire about the client's current relationship with the family of origin and assess with the client the appropriateness of involving the family in treatment. Families can be extremely supportive or overly hostile to involvement in their child's sexual orientation/gender identity and substance use disorder. In a study comparing family support of transgender persons, MSM, and bisexual women, transgender persons had the lowest levels of family and social supports (Bockting, Huang, Ding, Robinson, and Rosser 2005). They were also the most likely to be depressed and at risk for suicide.

Much depends upon the developmental stage of the family's own coming out process. Families, just as LGBT individuals, go through a process of dealing with their children's disclosure of sexual orientation/gender identity issues. For example, Crosbie-Burnett and colleagues (1996) identified three stages of adjustment for heterosexual families of origin: (a) performing incremental disclosure to others, (b) adjusting to the new role of parent or sibling of a gay or lesbian child, and (c) coming out as family members. Lev (2004) has conceptualized these family stages in regard to gender variance as discovery and disclosure, turmoil, negotiation, and finding balance. Ellis and Eriksen (2002) state that families' successful adaptation to transgender experiences progress through six stages. In addition to considering the family's developmental stage, the practitioner needs to understand the family's involvement in and view of the client's substance use disorder. Often, the difficulty of coming out to parents is compounded by revealing substance abuse, resulting in profound feelings of failure in the parents.

Families can receive information and enormous support from attending local meetings of Parents, Families, and Friends of Lesbians and Gays (PFLAG). This national nonprofit organization aims to promote the health and well-being of LGBT people and their families and friends. Their literature addresses most of the questions families ask when they first learn that their child is LGBT (www.pflag.org).

Families of choice—friends who are selected and counted as relatives— often play the most important ongoing supportive role in the lives of LGBT clients, and it is very important to understand the dynamics of these families and validate their importance. It must also be recognized that the grief of giving up drugs is often accompanied by that of losing significant others to the AIDS epidemic.

In sum, the practitioner needs to assess the client's current relationships with families of origin and choice. This will include the developmental stage of both regarding the client's sexual orientation/gender identity as well as their connections to the client's substance use and abuse.

Health-Related Factors

Psychiatric/Medical History and Current Condition

The practitioner will need to obtain a clear psychiatric and medical history and assess the client's current medical condition. The psychiatric history includes occurrence and treatment for ADHD, mood and anxiety disorders, suicidal thoughts and behavior, posttraumatic stress disorder (PTSD), eating disorders, conduct disorders, and substance use disorders. As discussed previously, LGBT clients frequently report depression and anxiety related to stress from discrimination and coming out issues (Hershberger and D'Augelli 2000). They also report higher rates of suicide symptoms than do heterosexuals (Cochran and Mays 2000), and lesbians and gay men report more frequent use of mental health services than do heterosexuals (Cochran, Sullivan, and Mays 2003).

In addition to a verbal psychiatric history, laboratory work can confirm certain medical and substance use disorders. When available, a physical examination and lab work would include the following: blood pressure and heart and respiratory rate, electrolytes, liver function tests, complete blood count, urine toxicology, breathalyzer, and blood toxicology.

Ryan (1994) has summarized the health concerns of lesbian, gay, and bisexual clients, and these should be explored when assessing LGBT clients. In youth and young adults, these include hepatitis, HIV, STDs, pregnancy, and eating disorders. In middle-aged adults, health concerns include anal cancer, cardiovascular disease, chronic liver disease, lung cancer, hepatitis, HIV, STDs, breast cancer, and gynecological cancers. In adults over age sixty, additional concerns include cerebrovascular disease and neurocogitive impairment. *

LGBT youth who are sexually active are at risk for a range of STDs, including HIV, herpes, and hepatitis. Hepatitis A and B are transmitted sexually and hepatitis C is transmitted primarily through contact with blood. Adult lesbian and bisexual women, compared with heterosexual women, more often use alcohol and cigarettes, consume fewer fruits and vegetables daily, and are more likely to be overweight (Valanis, Bowen, Bassford, Whitlock, Charney, and Carter 2000). In addition, lesbians are less likely to have ever used contraceptives and to have ever been pregnant or given birth to a live infant, all protective against ovarian cancer (Rosenberg 2001).

In assessing the client's psychiatric and medical history, it is equally important to explore and appreciate his or her strengths and resilience. Resilience is the capacity of a person to use challenges for psychological growth and to function at a level far higher than would be predicted from earlier developmental experiences (Baldwin, Baldwin, Kasser, Zax, Sameroff, and Seifer 1993). There has been little interest in exploring resilience in the LGBT populations, although it is logical that they may develop significant strengths through their struggles with oppression. Anderson and Sussex (1999) found that the resilient lesbians in their study dealt with prejudice and discrimination by placing them in a broader political

* Yvonne is a twenty-one-year-old pregnant lesbian who has been addicted to heroin for four years. Heroin use during pregnancy and its combination with lack of prenatal care are associated with low birth weight, a major risk factor for later developmental delay. For the pregnant heroin abuser, methadone maintenance, prenatal care, and a comprehensive drug treatment program can significantly improve outcomes. There is also preliminary evidence that buprenorphine is safe and effective in treating heroin dependence during pregnancy, although infants exposed to methadone or buprenorphine during pregnancy typically require treatment for withdrawal symptoms. For women who do not want or are not able to receive pharmacotherapy for heroin addiction, detoxification during pregnancy can be accomplished with relative safety (NIDA 2008b). In Yvonne's case, her nutrition is poor and she is not receiving prenatal care. She wants the baby, but still wants heroin in her life, and does not want to go through withdrawal during pregnancy. Her goal is to reduce or cease use, and then renew her habit at a lower dose. Yvonne's girlfriend, who is attempting to reduce her own heroin use, has continued to come to the syringe-exchange program to secure clean needles for both of them. She has not disclosed how Yvonne is faring with the pregnancy or addiction, and the agency staff is waiting for "word on the street" about the outcome.

context, not taking them personally, and engaging in social activism. The practitioner needs to fully assess clients' strengths and how they will be of assistance in achieving the therapeutic goals.

HIV-Infection Status

High-risk sexual behaviors are linked to the use of meth and recreational club drugs, increasing the susceptibility to acquiring HIV infection. The symptoms of HIV disease/AIDS range in severity, and early signs of HIV infection are not visible. Later symptoms include Kaposi's sarcoma (skin lesions), herpes, and wasting syndrome involving significant weight loss. Because HIV compromises the immune system, many individuals develop a variety of opportunistic infections that lead to other disorders. In addition to the symptoms of HIV/AIDS, intravenous-drug users may continue to have physical symptoms of drug craving. If they have shared dirty needles, they may have also developed additional systemic infections. It is not hard to understand why those with HIV/AIDS have increased rates of suicidal ideation, attempts, and completed suicide (Komti, Judd, Grech, Mijich, Hoy, Lloyd, and Street 2001).

Drug use is a major risk factor for acquiring HIV infection because of its direct relationship to unsafe injection and sexual practices (Plankey, Ostrow, Stall, Cox, Xiuhong, Peck et al. 2007). Alcohol and other drug intoxication affect judgment and inhibition, which can lead to high-risk sex behaviors and HIV transmission (Parsons, Vicioso, Kutnick, Punzalan, Halkitis, and Velasquez 2004). In addition, substance abuse facilitates the progression of HIV by further compromising the immune system.

According to the Centers for Disease Control and Prevention (CDC), approximately one million people in the U.S. are living with HIV/AIDS. In 2005 MSM accounted for 71 percent of all HIV infections among male adults and adolescents and 53 percent of all people receiving an HIV/AIDS diagnosis. This was an increase of 11 percent of MSM with HIV/AIDS since 2001 (CDC 2007). HIV infection is strongly associated with syphilis, and outbreaks of syphilis in MSM have been reported in numerous urban areas since 2001. These outbreaks are characterized by high rates of HIV and high-risk sexual behaviors (Ciesielski, Kahn, Taylor, Gallagher, Prescott, and Arrowsmith 2005; Paz-Bailey, Meyers, Blank, Brown, Rubin, Braxton et al. 2004). Hirschfield, Remien, Humberstone, Walavalkar, and Chaisson (2004) found in their study that the majority of HIV-positive gay and bisexual men with multiple sex partners reported unprotected sex with HIV-negative or status-unknown partners. This is a very alarming finding, as is that of Celentano, Valleroy, Sifakis, MacKellar, Hylton, Thiede et al. (2006) that the majority of very young MSM in their study reported unprotected receptive anal intercourse, in the prior six months, while under the influence of alcohol, cocaine, amphetamines, or marijuana.

Methamphetamine, a highly addictive stimulant drug, has been the drug of choice of many MSM (especially on the West Coast) since the early 1990s, and is associated with unprotected sex, multiple sexual partners, increased rates of HIV infection, and decreased HIV disclosure among sexual partners (Larkins, Reback, Shoptaw, and Veniegas 2005; Mimiaga, Fair, Mayer, Koenen, Gortmaker, and Tetu et al. 2008; Peck, Shoptaw, Rotheram-Fuller, Reback, and Bierman 2005b; Reback, Larkins, and Shoptaw 2004). MSM who also inject drugs are among the highest-risk groups for transmitting HIV. Bull, Piper, and Reitmeijer (2002) found that these men have multiple partners of both genders and that their condom use is inconsistent. Their injection drugs of choice are methamphetamine and cocaine. Ibañez, Purcell, Stall, Parsons, and Gómez (2005) found that, when compared to nonusers, more injection drug users reported unprotected sexual behaviors with partners who were of unknown serostatus and HIV-negative.

When compared with MSM, much less is known about HIV risk for lesbians, bisexual women, and transgender individuals. Although female-to-female HIV transmission is considered rare, vaginal fluids and menstrual blood *are* potentially infectious (CDC 1999). Lesbians are at risk when a mucous membrane comes into contact with vaginal or menstrual fluid, when they perform cunnilingus without a protective barrier, or when there are cuts or sores on the hand or mouth during vaginal masturbation, oral-vaginal, or oral-anal contact. As with other STDs, however, HIV infection in lesbians is usually related to sex with men, bisexual women, intravenous drug use, or sex with those who use intravenous drugs (Campos-Outcalt and Hurwitz 2002). Numerous studies have found sexual-minority women injectors to be more than twice as likely to be HIV-positive as other injectors, both male and female (Young, Friedman, Case, Asencio, and Clatts 2000). And women who have sex with both women and men are clearly at an increased risk for HIV. Compared to heterosexual women, bisexual women are more likely to have sex with HIV-positive men, multiple male sexual partners, sex with MSM, sex with injection drug users, and anal sex. They are also more likely to report recent injection drug use themselves (Scheer, Peterson, Page-Shafer, Delgado, Gleghorn, Ruiz et al. 2002) and a higher rate of substance use with sex (Koh, Gómez, Shade, and Rowley 2005).

In a large national study of male and female bisexual and heterosexual injector or crack users, Logan and Leukefeld (2000) found that bisexuals, in general, were more likely to be HIV-positive and to engage in high-risk sexual behaviors and injection practices. Bisexual women, in particular, were much more likely to exchange sex for drugs or money.

Transgender women are at high risk for HIV, substance use disorders, and mental health problems (Lombardi, Wilchins, Priesing, and Malouf 2001). Many transgender women are at risk because of sexual behaviors, but sharing needles during the injection of hormones or drugs is also a risk factor (Nemoto, Luke, Mamo, Ching, and Patria 1999). It appears that male-to female transgender persons are more likely to engage in receptive rather than insertive anal sex, a role considered more feminine. And inconsistent condom use during receptive anal sex is commonly reported (Clements-Nolle, Marx, Guzman, and Katz 2001). HIV prevalence and risky sexual behaviors are much less common among female-to-male transgender persons (Clements-Nolle et al.).

African Americans are being hit disproportionately by HIV, and they are at particularly high risk for developing AIDS. While African Americans make up 13 percent of the U.S. population, they accounted for more than half of the total AIDS cases diagnosed in 2004. African American females accounted for 68 percent of the female HIV/AIDS diagnosis, white females for 16 percent, and Hispanic females for 15 percent (Morbidity and Mortality Weekly Report 2005). HIV/AIDS is now the leading cause of death among all African Americans ages twenty-five to forty-four (Anderson and Smith 2002).

Arend (2005) notes that because of socioeconomic factors and stigma against homosexuality and HIV in communities of color, low-income lesbian and bisexual women of color are at very high risk for HIV. These women are affected by homelessness and drug addiction, and frequently engage in sex work involving unprotected sex and multiple sex partners. The primary cause of HIV infection among black men is having sex with other men, and bisexual activity is highly correlated with secrecy and unprotected sex (Lichtenstein 2000). In black communities men are the main source of sexually transmitted HIV infection for both black men and women. Miller, Serner, and Wagner (2005) found that black MSM were very reluctant to identify as gay, went to sex clubs where they used drugs, and sought sex partners on the Internet. Most tried to appear "straight" and masculine and preferred sex partners who appeared masculine as well. This phenomenon of maintaining a "straight" public appearance and having sex with men on the side is referred to in the media as black men on the "down low." Native American and Latino MSM are also at high risk of HIV infection (Fernandez, Perrino, Bowen, Hernandez, Cardenas, Marsh et al. 2005; Simoni, Walters, Balsam, and Meyers 2006).

Male-to-female transgender persons of color, particularly African Americans and Latinas, are at very high risk for HIV infection (Clements-Nolle, Marx, Guzman, and Katz 2001). Nemoto, Operario, Keatley, Han, and Soma (2004) note that because of discrimination, many MTFs of color live in poverty and engage in high-risk sex work. Some have sex with multiple partners to affirm their female gender identities and abuse substances to cope with stress and depression (Reback, Lombardi, Simon, and Frye 2005). Operario and Nemoto (2005) interviewed Asian Pacific Islander MTF transgender individuals in San Francisco, and found them at high risk for HIV. Nearly one-half had sex while under the influence of substances, and more than half used illicit drugs.

Patterns of Abusive and Dependent Behavior

Treatment History

The practitioner needs to obtain a complete history of substance use treatment. This includes the names of treatment providers, dates and levels of care, reasons for discharge, and what was helpful about each treatment episode. Prior to and between treatment episodes, did the client attempt to control or stop substance use without assistance? And has the client participated in a community support program such as Alcoholics Anonymous (A.A.), Narcotics Anonymous (N.A.), or Rational Recovery? If they participated, what was the length of involvement and did they have a sponsor?

Lesbians tend to use mental health services at higher rates and for longer duration than other women (Cochran, Sullivan, and Mays 2003), and lesbian and bisexual women are also more likely to have received treatment for alcohol-related problems (Cochran, Keenan, Schober, and Mays 2000). Based on data from the 2000 National Alcohol survey, Drabble and Trocki (2005) found past treatment and problems among current drinkers to be particularly high among lesbian and bisexual women. Interestingly, lesbian and bisexual women were also less satisfied with their treatment experience. Corliss, Grella, Mays, and Cochran (2006) found that one in six lesbian and bisexual women in their study who evidenced high-risk drug use had wanted but not received professional help. Finally, Cochran and Cauce (2006) compared a representative sample of LGBT and heterosexual clients receiving substance abuse treatment in Washington State. They found that LGBT clients enter treatment with more severe substance abuse problems, a history of more mental health treatment, and more medical service utilization than heterosexual clients.

DSM-IV-TR Criteria

In the latest edition of the APA manual (American Psychiatric Association 2000:197–199), *substance abuse* is defined as "a maladaptive pattern of substance use leading to clinically significant impairment or distress" in *one or more* of the following within a twelve-month time frame:

1. The continued use of psychoactive substances despite experiencing social, occupational, psychological, or physical problems.

2. Inability to fulfill major role obligations at work, school, or home.

3. Recurrent use in situations in which use is physically hazardous, such as driving while intoxicated.

4. Recurrent legal problems related to the use of a substance.

DSM-IV-TR differentiates substance *abuse* from substance *dependence*, which requires *at least three* of the following seven symptoms within a twelve-month period:

1. Tolerance, as defined by either a need for increased amounts of a substance to achieve a desired effect or a diminished effect with use of the same quantity of substances.

2. Withdrawal, as characterized by specific withdrawal symptoms defined for each substance, or using a substance in order to relieve or avoid withdrawal symptoms.

3. Taking the substance in larger amounts or over a longer period than was intended.

4. A persistent desire or unsuccessful efforts to reduce or control use.

5. A great deal of time spent obtaining, using, and recovering from substance abuse.

6. Important social, occupational, or recreational activities are given up or reduced because of the substance use.

7. The substance continues to be used despite knowledge of resulting serious physical or psychological problems.

Substance abuse and dependence often involve several substances used simultaneously or sequentially. For example, individuals with opioid or cannabis dependence usually have several other substance-related disorders, most often involving alcohol, amphetamine, or cocaine. When criteria for more than one substance-related disorder are met, multiple diagnoses should be given.

Once a person has been diagnosed with substance dependence, she or he will never be diagnosed with the less severe diagnosis of substance abuse. The diagnosis of either abuse or dependence requires one of six "course specifiers" delineating the longer-term outcome. Specifiers are given only *after* the client has stopped using the substance for at least one month. Specifiers include:

1. *Early full remission*, defined as being substance-free for more than one month but less than twelve months.

2. *Early partial remission*, when the client resumes some use of a substance and subsequently meets at least one criterion of abuse or dependence within the first year of recovery.

3. *Sustained full remission*, defined as being totally substance-free for more than one year.

4. *Sustained partial remission*, when the client resumes substance use after twelve months of not having any symptoms, and then meets at least one criterion related to substance abuse or dependence.

5. *On agonist therapy*, which refers to the use of agonist medication to treat the substance, such as using methadone as a replacement for opiates.

6. In a *controlled environment*, when the client is not using a substance due to living in a substance-free environment such as a treatment center or prison.

A complete DSM-IV-TR diagnosis will include existing Axis I disorders in addition to substance use disorders, Axis II disorders (personality disorders and mental retardation), Axis III conditions (general medical), Axis IV problems (psychological and environmental), and Axis V "Global Assessment of Functioning" (GAF) score.

Screening and Assessment Instruments

The practitioner may choose to use a standardized screening and/or assessment tool to aid in the overall assessment of a substance use disorder.

Among the most frequently used are the CAGE (for alcohol assessment), the CAGE-AID (which includes other drugs), the SASSI (Substance Abuse Subtle Screening Inventory), the MAST (Michigan Alcohol Screening Test), the AUDIT (Alcohol Use Disorders Identification Test), the DAST (Drug Abuse Screening Test), the ASI (Addiction Severity Instrument), and POSIT (Problem-Oriented Screening Instrument for Teenagers). Unfortunately, there continues to be a serious lack of LGBT-specific and culturally sensitive screening and assessment instruments. Any information gained from the use of a standardized tool needs to be integrated with the information gained through interview so that the treatment plan can be individualized (Olson 2000).

Assessment of Specific Drugs

Regardless of the method of ingestion, psychoactive drugs are absorbed into the bloodstream and carried to the central nervous system (CNS), causing the release of neurotransmitters in the brain. A commonly used classification of substances is based on their effect on the central nervous system (Straussner 2004).

Central Nervous System Depressants

This category includes alcohol, barbiturates, and nonbarbituate sedative-hypnotics (antianxiety and sleeping medications), benzodiazepines (minor tranquilizers), anesthetics, volatile solvents, and low doses of cannabinoids such as marijuana and hashish (marijuana is sometimes placed in a separate category or, in large or highly potent doses, categorized as a hallucinogen). The sedation from these drugs affects speech, vision, coordination, and judgment, potentially leading to inappropriate and high-risk behavior. *Marijuana* causes increased heart rate, bloodshot eyes, dry mouth, and increased appetite. It can impair short-term memory and comprehension, and can be psychologically addictive. High doses of CNS depressants slow down the heart rate and respiration, produce stupor, and may result in death. When two substances in this category are combined, it is even more likely to result in overdose and death.

Central Nervous System Stimulants

This category includes *caffeine, nicotine, cocaine* and *crack* (smoked cocaine), *amphetamines,* and *methamphetamine* (known as meth, tina, chandelier, speed, ice, chalk, fire, glass, crystal crank). Stimulants range from the mild, such as caffeine and nicotine, to the much more potent cocaine and amphetamines/methamphetamines. Nicotine is both psychologically and physically addictive, and significantly increases the likelihood of heart disease, emphysema, chronic bronchitis, and numerous cancers. Nicotine is highly toxic, and produces compulsive patterns of use, craving, and tolerance.

CNS stimulants can be snorted, smoked, injected, or swallowed, and result in increased heart and respiratory rates, dilated pupils, elevated blood pressure, insomnia, and decreased appetite. Users may experience sweating, headache, blurred vision, dizziness, and anxiety. As tolerance develops, substantial escalation of dose amount is common.

Cocaine is a white powder that is usually snorted, but can also be dissolved in water and injected or smoked as crack. Converting into crack involves cooking the cocaine in a mixture of water, ammonia, and baking soda, yielding a much more concentrated form of cocaine (crystal or rock). Whereas snorted cocaine takes several minutes to reach the brain, crack takes seconds, and is extremely addictive. The high lasts only about 15 minutes, but can be found in the urine for up to eight hours. Tolerance develops rapidly, and large doses can produce acute delirium, psychosis, seizures, and depression. The most common causes of death from cocaine are heart attacks, strokes, and respiratory failure.

Methamphetamine is a synthetic drug that can be orally ingested, snorted, injected ("slamming"), smoked, or used rectally ("booty bumped"). It works by entering the brain and causing a release of dopamine, norepinephrine, and serotonin. It has a long half-life (8–12 hours), is cheap to make, and the main ingredient, ephedrine or pseudoephedrine, is readily available. It is associated with a variety of well-documented physical harms, including weight loss, skin lesions, and tooth decay ("meth mouth"). Users stay awake for days and sometimes weeks at a time, in some cases developing depression, anxiety, violent behavior, hallucinations, delusions, and paranoia. The drug is psychologically and physically addicting, and can lead to stroke, heart damage, and neurological problems. It is detectable in the urine for 3–5 days, depending on route of administration. For a comprehensive discussion of the medical consequences of methamphetamine use, the reader is referred to Gay and Lesbian Medical Association 2006.

In spite of the potential dangers of this drug, methamphetamine remains the drug of choice of many MSM, and is linked with high-risk sexual behaviors and HIV infection (Halkitis, Green, and Carragher 2006; Halkitis, Moeller, Siconolfi, Jerome, Rogers, and Schillinger 2008; Hirshfield, Chiasson, and Remien 2006; Mayer 2006). Up to 84 percent of methamphetamine-using MSM engage in sexual risk behaviors when high (Semple, Patterson, and Grant 2002), including unprotected insertive and receptive anal intercourse ("barebacking") with casual partners (Reback, Larkins, and Shoptaw 2004). Researchers have found no differences of methamphetamine use based on race or income (Halkitis and Jerome 2008). Very little has been published about meth use among lesbians, but it is probable that the addictive and medical issues are the same as among MSM and that the HIV-transmission issues of lesbians may also be exacerbated with meth use (Wainberg, Kolodny, and Drescher 2006).

Methamphetamine is an especially appealing drug because it is inexpensive, induces prolonged euphoria, eliminates fatigue, and heightens libido (Peck, Reback, Yang, Rotheram-Fuller, and Shoptaw 2005a). Halkitis, Pandey Mukherjee, and Palamar (2007) found that the MSM in their study used methamphetamine to enhance sexual pleasure and to mask difficult emotions related to loneliness, sexual unattractiveness, internalized homophobia, and having HIV. Those who combined Viagra with methamphetamine ("trailmix") reported even higher rates of methamphetamine use. Viagra is used to counter erectile dysfunction experienced by some men after chronic methamphetamine use, further increasing the risk for HIV and other STDs. Protease inhibitors, taken by a large number of patients with HIV, may be fatal when combined with methamphetamine even after a single dose (DeSandre 2006). Because even intermittent, recreational use of meth may lead to high-risk sexual behavior, no level of use of this drug should be considered safe (Colfax, Coates, Husnik, Huang, Buchbinder, Koblin et al. 2005).

Methamphetamine is only one of many drugs being abused by MSM, and some of these other drugs are strongly associated with methamphetamine use, high-risk sexual behavior, and HIV transmission (Grov, Parsons, and Bimbi 2008). Patterson, Semple, Zians, and Strathdee (2005) found that 64 percent of the HIV-positive meth-using gay men in their study also used cocaine, heroin, hallucinogens, and ketamine. The use of multiple drugs is fairly consistent across all racial and ethnic gay male populations (Irwin and Morgenstern 2005).

Narcotics or Opiates

This category includes opium and its derivatives, such as *morphine, heroin,* and *codeine,* as well as synthetic drugs such as *methadone, LAAM, buprenorphine, Demerol, Darvon, Percodan, Percocet, OxyContin,* and *Vicodin.* Users snort, smoke, or inject the substance, and a powerful rush is followed by feelings of sedation and contentment. Some users mix heroin and cocaine and shoot it ("speedballing") and some mix heroin and crack ("chasing the dragon"). Tolerance for these drugs is strong, and withdrawal is painful but less dangerous than alcohol withdrawal.

Methadone is a long-acting synthetic opiate used for prolonged detoxification or treatment of persons addicted to heroin. This drug blocks withdrawal symptoms, reduces craving, and has less euphoric effect than heroin. *LAAM* is another synthetic opiate that blocks the effects of heroin for up to 72 hours, with few side effects, when taken orally. Finally, *buprenorphine* (Subutex and Suboxone), a semisynthetic opiate derivative, reduces heroin use and cravings and is less toxic than methadone and LAAM (Johnson, Chutuape, Strain, Walsh, Stitzer, and Bigelow 2000).

Hallucinogens

Drugs in this category include *LSD, Foxy, PCP, mescaline,* and *peyote.* They produce gross distortions of thinking and sensory processes, an altered sense of time, and often visual hallucinations. Less psychologically addictive than other substances, they can nonetheless cause extreme anxiety and psychosis in vulnerable individuals.

LSD (acid, boomers, yellow sunshines) is sold in tablet, capsule, and liquid forms, and is typically taken by mouth. The user usually feels the effects in 30 to 90 minutes, and may evidence dilated pupils, high temperature, increased blood pressure and heart rate, sweating, loss of appetite, sleeplessness, dry mouth, and tremors. The user may also report numbness, weakness, and nausea. Long-term disorders include persistent psychosis and hallucinogen persisting perception disorder ("flashbacks").

Foxy, another synthetic hallucinogen, belongs to a class of chemicals known as tryptamines. Other hallucinogenic tryptamines include psilocybin and psilocyn. Foxy is available as a powder, capsule, or tablet, and can be consumed by ingestion, snorting, or smoking. The drug's effects are felt within 20 to 30 minutes, peak after 60 to 90 minutes, and last for three to six hours. Physical effects include dilated pupils, nausea, vomiting, and diarrhea. Psychological effects include hallucinations, talkativeness, and emotional distress. Foxy diminishes inhibitions, often resulting in high-risk sexual activity.

PCP (angel dust) can be ingested, smoked, snorted, or injected, and has been associated with depression, psychosis, and violence. *Peyote* can be chewed or ingested in powder form, and *mescaline* occurs naturally in mushrooms.

Club Drugs

These drugs are very popular with young people (NIDA 2008a), and are frequently used at "raves" and circuit parties (Kipke, Weiss, Ramirez, Dorey, Ritt-Olson, Iverson et al. 2007). "Raves," unlike circuit parties that attract gay and bisexual men, are nighttime dance parties that attract primarily middle-class heterosexual fifteen- to twenty-five-year-olds. Although whites are more likely than others to use club drugs, use among Latinos and African Americans is not uncommon (Ompad, Galea, Fuller, Phelan, and Vlahov 2004). Among the most popular club drugs are MDMA, GHB, Rohypnol, and ketamine.

MDMA (Ecstasy, EXTC, X, Adam, Clarity, Hug Drug, Lover's Speed) is taken orally, usually in a tablet or a capsule. It can produce both stimulant and psychedelic effects within an hour that last three to six hours. Confusion, depression, sleep problems, anxiety, and paranoia can occur weeks after the drug is taken. MDMA can cause a significant increase in blood pressure and heart rate, and the stimulant effects can lead to dehydration, hypertension, and heart or kidney failure. In high doses, a great increase in body temperature can result in muscle breakdown, organ failures, and death. Strokes and seizures have also been reported at "raves." MDMA is neurotoxic, and some heavy users experience long-lasting confusion, depression, and impairment of memory and attention processes.

MDMA is very popular with MSM because of the initial positive effects of mental stimulation, emotional warmth, empathy, decreased anxiety, loosened inhibitions, and a general sense of well-being. Unfortunately, this often leads to unsafe sexual behaviors and increasing HIV incidence (Klitzman, Greenberg, Pollack, and Dolezal 2002). MDMA can be addictive and withdrawal symptoms include fatigue, loss of appetite, depressed feelings, and difficulty concentrating.

GHB (Grievous Bodily Harm, G, Liquid Ecstasy, Fantasy, Georgia Home Boy) can be produced in clear liquid, white powder, tablet, and capsule forms, and is often used by young adults in "date rapes." The drug has growth hormone-releasing effects that can build muscles as well as sedative/euphoriant properties. As a CNS depressant, it can relax the body, but at higher dose it can dangerously slow breathing and heart rate. Its intoxicating effects begin within 20 minutes and last up to four hours. It is cleared from the body relatively quickly. Overdose results in drowsiness, nausea, vomiting, headache, loss of consciousness, impaired breathing, and ultimately death.

Some researchers (Camacho, Matthews, Murray, and Dimsdale 2005) note the popularity of GHB among homosexual and bisexual respondents. Males tend to use the drug for energy and euphoria and females for weight loss. College students, who are frequent users, have little knowledge of the addictive potential and illegal status of GHB. Halkitis and Palamar (2006) found that almost half of the MSM who used GHB in their study combined the drug with methamphetamine, MDMA, or ketamine; about one-quarter also used GHB with alcohol. They also found that GHB is viewed unfavorably in many social circles and that frequent users tolerate side effects and choose it over other substances because of the short duration of action, energy boost, sleep assistance, and increase in libido (Palamar and Halkitis 2006).

Rohypnol (Roofies, Ropies, Roche, Forget-me Pill, Mexican Valium, Rope, Roaches) is a benzodiazepine drug not approved for prescription use in the U.S., but used in more than sixty countries as a sedative and pre-surgery anesthetic. The drug is tasteless and odorless, and dissolves easily in carbonated beverages. Its sedative effects are exacerbated by concurrent use of alcohol, and victims can be impaired for 8–24 hours. Rohypnol can cause profound anterograde amnesia, so victims do not remember sexual assaults experienced while under the effects of the drug.

Ketamine (Special K, K, Vitamin K, Cat Valiums, Horse Tranquilizer) is an injectible anesthetic widely used in veterinary practice, but also approved for human use. It is produced in liquid form or as a white powder that is snorted or smoked with marijuana or tobacco products. Ketamine induces states of euphoria and dissociation, and is relatively short acting. Low-dose intoxication results in impaired attention, learning ability, and memory. Larger doses cause dreamlike states and hallucinations, and higher doses can cause delirium, amnesia, impaired motor function, high blood pressure, depression, and potentially fatal respiratory problems. Copeland and Dillon (2005) note the evidence of psychological and physical dependence among recreational users and the drug's association with high-risk sexual behaviors.

There is impressive empirical evidence of the association of club drug use among MSM with unsafe sexual behaviors leading to increasing HIV incidence (Gorman, Nelson, Applegate, and Scrol 2004). "Party-n-play" is the colloquial term used by MSM to describe drug use before and during sexual activity (Hirschfield, Remien, Humberstone, Walavalkar, and Chaisson 2004). Clatts, Goldsamt, and Yi (2005) found high rates of unprotected anal intercourse among young MSM chronic club drug users in NYC, and Fernandez, Bowen, Vargo, Collazo, Hernandez, and Perrino (2005) found high rates of unprotected anal sex and multiple partners among Hispanic MSM club drug users in Miami. In another study of club-going young adults in New York City, Kelly, Parsons, and Wells (2006) found male gender predictive of methamphetamine, GHB, and ketamine use, and female gender predictive of cocaine use. Homosexual and bisexual patrons had higher rates of club drug use than heterosexual patrons. Parsons, Kelly, and Wells (2006) found that lesbian and bisexual women frequenting dance clubs in New York City had higher lifetime rates of methamphetamine, cocaine, ecstasy, and LSD use compared to heterosexual women.

Other Drugs and Polydrug Use

Anabolic steroids are synthetic substances related to the male sex hormones that promote the growth of skeletal muscle and development of male sexual characteristics in both males and females. Some of these drugs are taken orally, others injected, and some are creams that are applied to the skin. Steroids are frequently abused by means of "cycling," which involves taking multiple doses over a period of time, stopping for a period, then starting again. Users also "stack" drugs by taking two or more different steroids, mixing oral and/or injectable types. They also abuse steroids by "pyramiding," slowly escalating abuse then gradually tapering the dose. Steroid abuse can cause acne, testicular atrophy, male-pattern baldness, and breast development in men. In women, steroids cause a decrease in breast size and body fat, coarsening of the skin, enlargement of the clitoris, and deepening of the voice. There may also be excessive growth of body hair and loss of scalp hair. Abuse has been associated with heart attacks, strokes, liver tumors, and an increase in irritability and aggression.

Shernoff (2001) has discussed the pressure in gay male culture to have a "gym body," how this has become an unhealthy obsession, and how anabolic steroids are abused to gain a huge degree of muscle mass. Halkitis, Moeller, and DeRaleau (2008) found that 11 percent of their sample of MSM in New York City had used steroids in the past six months. Shernoff notes that many of these men who use steroids have distorted body images and develop eating disorders. As steroids exacerbate mood swings, there are inexplicable episodes of depression, mania, and rage. *

* Kelly is a twenty-year-old man who self-identifies as gay, and is very concerned about his body image. He likes to go dancing, and he uses methamphetamine to help him let loose on the dance floor, keep his energy up, and keep his weight down. Recently he got into trouble with the law for possession of meth. He is very worried about gaining weight now that he is not using, and says that he has been purging and using a friend's weight loss pills to try to keep his weight down.

The use of a combination of two or more drugs to achieve desired effects ("trail mix") is very common during "raves" and circuit parties, putting users at risk for even more negative consequences. In the past five years there has been growing concern about the role of *Viagra* in HIV and STD transmission, due to its use alone and in combination with illicit drugs. Kim, Kent, and Klausner (2002) found that gay or bisexual men were significantly more likely to use Viagra than heterosexual men. These Viagra users in San Francisco reported more recent sex partners, more unprotected anal sex with an HIV-positive partner, and more STDs than nonusers. Purcell, Wolitski, Hoff, Parsons, Woods, and Halkitis (2005) found that Viagra was associated with using ketamine and engaging in unprotected insertive oral intercourse with HIV-negative/unknown-status casual partners.

It is clear that polydrug use, which reflects serious substance abuse problems, is linked with high-risk sexual practices, particularly among gay and bisexual men (Lee, Galanter, Dermatis, and McDowell 2003). The reasons for polydrug use are to get a better high, extend sexual performance, or to counterbalance negative effects from another drug. For example, methamphetamine in combination with other drugs is the rule rather than the exception, and marijuana is smoked to reduce the effects of "crashing" on methamphetamine. Amyl nitrates ("poppers") are used by gay men to extend sexual endurance, and cocaine sustains the body rushes associated with ecstasy (Patterson, Semple, Zians, and Strathdee 2005).

Methamphetamine is related to the use of both ecstasy and GHB (Halkitis, Palamar, and Pandey Mukherjee 2007), and MSM who use Viagra with crystal methamphetamine engage in HIV risk behaviors and have high prevalence rates of HIV (Spindler, Scheer, Chen, Klausner, Katz, Valleroy et al. 2007). MSM also use Viagra in combination with "poppers," ecstasy, ketamine, cocaine, and GHB, and these combinations are strongly associated with circuit and sex parties. Viagra is used by MSM as a recreational drug, regardless of physiological need, increasing the rates of unprotected sex and the transmission of HIV and STDs (Fisher, Malow, Rosenberg, Reynolds, Farrell, and Jaffe 2006; Halkitis and Green 2007).

Recreational drugs pose serious risks when combined with the life-saving medications of highly active antiretroviral therapy (HAART), which are used to treat HIV disease. Polydrug use, including club drugs as well as Viagra, can interfere with their effectiveness (Comacho, Matthews, and Dimsdale 2004; Romanelli and Smith 2004; Romanelli, Smith, and Pomeroy 2003). For an extensive discussion of antiretroviral medication interactions with substances of abuse, the reader is referred to Wynn, Cozza, Zapor, Wortmann, and Armstrong 2005.

When taking a substance abuse history from a client, the practitioner needs to obtain the following for each substance (Olson 2000:74):

- Age at first use, length of time to second use
- Pattern of use: amount, frequency, fluctuation (maximum, abstinence), setting, route
- Means of acquiring the substance
- Effect: psychological and physiological, during and after use, positive and negative
- Tolerance, withdrawal, blackouts

- Behaviors when high, including unprotected sex
- What triggers use, relapse potential
- Treatment history, attitude toward treatment
- Attempts to reduce or stop use

DiClemente (2006) points out that there are important differences in the lifetime careers of substance abusers. Some exhibit a pattern of abuse or binge use over long periods without developing severe dependence, some continue daily use for many years, and some have a variable pattern with periods of nonabusive use mixed with periods of dependence and abstinence. Patterns can change as social networks shift, stressful events are resolved, and consequences become more relevant. Changes in substance use, however, are not always to total abstinence.

DiClemente (2006) also notes that problematic use that continues from adolescence into middle adulthood is less likely to respond to self-change. These patterns usually meet the criteria of dependence, and these are the clients most typically seen in treatment programs. Longitudinal studies of chronic substance abusers show that, with some treatment, some achieve complete permanent abstinence and some achieve abstinence and then relapse. Others with long histories of abuse have been able to achieve complete abstinence without any treatment or organized support groups. For this reason, DiClemente believes it is inappropriate to place natural or self-change in opposition to treatment-assisted change, since both involve the same process of change.

Motivational Readiness to Change

The "stages of change" model (Prochaska and DiClemente 1982) is a framework for assessing clients' readiness to change. The five steps of change support the social work principle of "starting where the client is," applying motivational strategies that are matched to the client's current stage of readiness. Most clients move through the stages in a cyclical fashion: precontemplation, contemplation, preparation, action, maintenance. Relapse and recycling often occur before the client is ready for termination. Brief screening instruments that assess motivational stage are described in detail in appendix B of *Enhancing Motivation for Change in Substance Abuse Treatment* (CSAT 1999a).

American Society of Addiction Medicine (ASAM) Levels of Care

At the completion of the assessment, the ASAM adult placement criteria can be helpful in determining the appropriate level of care for the client. Several studies have shown better retention and posttreatment improvements in clients whose placement was consistent with the ASAM criteria (McLellan 2006).

The criteria contain six dimensions for assessment, leading to one of four levels of care, with sublevels within these. The dimensions are

1. Acute intoxication or withdrawal potential
2. Biomedical conditions or complications
3. Emotional, behavioral, or cognitive conditions or complications
4. Readiness to change
5. Relapse, continued use, or continued problem potential
6. Recovery environment

The levels of care include

0.5:	early intervention
I:	outpatient treatment
II.1:	intensive outpatient
II.5:	partial hospitalization
III.1:	clinically managed low-intensity residential services
III.3:	clinically managed medium-intensity residential treatment
III.5:	clinically managed high-intensity residential treatment
III.7:	medically monitored intensive inpatient treatment
IV:	medically managed intensive inpatient treatment

For details on the relationship between the dimensions and recommended levels of care, see Mee-Lee, Shulman, Callahan, Fishman, Gastfriend, Hartman et al. 2001.

Practice with Individuals

This chapter covers the formation of a therapeutic alliance, motivational interviewing, the stages of change, and behavioral therapies for working with individual LGBT clients. Therapeutic issues, including those unique to transgender clients, are also discussed.

Forming a Therapeutic Alliance

In order to tailor treatment to the LGBT client's current stage of change, the practitioner must first form a solid therapeutic alliance with him or her. Bien, Miller, and Tonigan (1993) have identified six practitioner skills that are relevant to the therapeutic alliance and to the development of motivation to change:

1. *Feedback*. Based on the assessment, the therapist is empathic and provides personalized feedback about the client's current circumstances related to substance abuse.

2. *Self-responsibility*. The therapist stresses that, ultimately, responsibility for change rests with the client and that he or she has choices about the strategies to be implemented.

3. *Advice.* The therapist, with permission, offers clear and specific advice about the advantages of changing addictive patterns and the different ways that change can occur.

4. *Menu.* After exploring what the client has tried or considered, the therapist asks permission to provide a range of appropriate strategies and modalities for changing addictive behaviors.

5. *Empathy.* The therapist demonstrates concern for clients, validates their experiences, and supports their changes.

6. *Self-efficacy.* The therapist expresses confidence in the client's ability to carry out therapeutic tasks.

These six components have been shown to be present in effective brief interventions with problem drinkers. According to Miller (2006), "Noticeably absent in effective brief interventions are general education, confrontation, or efforts to teach specific change skills" (p. 146.). Brief interventions utilize *motivational interviewing* (MI), a client-centered approach that facilitates change through exploring and resolving ambivalence.

Motivational Interviewing

Developed by William Miller (Miller and Baca 1983), motivational interviewing (MI) is a person-centered, goal-oriented approach for facilitating behavior change through exploring and resolving ambivalence. It is typically offered in one to four sessions and focuses on the client's own statements regarding the benefits and consequences of making a change. The clinician is empathic, nonjudgmental, and accepting of the client's ambivalence about behavior change. The work is collaborative and respectful of the client's autonomy and decision making. A range of possible goals, not necessarily including formal treatment or abstinence, are discussed with the client. Unlike the expectations of traditional treatment programs, clients are not required to attend education groups and self-help meetings or commit to a goal of abstinence (Carroll and Rounsaville 2006).

Motivational interviewing consists of basic therapeutic *skills* utilized in two treatment *phases*. The skills consist of asking open-ended questions, listening reflectively, affirming, summarizing, and eliciting self-motivated statements (Rollnick and Morgan 1995).

• *Asking open-ended questions.* Open-ended questions encourage client elaboration and openness and create an atmosphere of acceptance. A question such as "What brings you in today?" can be followed by more open-ended questions about the history and current status of substance use concerns. When clients express ambivalence, therapeutic questions should reflect both sides of the ambivalence. For example, "What do you like about snorting cocaine?" and "What worries you about doing it?" The clinician needs to be both curious and nonjudgmental in eliciting the client's story about the substance use.

• *Listening reflectively.* Reflective listening aims at understanding the meaning of the client's story. The clinician listens, then makes a brief comment that allows the client to confirm, correct, or develop more fully their story. Advice, interpretation, and extreme support are not helpful and usually divert the therapeutic process.

• *Affirming clients' concerns.* Clinicians need to be supportive to clients as they tell their stories. Appreciation of the client's efforts to be present and discuss their substance use should be stated consistently.

• *Summarizing.* Summary statements tie together the client's comments and verify the accuracy of the clinician's impressions. For example "What I understand you're saying so far . . ." encourages the client to move on and can accentuate the client's ambivalent thoughts and feelings. The clinician attempts to create and amplify the discrepancy between the client's current behavior and important personal goals.

• *Eliciting self-motivational statements.* When elicited, these statements from clients express their reasons for change. These statements either recognize that substance use is problematic, express concern about the current situation, indicate a desire to change, or reflect optimism about change (Miller and Rollnick 2002). For example, "I notice when I drink less I feel less irritable and get more done at work" reflects recognition that alcohol use is problematic. Clinicians elicit these statements through therapeutic open-ended questions, which continue after the self-motivating statements are made. A curious "tell me more" approach helps clients clarify their ambivalence and increase their motivation for change.

The motivational interviewing process consists of two phases: phase one, in which motivation for change is cultivated, and phase two, in which commitment to change is strengthened (Miller and Rollnick 2002).

- *Phase 1: Enhancing motivation for change.* In this phase, the therapist starts with open-ended questions, utilizes reflective statements, affirms and supports, and elicits self-motivated statements ("change talk"). In eliciting change talk, the therapist asks open-ended questions about the disadvantages of the status quo (current situation), the potential advantages of change, intentions to change, and the client's thinking about self-efficacy in the change process.

    In this process, resistance is handled by "rolling with" or reframing it. In rolling with the resistance, ambivalence is understood to be a natural part of the change process, and resistance is not challenged aggressively. Instead, it is reflected back to clients in a way that states both sides of the conflict. For example, "You like the feeling of getting high, but you're worried that your partner is going to leave you because you get irritable and argumentative with her after you drink. That's a real dilemma." Unlike more traditional approaches, clinicians who utilize MI do not confront or try to persuade clients that they are in terrible trouble and need to give up their addiction. The use of confrontation to "break through denial" can actually increase resistance and decrease the likelihood of change.

    The other way to handle resistance in MI is to reframe it. By offering an alternative interpretation of an issue, the client can get unstuck and move forward in the change process. For example, "You say that your partner nags and threatens you about your substance use, and that causes you to use more heavily. What if you learned that she nags and threatens because she loves you, is scared for you, and doesn't know how else to show her worry to you?"

    In Phase I of MI, clients are encouraged to explore both the costs and benefits of maintaining their addictive patterns. It is important to recognize the positive effects clients get out of drug use, determine if they are worth the costs, and begin to consider alternative ways of achieving the benefits.

- *Phase 2: Strengthening commitment for change.* Once the client has entered the preparation stage of change, commitment is strengthened by exploring different treatment options, creating a clear plan, and seeking verbal commitment. A change plan typically involves specifying the target substance problem, important incentives, action steps, resources, and potential barriers to change.

Brief MI has been shown to instigate change in clients who appear completely unmotivated. Miller and Carroll (2006) point out that "the idea that there is nothing one can do until a person 'hits bottom' is simply mistaken" (p. 298). Motivational interviewing/enhancement therapy as an empirically supported treatment (EST) for substance use disorders in LGBT clients is discussed in chapter 9.

Stages of Change

Motivational interviewing strategies can be well integrated into the stages of change model, and MI skills are appropriate for working with clients in all stages. The early stages of change are most affected by motivational considerations, and knowing what stage the client is in provides direction on which strategies to use to further enhance change. DiClemente (1991) discusses how clinicians can more fully integrate MI with the stages of change model.

- In the *precontemplation* stage, clients may not see the behavior as a problem, and are often labeled "resistant" or "in denial." Clinicians who are empathic, reflective listeners can be of most help in this stage. Clients may benefit from nonthreatening information and feedback, but not from confrontation.
- In the *contemplation* stage, MI strategies are particularly important, because the client is willing to consider the problem and the possibility of change. Accurate information about the addiction and focus on incentives to change are key strategies. Exploring problems with previous change efforts is also helpful. Continued ambivalence is normal in this stage, and if clinicians challenge it too aggressively, the client may become defensive and more resistant. In this stage, all of the MI strategies are used to work through the ambivalence, anticipate barriers, decrease the desirability of continuing the problem, and increase the client's sense of self-efficacy.

TABLE 5.1

Motivational Readiness to Change

STAGE OF CHANGE	CLIENT CHARACTERISTICS
Precontemplation	Not yet considering the possibility of change, although others are aware of the problem; does not link problems to substance use; seldom appears for treatment without coercion.
Contemplation	Ambivalent, vacillating between whether he/she really has a "problem" or needs to change; wants to change, but this desire exists simultaneously with resistance to it; may seek professional advice to get objective assessment; many have indefinite plans to take action in the next six months or so.
Preparation	Has increasing confidence in the decision to change; most clients at this stage are planning to take action within the next month, making final adjustments before they begin to change their behavior.
Action	Specific actions intended to bring about change; overt modification of behavior and surroundings; most busy stage of change, requiring the greatest commitment of time and energy.
Maintenance	Sustains the changes accomplished by previous action and prevents relapse; requires different set of skills than those needed to initiate change; consolidation of gains attained; not a static stage and lasts as little as six months or up to a lifetime; learns alternative coping and problem-solving strategies; replaces problem behaviors with new, healthy lifestyle; works through emotional triggers of relapse.
Relapse and Recycling	Expectable, but not inevitable setbacks; avoids becoming stuck or demoralized; learns from relapse before committing to a new cycle of action.
Termination	This stage is the ultimate goal for all changers; person exits the cycle of change without fear of relapse.

- In the *preparation* stage, the client appears to be ready for and committed to change, but needs to increase investment in a particular plan of action after exploring a range of goals and action plans. The clinician can assist the client in anticipating problems, finding alternative behaviors to replace substance use, and developing coping skills and activities that will support the action plan.

- In the *action* stage, clients take more decisive steps to modify their addictive behaviors and develop goals that are more acceptable to others. The clinician's continued support is critical during this stage, and focusing on the client's successful activities helps them increase their sense of self-efficacy.
- In the *maintenance* stage, the new behavior is becoming firmly established, with the test being long-term sustained change over several years. Clients consolidate coping strategies, replace problem behaviors with healthy ones, and work through emotional triggers to relapse. If relapse occurs, the client is helped to assess all reasons for it before committing to a new action plan.

See table 5.1 for a summary of client characteristics in each stage of change.

Behavioral Therapies

In the action and maintenance stages, the clinical focus is on the client's acquisition of strong coping skills and on mobilizing resources that can help prevent relapse. In this effort, behavioral interventions have been shown to be effective across the major classes of substance use. This is important because "pure" forms of substance use are rare and these interventions target the commonalities across the various classes of substance use. They are also effective in treating other psychological problems, which is important because of the high level of comorbidity among substance users (Carroll and Rounsaville 2006).

There are several classes of effective behavioral therapy for substance use disorders. Currently, the highest level of empirical support is for brief motivational therapies, cognitive-behavioral approaches, contingency management approaches, and couple/family approaches. The approaches are not universally effective, however, and tend to be more effective with clients who have less chronic substance use, more supportive families and social networks, fewer psychological disorders, and fewer medical problems. What these effective approaches have in common is their ability to increase motivation, reinforce behaviors incompatible with substance use, and change reinforcement contingencies so that abstinence is rewarded (Carroll and Rounsaville 2006).

In this chapter on practice with individuals, cognitive-behavioral therapy will be addressed. Later chapters will address other empirically supported treatments that have been incorporated into effective treatment *programs*. These include motivational enhancement therapy, contingency management approaches, the community management approach, and the matrix model.

In reviewing effective behavioral therapies, Carroll and Rounsaville (2006) point out that:

> With few exceptions, however, progress in the development of effective behavioral therapies has not been met by adoption of these approaches in clinical practice. The treatment system, with some exceptions, is dominated by the delivery of approaches of unknown efficacy and often by treatments demonstrated to be of little or no benefit.   (p. 224)

Carroll and Rounsaville view substance use disorders as impulse control disorders associated with excessive craving for drugs and poor behavioral controls. The individual has not learned healthy coping strategies and does not seek rewards incompatible with drug abuse. Substances are powerful reinforcers, and change is more likely when countervailing reinforcers such as families and jobs are threatened. "Poor behavioral controls or 'bad breaks' can result from preexisting or substance-induced impairment in the brain regions responsible for impulse control and emotional regulation" (p. 226).

Cognitive-behavioral therapy aims at identifying behavior that sustains substance use and learning effective alternatives. There is a focus on building practical skills to deal with problems and cravings that could lead to relapse. This involves changing cognitive distortions, learning to avoid situations associated with substance use, learning to delay impulsive behavior, reducing stress, and increasing social support from networks that discourage substance use. In essence, clients are helped to achieve better control by changing the reinforcing aspects of drugs and by strengthening connection with countervailing reinforcers such as the biological or chosen family. Clients learn to interrupt the connection between substance cues and use and tolerate unpleasant feelings.

Carroll and Rounsaville (2006) also conclude that "the most potent avenue for behavioral therapies to foster drive reduction is through combination with pharmacological treatments for drug abuse, most of which have their primary impact on drive reduction" (p. 233). Thus, for example, using methadone for heroin addiction avoids withdrawal symptoms and reduces craving, and bupropion for smoking and naltrexone for alcohol dependence also reduce craving. Antagonists like naltrexone for opioids that block the reinforcing effects of drugs and drugs like disulfiram for alcohol that cause aversive responses to use help achieve better behavioral control.

Therapeutic Issues

Substance abuse treatment for LGBT clients cannot focus solely on substance abuse, but must also address the psychosocial aspects of being LGBT. In addition to being knowledgeable about substance abuse treatment, the practitioner must be aware of issues unique to the LGBT population. These include coming out, dealing with antihomo/bi/trans violence, and internalized homo/bi/transphobia. Transgender clients who desire sexual reassignment surgery have additional unique issues. Other therapeutic issues, shared with heterosexual clients, include dealing with co-occurring disorders, managing HIV disease, resolving family of origin issues, and parenting and raising children. In addressing their substance use disorder, LGBT clients will need to deal with their identity as a clean and sober person and learn to participate in clean and sober safer sex and socializing.

Coming Out

Coming out is a highly significant, ongoing process in the lives of LGBT people, and therapists need to understand the relationship between coming out and the client's substance use disorder. As pointed out by Senreich and Vairo (2004), the coming out process can be supportive of recovery as the client works through issues of secrecy and shame, but it can also engender anxiety and trigger relapse. Practitioners should respect the wishes of the client who does not view coming out as part of recovery. Most research on coming out has involved gay men, so much less is known about the process for individuals who are lesbian, bisexual, or transgender.

Since the APA deleted homosexuality from its list of mental disorders in 1973, practitioners have increasingly associated problems faced by LGB clients with being covert about their identity, rather than with the identity itself; coming out began to be equated with good mental health and authentic interpersonal relationships, and covertness began to be associated with a range of social and psychological problems (La Sala 2000). Consistent with this position, therapists have been advised to discuss with covert clients the advantages of being open and ways of coming out to others (Woodman and Lenna 1980). This link between a healthy identity and self-disclosure assumes that decisions around disclosure are based on individual psychological rather than social influences and that these decisions are relatively unproblematic. While it is certainly true that being closeted involves constant vigilance and denying and concealing true feelings, self-disclosure can also be risky. As summarized by Green, Causby, and Miller (1999): "(Coming out) may result in ostracism by one's friends; alienation from one's family; the loss of one's job, housing or child custody; and subjection to gay bashing or other forms of harassment and abuse" (p. 80).

In a study of disclosure by gay men, Schope (2002) found that all respondents were out to friends, but a quarter remained closeted with siblings, at work, and in their neighborhoods, and over a third remained closeted with parents. Those who remained most closeted were older and resided in a rural or suburban area. Anderson and Holliday (2004) found that the lesbians in their study all "pass" as heterosexual at some times and view this as a necessary evil, an understandable response to a lack of civil rights, often essential to safety and survival in their jobs, religious settings, and families.

Green (2000) argues that in some situations passing is a sign of differentiation and positive coping with a hostile environment:

> Many people of color whose families are immigrants, many people in homophobic occupational settings, and many people living in smaller conservative towns face extreme discrimination or violence if they come out. . . . To label such people "immature" or "lacking differentiation" or "psychologically maladjusted" seems just plain ethnocentric.   (p. 263)

Green's comments are just as relevant to bisexual and transgender clients as they are to gay and lesbian clients.

Coming out as bisexual involves special challenges, since this sexual identity may be viewed as nonexistent or as a transitional phase on the way to being lesbian or gay. In fact, many women experience fluidity in their sexual identity, and women tend to come out as bisexual later than men.

Bisexuals often begin identifying as heterosexuals and later add same-gender relationships, resulting in bisexual identification (Dworkin 2001). Practitioners need to understand that the coming out process for bisexual clients is usually more difficult and complicated than for lesbian and gay clients, and many clients functioning as bisexual never identify as bisexual or actually come out (Reynolds and Hanjorgiris 2000).

Coming out as transgender or transsexual is even more complicated, since these clients often do not have the opportunity to become comfortable with their new identity before coming out to family, friends, and co-workers. Practitioners need to help these clients develop a coming out plan in various areas of their lives as well as contingency plans for dealing with rejection. In addition, clinicians should discuss sexual orientation with transitioning clients, as this may unexpectedly change during the transition process. In essence, some clients may need to come out in both gender expression and sexual orientation (Lombardi and Davis 2006). As in work with LGB clients, the practitioner must continually assess how recovery is affected by the presence or absence of the coming out process (Senreich and Vairo 2004).

Stage Models of Identity Development

A number of models for describing the process of developing a LGBT identity have been proposed. Before reviewing these models, it should be recognized that all have been criticized for being too linear and insensitive to unique variations in identity (Fassinger 1991). Devor (2004) notes that some people never experience some stages. People pass through the stages at different rates, some repeat some stages several times, and the models may be totally inapplicable to others. Dworkin (2001) also points out that identity commitment, the last stage of many models, precludes the idea of identity fluidity and the movement from a lesbian or gay identity to a bisexual identity. In addition, most models do not recognize ethnic and cultural differences or a healthy decision to not come out at all.

When stage models are not viewed as linear, however, they can be clinically useful in understanding the client's location in the identity process. Finnegan and McNally (2002) point out that many of these models can also be applied to the experiences of some substance abusers when they stop using drugs and seek their identity as a recovering person. Prior to beginning the process, the reference point for lesbian and gay people is heterosexuality and the reference point for substance abusers is social drinking and/or recreational drug use.

As mentioned, a number of LGBT identity-development models have been proposed. Those addressing lesbian and gay identity were developed by Cass (1979, 1984), Troiden (1979), Coleman (1982), and Minton and McDonald (1984). McCarn and Fassinger (1996) developed a model of lesbian identity development. The Cass model, which has received the most empirical support to date, is a six-stage model of gay and lesbian identity development. The following is a summary of this model.

- *Stage 1: Identity confusion.* Includes conscious awareness that homosexuality has personal relevance, dissonance regarding presumed heterosexuality, and/or beginning awareness of self as possibly gay or lesbian. The possibility of homosexuality and substance abuse problems may be denied in this stage, and therapists are ill-advised to attempt to break through this defense system. Finnegan and McNally (2002) note that many clients will not move into stage 2 until they have been clean and sober for several years.

- *Stage 2: Identity comparison.* Includes recognition of the probability that one is lesbian or gay and continued dissonance and feelings of social alienation. Individuals may view this only as a "phase" in their sexual orientation and may rationalize their drinking and/or drug use or attempt to control it. Direct confrontation continues to be contraindicated in this stage, as the client is still confused and very vulnerable.

- *Stage 3: Identity tolerance.* Includes reasonable certainty of a lesbian or gay identity and tolerance, without acceptance, of that identity. The individual seeks out other lesbian and gay people, but continues to "pass" in heterosexual culture. Substance abusers in this stage may immerse themselves in A.A. or N.A. and exclude all other activities. They may want to tell everyone they are in recovery or they are lesbian or gay. Therapists need to help clients in this stage examine the consequences of such actions and become more reflective. McNally (1989) found that none of the lesbians in her study were able to go beyond stage 3 while they were active in their addiction. Kuss (1988) found the same in his study of gay men in recovery.

- *Stage 4: Identity acceptance.* Includes positive acceptance of self as lesbian or gay and more social interaction with other lesbian and gay people. The individual is more open with others regarding identity, and there is development of a passing strategy. Recovering substance abusers in this stage have begun to accept their identity as substance abusers. Lesbians and gay men may grieve the loss of heterosexual privilege, and clients who are substance dependent mourn the loss of being social drinkers and recreational drug users. Practitioners need to be supportive of the grief process and, when appropriate, refer clients to lesbian/gay A.A./N.A. meetings.
- *Stage 5: Identity pride.* There is immersion in lesbian/gay culture and association primarily with gay/lesbian people. There is also growing anger with dominant, oppressive heterosexual culture. The practitioner needs to help the client in this stage work with this anger so that he or she is able to move on to the final stage of identity development.
- *Stage 6: Identity synthesis.* Includes integration of being lesbian or gay with other aspects of personal identity. Interactions involve both gay/lesbian and heterosexual people. The individual is clearer about appropriate anger, and there is more synthesis between public and private identities. According to Finnegan and McNally (2002), when lesbians or gay men are in this stage, their substance addiction requires primary attention. Some, however, will need to go back to an earlier stage and come out again in recovery.

Morrow (2006) points out that individuals in the first few stages of identity development may be at greater risk for substance abuse, depression, or even suicide. These risks exist not because the lesbian or gay person is inherently less stable, but because of the stresses of living in an oppressive, heterosexist environment.

Bisexual identity development is not adequately described by models of coming out as lesbian or gay. Weinberg, Williams, and Pryor (1994) point out that bisexual identity tends to be more fluid, bisexuals tend to be older than lesbians and gay men when they come out, and they do not have the benefits of a large supportive community. In addition, bisexual people face biphobia as well as homophobia and have to come to terms with both the lesbian/gay and heterosexual parts of their identity. Bisexual people are extremely diverse, and they do not have one, typical pattern of identity development. They may arrive at their identities by a number of possible routes (Fox 1995).

That said, the four-stage model of bisexual identity development proposed by Weinberg, Williams, and Pryor (1994) is the best known. The following is a summary of this model.

- *Stage 1: Initial confusion.* Includes stress and dissonance over the inability to declare either a gay/lesbian or a heterosexual identity. This period can last for years, and substances may be abused to help cope with the anxiety and confusion.
- *Stage 2: Finding and applying the label.* There is relief in finding that bisexuality is a legitimate sexual orientation. This stage can be quite long in duration.
- *Stage 3: Settling into the identity.* There is increasing comfort and self-acceptance as a bisexual person. Finnegan and McNally (2002) note, however, "that it is difficult, if not impossible, to fully internalize and develop one's identity while in the throes of substance abuse" (p. 192).
- *Stage 4: Continued uncertainty.* Continued occasional periods of doubt about sexual orientation due to a lack of social validation and social pressures by both homosexual and heterosexual communities. In the context of a long-term monogamous relationship, the bisexually identified person may begin to identify as gay/lesbian or heterosexual, but this does not mean that bisexuality is just a transitional stage to these identities. Finnegan and McNally (2002) point out that the uncertainty and stress of bisexual identity development can contribute to substance abuse and risk of relapse in recovering people.

Transgender *emergence* (Lev 2004) refers to developing a gender identity as a transgender or transsexual person. Although there are similarities to coming out as lesbian/gay or bisexual, there are also profound differences because there are more transgender identities and paths to resolution. Lev has proposed a six-stage model of transgender emergence, and the following is a summary of that model:

- *Stage 1: Awareness.* Involves a sense of feeling different, a discomfort with the birth sex, and confusion about what this means.

In discussing her transition from male to female, Boylan (2003) recalls "the awareness that I was in the wrong body, living the wrong life, was never out of my conscious mind" (p. 19). She asked herself, "What was I? What was going to happen to me if I didn't stop wanting to be a girl all the time?" (p. 23). Individuals may feel anxious, depressed, and overwhelmed. Alcohol and other drug use may increase, and those in recovery become prone to relapse. The practitioner needs to normalize gender identity issues, create a safe environment, and slow down any decision-making about the irreversible aspects of transitioning.

• *Stage 2: Seeking information/reaching out.* Involves becoming educated and coming out to others like themselves. The strong desire to move forward can lead to very risky behavior, like cutting off old friends and family, seeking black market hormones, self-mutilation, and abusing substances as a way to connect with others. The practitioner's role is to help clients engage with clean and sober people and slow down enough to evaluate the consequences of their behavior. Supportive couple or family therapy may also be appropriate.

• *Stage 3: Disclosure to significant others.* This may be the most difficult stage, sometimes leading to anxiety, depression, and substance abuse. Families of origin are often rejecting, and partners may feel hurt and betrayed. The practitioner must not collude with either the client or his/her partner, but instead continue to support the client's integration into the family or, if necessary, into relationships with more appropriate support surrogates.

• *Stage 4: Exploring identity and transition.* Includes resolution of gender dysphoria and exploration of various gender identities. There is also exploration of future options for transition and occupational and financial needs. Individuals focus on decisions regarding clothing, mannerisms, taking hormones, and beginning electrolysis. This can be the most dangerous stage for many clients, who may experience terrible losses, leading to depression and substance abuse. Practitioners need to advocate for clients, address depression and substance abuse, and continue to work with the family.

• *Stage 5: Exploring transition and possible body modification.* Some individuals begin hormones, prepare for surgeries, complete electrolysis, and begin the "real-life experience" of living full-time in the opposite sex. Some choose to live in the opposite gender role without the full range of body alterations, and some choose to switch back and forth between genders or stay in neither of the supposed binary options. Clients have major concerns about passing during this stage, more easily accomplished in most cases by FTMs taking testosterone. Some MTFs need to accept that they will never pass well, and many are now choosing to be completely open about their gender transition. The practitioner needs to validate the range of choices available, deal with ongoing losses, and continue to work with the family during this stage.

• *Stage 6: Integration and pride.* Individuals are fully integrated into their new identity choice and are comfortable with that status. It is possible, however, to still be grieving some losses or to be depressed that transition did not solve all existing problems. In these cases, it should always be possible to return to therapy.

Finnegan and McNally (2002) caution that substance abuse interferes with the cognitive and affective skills needed to develop a positive gay/lesbian/bisexual or transgender identity. Because of this, true self-acceptance cannot occur without sobriety, and transgender clients who are substance abusers may have to return to stage 2 and rethink their identity development when in recovery.

Managing External and Intimate Partner Violence

Another therapeutic issue that is unique to LGBT clients is dealing with antigay/trans violence. Hate crimes involve direct violence against individuals because of apparent sexual orientation or gender expression (Swigonski 2006). According to Mason (2002), 70–80 percent of lesbians and gay men have experienced public verbal abuse, 30–40 percent have received threats of violence, and 20 percent of gay men and 10–12 percent of lesbians have experienced physical violence. Little is known about violence toward bisexual individuals, but 60 percent of transgender individuals have experienced some form of harassment and/or violence (Lombardi, Wilchins, Priesing, and Malouf 2001). Many of these victims experience depression, anxiety, and symptoms of posttraumatic stress disorder, all of which can result in excessive substance use. Practitioners working with these clients need to frame these symptoms as normative consequences of trauma and support clients in discussing and working through specific episodes of violence.

The rates of intimate partner violence are higher in couples in which one partner has a substance use disorder, and this must be dealt with as part of substance abuse treatment. The perpetrator may be male or female, and is engaged in behavior of dominating and isolating the partner in order to maintain power and control. The practitioner also needs to recognize that domestic violence occurs in families engaged in transition issues and transgender clients can become targets for the family's stress (Lev and Lev 1999). *

Research indicates that LGBT clients face significant barriers to accessing services for intimate partner violence. For example, Simpson and Helfrich (2005) found that lesbian domestic violence survivors faced systemic, institutional, and individual barriers. There appears to be a double standard in which heterosexual women have greater access to services than do women who have sex with women (Hassouneh and Glass 2008). Turell and Cornell-Swanson (2005) found that lesbians were more likely to seek help than gay men or bisexual people, and women were more likely to seek counseling than men. African American and Latino individuals utilized services the least, with relatively few seeking medical help or assistance from a domestic violence agency.

---

* Mary is a thirty-seven-year-old lesbian who is a self-employed financial advisor. She states that she is a very heavy drinker and uses alcohol to stabilize her mood and push away uncomfortable emotions. Her parents had a very chaotic, crisis-ridden relationship and divorced when she was ten. Her mother had several affairs during the marriage and is described as alcoholic, critical, and emotionally unavailable. Her father is described as alcoholic, controlling, and opinionated. Mary states that she is moderately anxious and depressed, and feels lonely and invisible. In relationships she is constantly fearful of abandonment, assumes a caretaker role, and has difficulty being direct about her own needs. She is attracted to highly emotional, reactive women and often provokes chaos that resembles the fights she observed between her alcoholic parents. As a result, several of these relationships have been quite violent, often made even more dangerous because of excessive alcohol use.

Managing Internalized Homo/Transphobia

A final therapeutic issue that is unique to LGBT clients is managing internalized homo/transphobia as well as external, such as religion-based, sources of guilt and shame. Negative societal messages are internalized by LGBT individuals and can contribute to anxiety, depression, and substance abuse. Internalized homo/transphobia leads to fear, guilt, and isolation, and is a major relapse trigger in recovering LGBT clients. Finnegan and McNally (2002) point out that "transgendered people—*whatever* their sexual orientation—are likely to be subjected to homophobia because of this culture's powerful stereotype that homosexuality is indicated by gender non-conformity" (p. 91). The practitioner must address these internalized negative feelings, but in a way that will not elicit too much anxiety when abstinence is tenuous. Careful timing is critical in this regard (Cabaj 1995). Self-acceptance is crucial to recovery, even if the client decides not to come out to certain people (Cabaj 2000).

In their study of lesbians' recovery from addiction, Matthews, Lorah, and Fenton (2005) found that substances were used to cope with the shame associated with internalized homophobia, and that traditional "religion that felt punishing exacerbated shame rather than supporting recovery" (p. 67). When appropriate, clients can be referred to the Metropolitan Community Church, a gay-positive Christian church that ministers primarily to the LGBT community. Rodriguez and Ouellette (2000) found that a majority of its members in their study had successfully integrated their homosexual and religious identities.*

Cabaj (2000) cautions that traditional psychotherapy with active substance abusers is usually contraindicated because insight does not neces-

---

* Jessica is a twenty-five-year-old lesbian whose parents did not attend church and abused alcohol, but insisted that she and her sister attend church regularly. She felt that the teachings of the church led to her feeling shame about being a lesbian. She eventually left home and became involved in a chaotic lifestyle that included risky sex and polydrug use. She was not able to benefit from a program with a "higher power" component, but did become involved in a drop-in program aimed at HIV prevention. Three years later she reports that the novelty of drug use is gone, she drinks moderately, and has a good job.

sarily lead to recovery and can, in fact, lead to rationalizations for continued abuse. Instead, supportive motivational therapy can serve as a bridge into addiction treatment. Psychotherapy can begin in the early recovery period when the practitioner is reasonably sure of the stability of sobriety and strength of the client's support system. Relapse is always a possibility, however, so the challenge is to know how soon to explore shame and internalized homophobia. Gair (1995) states that the shame created by hiding one's true self is an overriding factor in the development of the self, which can result in alcoholism, depression, or suicide. Because LGBT clients lack mirroring for their developing selves in heterosexist society, this becomes the role of the therapist. The empathic and mirroring functions of the therapist enable the client to become aware of and comfortable with the true, authentic self.

Co-occurring Disorders and HIV Disease

The term *co-occurring disorders* (COD) will be used to refer to co-occurring substance use (abuse or dependence) and mental disorders. Individuals with substance use disorders are subject to higher rates of psychiatric disorders than the rest of the population, and those with COD have poorer substance abuse and mental health treatment outcomes and higher treatment costs than those without comorbid conditions (Watkins, Burman, Kung, and Paddock 2001). The rate of hospitalization for clients with both a mental and a substance use disorder is more than twenty times the rate for substance abuse–only clients and five times the rate for mental disorder–only clients (Coffey, Graver, Schroeder, Busch, Dilonardo, Chalk et al. 2001). The more severe psychiatric disorders are associated with higher rates of substance abuse problems than are the less severe disorders. For example, the lifetime prevalence of substance use disorders in clients with schizophrenia or bipolar disorder is 50 percent, with depressive or anxiety disorders 25–30 percent, and with no psychiatric disorder 10–15 percent (Mueser, Drake, Turner, and McGovern 2006).

Seven meta-theories have been proposed to explain the high comorbidity between substance use and psychiatric disorders (Mueser et al. 2006):

1. *Secondary psychopathology* models attribute comorbidity to substance use being the cause of psychiatric disorders in vulnerable in-

dividuals. For example, alcohol and stimulants can lead to prolonged periods of depression in some vulnerable individuals.

2. The *self-medication* hypothesis states that people with psychiatric disorders use substances to ameliorate the symptoms of their mental disorders. The evidence for this hypothesis is weak for most disorders, but posttraumatic stress disorder (PTSD) does tend to precede alcohol abuse.

3. The *general dysphoria* theory states that people who suffer from unhappiness or pain of any kind use psychoactive substances repeatedly and develop addictions. This theory has little application to specific psychiatric disorders.

4. The *supersensitivity* model states that specific psychiatric disorders predispose people to be more sensitive to the effects of psychoactive substances. Evidence supporting this model is limited to schizophrenia.

5. The *secondary psychosocial effects* model posits that the psychosocial consequences of mental illness predispose people to substance abuse. There is little research on the role of adversity in the high rate of substance abuse in people with mental illness.

6. *Common factor* models state that another underlying variable independently increases risk for both mental illness and addiction. These common variables could be genetic, familial, or environmental, but there have been few attempts to test this model.

7. *Bidirectional* models posit that different factors related to mental illness and substance abuse contribute to the onset and maintenance of comorbid disorders. For example, PTSD is associated with the subsequent development of substance use disorders, which in turn can worsen PTSD symptoms.

In summary, Mueser et al. (2006) note that while a number of models have been proposed to explain the co-occurrence of psychiatric and substance use disorders, no model has received strong support. Because of this, no treatment program based on a single theory can be effective for the broad range of individuals affected. According to Mueser et al., "The basic monolithic fact is that we understand relatively little about the etiologies of individual psychiatric and substance use disorders. Therefore accounting for comorbidity is a complex conundrum" (p. 122).

The *assessment* of co-occurring disorders involves all of the components of substance abuse–only assessment as well as the following (CSAT 2005a):

- A detailed chronological history of past psychiatric symptoms, diagnosis, treatment, and impairment, particularly before the onset of substance abuse, and during periods of extended abstinence.
- A detailed description of current strengths, limitations, and cultural barriers related to following the treatment regime for any disorder.
- The stage of change for each substance use and psychiatric disorder.

Orlin, O'Neill, and Davis (2004) delineate two categories of clients with co-occurring disorders: the primary psychiatric client and the primary substance abuser. The primary psychiatric client uses substances in response to the discomfort of mental illness, and must be treated for both disorders to stop decompensation. The primary substance abuser may have hallucinations and delusions secondary to substance abuse. If a urine toxicology is ordered and antipsychotic medication is delayed, the client can be observed in a drug-free state. Symptoms of psychosis will persist if unmedicated and symptoms due to substance abuse will abate with abstinence.

Although there is little research specific to assessing comorbidity in LGBT clients, assumptions continue to be published about these clients. The most severe psychopathology is attributed to transsexual individuals. As Lev (2004) points out, "Gender-variant people are identified as impulsive, depressed, isolated, withdrawn, anxious, thought-disordered, and suffering from narcissistic, schizoid, and borderline personality features" (p. 189). She stresses the importance of making a distinction between psychiatric disorders that are independent of gender issues and those that result from living with transphobia and oppression. In fact, transgender people do not appear to have higher rates of mental disorders than nonclinical populations (Carroll 1999), with fewer than 10 percent having a history of mental illness (Cole, O'Boyle, Emory, and Meyer 1997). In a study of suicidality and psychiatric history, Mathy (2002) found that, despite the greater sexism and heterosexism endemic to transgender identity, the majority of transgender individuals do not suffer from the comorbidity of suicidality or substance abuse.

It is known that lesbians use mental health therapy at high rates, with depression and relationship problems the most frequently reported reasons for seeking care (Roberts, Grindel, Patsdaughter, Reardon, and Tarmina 2004b). Lesbians are three and one-half times more likely than heterosexual women to report using mental health services (Razzano, Cook, Hamilton, Hughes, and Matthews 2006), and some studies suggest that bisexual women and men have more mental health risk factors than heterosexual, gay, or lesbian individuals (Cochran, Sullivan, and Mays 2003; Jorm, Korten, Rodgers, Jacomb, and Christensen 2002). It is certainly possible that stressors such as discrimination and potential victimization from hate crimes account for this higher risk and service utilization.

After assessment clients with COD should ideally receive *integrated* treatment. In contrast to parallel or sequential treatment, integrated treatment provides mental health and substance abuse services by the same team of clinicians in the same setting. Research indicates that clients receiving integrated treatment have better substance abuse outcomes, and cognitive-behavioral group modalities are favored. Finally, many individuals with COD require long-term residential treatment (Mueser, Drake, Turner, and McGovern 2006).

Another model, utilized by some treatment agencies, is the *quadrant* model, which conceptualizes different subgroups of clients with COD in terms of the severity of each disorder. Although this model is in wide use, Mueser et al. (2006) point out that it has not been empirically validated and "breaks down immediately when it is applied to routine clients or treatment settings" (p. 126).

CSAT (2005a) has identified five strategies for working with clients with co-occurring disorders: motivational enhancement, contingency management, cognitive-behavioral techniques, relapse prevention, and dual recovery self-help groups. Motivational interviewing accepts the client's level of motivation, whatever it is, as the starting point of change, and *motivational enhancement therapy* (MET) combines motivational interviewing with systematic feedback of assessment results. The practitioner accepts ambivalence about change as normal, notes discrepancies between present problems and important goals, rolls with resistance, and supports self-efficacy. Every attempt is made to match motivational strategies with the client's stage of change. Samet, Rollnick, and Barnes (1996) have summarized motivational approaches to be used with clients with COD at different stages of readiness.

- *Precontemplation.* The clinician expresses concern about the client's substance use or symptoms of psychiatric disorder and acknowledges nonjudgmentally that either is a problem; explores the client's perception of a substance use or psychiatric problem; suggests a trial of abstinence to clarify the issue; suggests bringing a family member to an appointment; emphasizes willingness to try to help.

- *Contemplation.* The clinician elicits positive and negative aspects of past and present substance use or psychiatric symptoms; summarizes the client's comments on substance use and psychological issues; explicates discrepancies between actions and values; suggests a trial of abstinence and/or psychological evaluation.

- *Preparation.* The clinician recognizes the importance of deciding to seek treatment for each of the COD; helps the client decide on achievable action for each of the COD; explains that relapse should not disrupt the therapeutic relationship.

- *Action.* The clinician is supportive and acknowledges the painful aspects of withdrawal and/or psychiatric symptoms; reinforces the importance of remaining in recovery from all problems.

- *Maintenance.* The clinician anticipates and addresses difficulties as a measure of relapse prevention; recognizes the client's struggles and supports the client's resolve; reiterates that relapse should not disrupt the therapeutic relationship.

- *Relapse.* The clinician expresses concern and explores what can be learned from the relapse; supports the client's self-efficacy so that recovery seems achievable.

The effectiveness research on motivational enhancement therapy for COD is promising, and Carey, Purine, Maisto, and Carey (2001) have developed a four-session intervention to enhance readiness for treatment for people with schizophrenia and substance use disorders.

The second effective strategy for working with clients with COD is *contingency management* (CM), which posits that behavior can be altered through a system of positive and negative consequences. In substance abuse treatment, this might involve regular drug testing, positive reinforcement (cash, vouchers, prizes, privileges) when abstinence is demonstrated, and withholding reinforcers when substances are detected (Higgins and Petry 1999). CM can also be applied to treatment participation, appropriate behavior, and medication adherence.

The third effective strategy for working with clients with COD involves the use of cognitive-behavioral techniques (CBT). The underlying assumption of this therapy, as discussed previously, is that the client's distorted thinking (about the self, world, and future) creates behavioral problems, and irrational beliefs need to be replaced with rational ones. In substance abuse treatment, clients learn how to recognize and avoid situations in which they are likely to use substances and learn better coping skills to deal with thoughts and feelings that might lead to substance use (Carroll 1998). According to CSAT (2005a), thinking distortions are even more severe in individuals with COD, some of whom have experienced trauma or sexual abuse. These clients can be triggered by small events, setting off a strong craving to use substances. Najavits (2002) recommends teaching a skill called "grounding," which soothes and distracts the client and helps him or her anchor in present reality. Grounding is effective with substance craving, PTSD, and other intense negative feelings expressed by clients. For other specific CBT strategies for programs working with clients with COD, the reader is referred to Peters and Hills 1997.

The fourth effective strategy for working with clients with COD is the use of *relapse prevention techniques* (RPT). Because relapses are preceded by triggers or cues, clients need to learn to anticipate and label high-risk situations and develop strategies to cope with them without having a lapse. Irvin, Bowers, Dunn, and Wang (1999) found in a meta-analytic review of studies that RPT were most effective when applied to alcohol or polysubstance use disorders, combined with medication. Orlin, O'Neill, and Davis (2004) note that the newer antipsychotic medications target negative symptoms (depression, low energy, anxiety) as well as positive ones (paranoia, delusions, hallucinations). This makes them much more useful for clients with COD because negative symptoms are significant triggers for substance use and abuse.

Finally, the fifth effective strategy for working with clients with COD is facilitating client participation in mutual *self-help groups*. Clients can be helped to find an appropriate dual recovery group and sponsor, tasks that are much easier in larger communities. After attendance, clinicians can debrief with clients and help them process their reactions. LGBT clients are frequently resistive to self-help groups, and this situation will be addressed in chapter 9.

Orlin et al. (2004) stress the fact that treatment that targets only one disorder in clients with COD will not be successful. These authors also note that both substance treatment providers and mental health providers must make modifications in their typical single diagnosis strategies to effectively treat these clients. Drug and alcohol treatment providers need to do the following: expect more relapses and a longer timeframe to achieve resolution; appreciate the value of psychotropic medication in preventing relapse; modify traditional confrontation techniques to be gentler and directed only at behaviors; reframe the concept of enabling so that therapy can be more active and supportive when the client is at risk for relapse; have psychiatric availability to monitor mental status, prescribe and use injectable medication when available; and use harm reduction approaches. Mental health providers need to do the following: fully assess and monitor substance abuse; utilize urine monitoring and breathalyzers, and actively encourage participation in self-help programs for clients and their families. Because the highest dropout rate occurs in the first few sessions, the use of motivational interviewing to engage clients is extremely important.

All clinicians who work with clients with COD need to recognize that suicidality is a high-risk behavior associated with COD. Most people who kill themselves have a diagnosable mental or substance use disorder or both, and the risk of suicide is greatest when relapse occurs after a significant period of abstinence (CSAT 2005a).

For an overview of working with substance abuse treatment clients with *specific* psychiatric disorders, the reader is referred to chapter 8 and appendix D of CSAT 2005a, which reviews the most commonly observed DSM-IV disorders (APA 2000) seen in clients who are substance abusers. For the most common medications for psychiatric disorders, the reader is referred to appendix F of CSAT 2005a and to *Psychotherapeutic Medications: What Every Counselor Should Know,* a publication of the Mid-America Addiction Technology Transfer Center (MATTC) that is updated annually and available at www.mattc.org. For discussion of the co-occurrence of borderline personality disorders and substance abuse, the reader is referred to Goldstein 2004. And for discussion of an evidence-based model for treating trauma/PTSD and substance abuse, the reader is referred to Najavits 2007. Kolodny (2006) addresses the co-occurrence of methamphetamine dependence and psychiatric disorders, and Bostwick, Hughes, and Johnson (2005) discuss the co-occurrence of alcohol dependence and depression.

It is also important for clinicians to recognize that the effects of substances can mimic psychiatric disorders and result in assessment and treatment errors. These substance-induced disorders are the result of substance abuse, intoxication, or withdrawal, and are distinct from co-occurring psychiatric disorders. Most of these symptoms begin to improve within hours or days after the cessation of substance use, but there are exceptions. For example, long-term methamphetamine abuse can cause psychotic symptoms that last for weeks, months, and years. And alcohol, inhalants, and amphetamines can cause dementias that are not entirely reversible even with sobriety. For a review of common substance-induced mental disorders, the reader is referred to chapter 9 of CSAT 2005a.

In addition to dealing with co-occurring or substance-induced disorders, many LGBT clients have to manage HIV disease. The risk for HIV infection is increased by substance use before and during sexual activity and by sharing needles for injection drug use. Gay and bisexual men represent 68 percent of men with AIDS in the United States. Men of color represent more than half of new AIDS cases among MSM in the U.S. every year (CDC 2007). HIV-positive MSM evidence high rates of alcohol use (64 percent), marijuana (36 percent), nitrate inhalants (27 percent), cocaine (13 percent), and amphetamines (12 percent) (Purcell, Parsons, Halkitis, Mizano, and Woods 2001).

Substance use also plays a significant role in the high HIV prevalence in MTF transgender clients, whose rate of approximately 35 percent is much higher than the 2 percent rate of FTM individuals. Among the MTFs in a San Francisco study, HIV prevalence for African Americans was over 60 percent (Clements, Marx, Guzman, Ikeda, and Katz 1998). Transgender people of color are at very high risk for both HIV/AIDS and substance abuse. Xavier, Bobbin, Singer, and Budd (2005) found that 48 percent of the transgender people of color in their sample had substance abuse problems, and 72 percent of those who were taking hormones acquired them from friends or on the street.

Substance use appears to have a greater effect on sexual risk with casual compared to primary partners (Purcell, Parsons, Halkitis, Mizano, and Woods 2001), so it is important to discuss serostatus disclosure with HIV-positive clients. Kalichman, Rompa, Cage, DiFonzo, Simpson, Austin et al. (2001) found that interventions that encourage disclosure to sexual partners actually do reduce risk. Failure to discuss HIV may be construed as an indication to a casual partner that one is HIV-negative (Serovich, Oliver, Smith, and Mason 2005). Interestingly, in a recent study of methamphetamine-dependent gay men, both HIV-positive and HIV-negative men believed the obligation to disclose HIV status and initiate condom use was the responsibility of the HIV-negative partner

(Larkins, Reback, Shoptaw, and Veniegas 2005). Practitioners need to be aware of this norm when discussing safe sex practices with their HIV-negative substance-abusing clients.

It has become clear to researchers and practitioners that psychiatric disorders are common in individuals with HIV/AIDS. In a study of HIV-infected clients in North Carolina, Whetten, Reif, Napravnik, Swartz, Thielman, Eron et al. (2005) found that 60 percent reported symptoms of mental illness, 32 percent reported substance use problems, and 23 percent identified both psychiatric and substance use problems. Substance use and psychiatric problems are underlying factors in both the spread of HIV disease and the difficulty in treating those affected (Avants, Warburton, Hawkins, and Margolin 2000). The Center for Substance Abuse Treatment (CSAT 2000) points out that psychiatric symptoms may be caused by preexisting psychiatric disorders, substance abuse, HIV/AIDS, or the medications used to treat HIV/AIDS.

The most common psychiatric disorders found in clients with HIV disease are as follows:

- Adjustment disorders, time-limited responses to acute stresses characterized by anxious or depressed mood
- Sleep disorders, resulting from substance abuse, depression, anxiety, or HIV disease itself
- Mania, caused by the HIV infection or use of stimulant drugs
- Dementia, caused by HIV disease or chronic alcoholism
- Delirium, more common than dementia in HIV-positive substance abusers, caused by substance intoxication or withdrawal or toxicity from medications
- Psychosis, caused by advanced HIV/AIDS dementia or substance usage
- Depressive disorders, common among clients with substance use disorders and common after withdrawal from some substances

Depression is one of the most prevalent psychiatric disorders among clients with HIV/AIDS, ranging from 22 to 32 percent (Bing, Burman, Longshore, Fleishman, Sherbourne, London et al. 2001). Up to 60 percent of HIV-infected women in one study reported depression (Levine 2002). Depression can impair the client's overall quality of life and can also diminish compliance with HIV medications (Angelino and Treisman 2001).

It is often difficult to determine whether substance abuse preceded a client's psychiatric disorder or vice versa. Substance abuse may be an attempt to self-medicate an underlying disorder or, more frequently, it may occur before any obvious psychiatric symptoms. To further confuse the situation, drugs used to treat HIV disease—highly active antiretroviral therapy, or HAART—can have side effects of depression, paranoia, insomnia, and hallucinations. And there can also be adverse interactions between HAART and psychiatric medications and between HAART and medications used in the treatment of substance abuse (e.g., methadone, LAAM, naltrexone, and bupropion).

Clearly, a complete history is critical in sorting out comorbidity issues with HIV disease. Table 5.2 delineates assessment factors for the HIV-infected substance abuse treatment client. After the assessment is completed, it is important to set realistic treatment goals with the client. In psychiatrically impaired substance abusers, immediate abstinence from substances may be unrealistic, and flexibility is essential with HIV-infected clients because of the public health importance of keeping them in treatment. The harm reduction model will emphasize incremental decreases in substance abuse and HIV-risk behaviors and keeping the client involved even if complete abstinence is not achieved. For example, focus may be on using condoms, reducing the number of sex partners, avoiding venues that might increase drug use, sterilizing syringes with bleach, et cetera. Any move toward lowering risk is helpful, and this approach is not incongruous with abstinence if this is the client's ultimate goal.

Standard pharmacologic approaches may be used to treat psychiatric disorders in LGBT clients who are HIV-infected and substance dependent. In addition, individual therapy can be particularly useful in helping these clients deal with issues related to HIV infection, substance use disorders, and sexual identity. Specific therapeutic issues of LGBT clients who are HIV-positive include the following: rage and depression; self-blame and guilt; and fears of physical deterioration, death, and toxicity to others (Gant and Strom 2004). Clients also struggle with feelings about drug treatment and drug-related side effects, changes in social status, and apathy (Frederick 2004). Transgender clients who are HIV-positive and in substance abuse treatment often face additional issues. They may suffer from internalized transphobia, low self-esteem, isolation, and lack of family and social supports. In addition, they may be undergoing hormone therapy and dealing with denial of sex reassignment surgery due to their HIV status.

TABLE 5.2
Initial Mental Health Assessment for the
HIV-Infected Substance Abuse Treatment Client

1. DEVELOPMENTAL/SOCIAL HISTORY
   a. Childhood trauma or illness
   b. Education
   c. Employment
   d. Sexual orientation
   e. Relationship history
   f. Current support system/social network

2. FAMILY
   a. Family relationships
   b. Family psychiatric history
   c. Family substance abuse history

3. MEDICAL HISTORY
   a. HIV history: Date of diagnosis
   b. Stage of disease according to CDC classification system
   c. Most recent CD4 + T-cell count
   d. Most recent viral load
   e. HIV-related illnesses
   f. Other medical illnesses
   g. Current medications

4. SUBSEQUENT ABUSE HISTORY
   a. Age of onset of substance abuse
   b. Substance abuse description:
      –Types of substances
      –Amounts
      –Frequency
      –Route of administration
   c. Past or current substance abuse treatment
   d. Involvement with self-help (e.g., Alcoholics Anonymous, Narcotics Anonymous)

5. PSYCHIATRIC HISTORY
   a. Age of first psychiatric problems
   b. Outpatient treatment
   c. Inpatient treatment
   d. Past and current diagnosis/diagnoses
   e. Past and current medications and responses

6. CURRENT PSYCHIATRIC SYMPTOMS
   a. Behavior (e.g., agitation)
   b. Appearance of psychomotor retardation

c. Cognitive:
  –Level of arousal/alertness
  –Attention/concentration
  –Orientation
  –Memory
  –Calculation
d. Mood (e.g., depression)
e. Mania
f. Emotional instability
g. Anxiety (acute or chronic)
h. Symptom pattern (episodic [e.g., panic attacks] vs. generalized)
i. Psychotic symptoms (e.g., thought disorder)
j. Hallucinations
k. Delusions

7. DANGER TO SELF OR OTHERS
  a. Ability to care for self
  b. Suicidality
  c. Assaultive/homicidal ideation

Source: Center for Substance Abuse Treatment, *Substance Abuse Treatment for Persons with HIV/Aids* (Treatment Improvement Protocol [TIP] 37; DHHS Pub. No. (SMA) 06-4137) (Rockville, MD: Substance Abuse and Mental Health Services Administration, 2000), p. 76.

Because of discrimination, many transgender clients lack formal education and have great difficulty maintaining gainful employment (CSAT 2000).

Family and social support are critical to the coping success of LGBT clients who are HIV-positive. Those who receive support from their families are less likely to be depressed (Serovich, Esbensen, and Mason 2005) and less likely to engage in risky sexual behaviors (Kimberly and Serovich 1999). While LGBT clients usually turn first to partners and friends for support, they are likely to turn to their families of origin as their disease progresses and their needs become greater. This often requires simultaneous disclosure of sexual orientation/gender identity and HIV status, resulting in tremendous stress to both clients and their families. Parents may experience grief and guilt and engage in intrusive, infantilizing behavior. Or they may be completely rejecting (Kadushin 1996). Gay men frequently come out to siblings before parents, and sisters and mothers are perceived as more supportive about sexual orientation and HIV status than brothers and fathers (Fisher, Goldschmidt, Hays, and Catania 1993). Practitioners can view families of origin as untapped sources of support for clients, and can assist them in functioning more effectively in this role.

Gant and Strom (2004) point out that:

> Intravenous drug users who are HIV-infected are an exceedingly difficult population with which to work. . . . [and] Negative countertransference can lead to an irrational fear and loathing of the client, the client's situation, and to working with him or her. (p. 464)

Common countertransference reactions include fear of contagion, blaming the victim, obvious or subtle rejection, homo/transphobia, hopelessness, grief, rage, and guilt. In addition, Frederick (2004) points out that anxieties around loss and death are common, as is overidentification among LGBT therapists. Countertransference can be managed by ongoing participation in peer supervision and consultation groups, limiting the number of clients with HIV disease, developing the social support of family and friends, and seeking personal psychotherapy if appropriate (Gant and Strom 2004).

Family of Origin Issues

The clinician will have assessed the client's early family experiences, including relationship with parents, stepparents, siblings, and extended family members. There will also be knowledge of family dynamics, cultural factors, and coming out experiences in the family. Family history of substance abuse is also important because of the high correlation between drug abuse and domestic violence and chemical dependency in offspring. Any of these issues may represent "unfinished business" for the LGBT client who is abusing substances. In addition, there are some similarities among racial/ethnic groups that negatively affect clients' attitudes about being LGBT (Finnegan and McNally 2002), and these factors may become important therapeutic issues. For example, while white LGB communities emphasize independence from the family of origin as the way to come out and identify as LGB, most minority groups value the heterosexual family as the key to survival and well-being (Smith 1997). And LGBT identities challenge traditional gender roles and can threaten the basic structure of the minority family/culture (Bohan 1996). Finally, religion plays a central role in the lives of many minority cultures and most continue to teach homo/transphobia values.

Another family of origin therapeutic issue for many LGBT clients is childhood sexual abuse. Between 40 and 75 percent of adolescent and adult women who abuse substances have been sexually abused or neglected during childhood (Karageorge and Wisdom 2001). Some clients, in fact, erroneously believe that sexual abuse *caused* their homosexuality or bisexuality, and this can become a complex therapeutic issue. Kort (2007) offers the following explanation of this issue:

> Many males who were physically and/or sexually abused as boys or teenagers may reenact that trauma by engaging in homosexual behaviors as adults. At first glance, they may appear to be in early denial about their homosexuality. I think of these men as being homosexually imprinted—they're innately heterosexual boys who were molested or physically abused by another male and keep "returning to the scene of the crime" to defuse and desensitize their emotional pain and trauma. When the original trauma is resolved, they stop having sex with men, if they're straight. If they're really gay, they continue having sex with men, which is an expression of their core identity. After the haze of trauma is lifted, they discover that they're romantically interested in men and want to make an intimate connection with other men.   (p. 68)

Parenting and Raising Children

This section will address the following therapeutic issues: LGBT couple relationships, LGBT parenting, and children of LGBT clients. Particular attention will be given to parenting issues of LGBT clients who have substance use disorders.

The majority of gay and lesbian couples are currently involved in primary romantic relationships and 22 percent of male couples and 34 percent of female couples are raising children (Gay Demographics 2003). Peplau and Cochran (1990) found no differences between lesbians, gay men, and heterosexual men and women on any measure of relationship quality. The conflicts unique to lesbian and gay couples appear to be created by societal homophobia, and disagreements about the extent of disclosure or being "out" about their relationship are not uncommon (James and Murphy

1998). In addition to dealing with negative societal attitudes, many LGBT couples have been stressed by an inordinate number of losses due to the HIV/AIDS epidemic.

As Patterson (2000) points out, the children of LGBT parents can be born or adopted in the context of heterosexual marriages that later dissolved or after parents have affirmed LGBT identities. Most parenting research has focused on comparisons between divorced lesbian mothers and heterosexual mothers, and few differences have been found. Patterson (1997) found no differences in self-concept, happiness, or psychiatric status between lesbian and heterosexual mothers.

There are relatively few studies of gay fathers and their children, and none comparing their psychological adjustment with heterosexual fathers. There is even less research on couple relationships and parenting of bisexual and transgender individuals.

Most studies of children born in the context of heterosexual relationships involve white, middle-class families. Research on these families has found that lesbian and bisexual women who had children before coming out were likely to be older when they self-identified as lesbian or bisexual and were less likely to be out to others compared to similar women without children (Morris, Balsam, and Rothblum 2002). An important therapeutic issue for these parents, whether they are lesbian, gay, bisexual, or transgender, is how to come out to their children. Barret and Logan (2002) stress the importance of parents being clear about their own sexual orientation or gender identity before disclosing to their children. Once the parent is clear, children are never too young to be told. Patterson (1995) found that disclosure to children is less difficult either before or after early adolescence. After divorce, children of lesbian mothers have more frequent contact with their fathers than children in the custody of heterosexual mothers (Hare and Richards 1993).

Overall, research indicates that children growing up in lesbian and gay households are as psychologically healthy as children reared in heterosexual households and show few, if any, developmental differences. There are no differences between the groups in peer relationships, academic and occupational development, or satisfaction with life (Wainwright, Russell, and Patterson 2004). Children from gay and lesbian families do tend to be more tolerant of others and more open to new experiences (Brooks and Goldberg 2001), and children reared in LGBT households are more likely to have accepting attitudes toward people with a sexual minority status

(O'Connell 1999). Finally, no study has shown that same-sex couples affect the sexual orientation of their children (Hicks and Wise 2000).

There is very little research focused on children raised by bisexual parents. The few studies that have addressed children being raised by a transgender or transsexual parent have not found any mental health or gender identity disturbances in the children (Ettner and White 2000). Adolescents have the most difficulty with a parent's transition, and preschool children do by far the best. The most protective factors for the child are a close emotional tie with the transitioning and the nontransitioning parent, cooperation between the parents regarding child rearing, extended family support of the transitioning parent, and ongoing contact with both parents. Practitioners need to focus on promoting this collaborative relationship between the parents and with extended family if possible (White and Ettner 2004).

When LGBT parents have substance use disorders, they have the same parenting and couples issues faced by other coupled clients, as well as issues related to societal and internalized homo/transphobia and disclosure. The practitioner must assess how the substance abuse is affecting the children, as the children have often been replaced by the parent's attachment to the drug. Markowitz (2004) notes that the parent is often withdrawn, emotionally unavailable, anxious, depressed, and irritable, leading to confusion and anger in the children. There is active discouragement of the expression of any feelings, and children become overly attuned to the parent's needs and desires. Given this situation, clinicians are often in the position of helping LGB clients make the changes necessary to keep or regain custody of their children.

Issues Specific to Transgender Clients

Lev (2004) points out that gender-variant individuals who are seeking services fall into three categories: (1) those who are struggling with genderdysphoric feelings, (2) those who are seeking referral letters for medical treatment, and (3) those who are presenting with family-related issues. Clients in the first category have generally experienced gender confusion since early childhood and feel great shame and emotional distress. Therapists can educate these clients about gender dysphoria, explore various options, and assist clients in the emergence of an authentic self. In a study of the psychotherapy experiences of transgender and transsexual clients, Rachlin (2002) found that 87 percent reported positive changes. Helpful therapists were flexible in their treatment approach and showed respect for the client's gender identity. Negative experiences were associated with therapists who were not current on transgender issues and/or were extremely passive or distant. For discussion of the proliferation of identifying terms and the evolving nature of the transgender community, the reader is referred to Carroll, Gilroy, and Ryan 2002.

Some of the clients in this first category are quite transphobic and have lived in the "wrong" gender because they cannot deal with the oppression of being transgender. They may have denied their true self by marrying and living as their birth sex. And they may have histories of abusing substances to deal with their pain (Finnegan and McNally 2002).

The second category of clients are those seeking referral letters for medical treatment. The Harry Benjamin International Gender Dysphoria Association (HBIGDA) is an organization of professionals working to assist transpeople transition to their new gender. One of the ways HBIGDA has done this is through its Standards of Care (SOC) for Gender Identity Disorders, now in its sixth version (Meyer, Bockting, Cohen-Kettenis, Coleman, Di Ceglie, Devor et al. 2001). The SOC require referral letters from clinical psychotherapists in order for clients to be approved for hormonal treatment and surgery, and also require the "real-life" experience of living as the preferred gender prior to genital surgery. The latest version allows clients who are born female to be approved for breast reduction/chest reconstruction and hormone treatment *before* beginning the "real life experience," since living successfully as a man without these treatments would be quite difficult. In spite of this revision, the SOC have been strongly criticized for restricting surgical interventions without empirical evidence that these rules are necessary. Cole, Denny, Eyler, and Samons (2000) note that requiring people to live as the other gender before surgery is dangerous for clients, making them vulnerable to discrimination and hate crimes. A related debate is about the medicalization of transsexualism and the inclusion of gender identity disorder (GID) in the DSM. Some believe that GID incorrectly pathologizes being transgender, which they argue is a variance as normal as homosexuality. Others, however, point out that having GID in the DSM allows access to costly medical care that would otherwise be unavailable to most. Still others have suggested replacing GID with a term that carries less stigma, such as gender dysphoria or gender dissonance.

For a more extensive discussion of this debate, the reader is referred to Kirk and Kulkarni 2006, Lombardi and Davis 2006, and Raj 2002.

Clients in both of these categories have undoubtedly struggled with discrimination and trauma. Lombardi, Wilchins, Priesing, and Malouf (2001) found that over half of the transgender people in their study had experienced some form of harassment or violence in their lifetimes, and Nemoto, Sausa, Operario, and Keatley (2006) found that MTF transgenders of color—African American, Latina, and Asian Pacific Islanders—experience even more risk due to multiple stigmas. Finnegan and McNally (2002) note that the LGB and transgender communities, like the larger society, tend to be racist and homo/bi/transphobic. And because all variations from prescribed gender roles are seen as reflecting homosexuality, transgender people—regardless of their sexual orientation—are subject to homophobia if they do not pass (Bohan 1996). According to Brown and Rounsley (1996), the ability to pass is very important to transsexuals, and many experience tremendous anxiety, depression, and shame around passing. Kirk and Kulkarni (2006) note that FTM (transmen) are less focused on passing because testosterone allows them to pass fairly well. And because they often identify as heterosexual, their adjustment to transitioning is less difficult. MTF (transwomen), on the other hand, tend to be more focused on passing and their sexual orientation tends to be more flexible.

Practitioners working with transsexual clients need to support and help them develop a coming out plan for family members, friends, and coworkers. This will include contingency plans for dealing with anger, rejection, and legal issues such as child custody. Many clients will also want to discuss their sexual orientation, which may change unexpectedly during the transition process. As Lombardi and Davis (2006) point out, "Sexual orientation depends largely on a stable gender identity, and when the gender identity of a client changes, an alteration in sexual orientation may follow" (p. 358). So, in addition to coming out as transsexual, some clients will need a plan for coming out in a different sexual orientation. Seil (2004) believes that, for some, sexual orientation only firmly develops postsurgically when the client receives validation by the sexual interest of others. Psychological function generally improves after sex-reassignment surgery (Mate-Kole, Freschi, and Robin 1990), and the incidence of regret is very low (Carroll 1999).

The third category of gender-variant individuals seeking services are those presenting with family-related issues (Lev 2004). Regardless of presentation, clients should be addressed in the gender pronouns and names that they identify. Younger clients may be seeking assistance with rejecting families and educational systems, and older clients with unaccepting spouses, partners, children, siblings, inlaws, and aging parents. Partners often experience confusion, anxiety, depression, rage, and a sense of betrayal. Clinicians need to address the crisis in the relationship as well as attempt to normalize the experience of the transsexual. Therapy with couples and families will be addressed in chapter 10.

Many transgender individuals present with physical and mental health problems related to stress and lack of access to services. Clinicians must differentiate between mental health disorders symptomatic of oppression and those that are independent of gender issues. Disorders that began prior to or concurrent with gender issues need to be assessed and treated. Xavier's (2000) study of transgender individuals found that 35 percent reported suicidal ideation and almost half of these had attempted suicide. Many transgender clients lose their jobs and turn to commercial sex work for survival, becoming at even higher risk for substance abuse and violence. *

Unfortunately, all of these struggles are compounded by poor access to psychiatric and medical care as well as transphobic treatment. Many transgender people avoid medical treatment and are very reluctant to reveal their history. Barriers to health care include blatant refusal to treat, inappropriate intake forms, and lack of insurance coverage for SRS (Sperber, Landers and Lawrence 2005). Xavier (2000) found that 58 percent of those currently using hormones acquired them from friends or on the street. Many transgender individuals also obtain needles from nonmedical sources, and report provider insensitivity as the most common barrier to receiving care.

---

* R. J. is a sixteen-year-old youth who identifies as trans (male to female). She ran away from home when she was thirteen and has been living on the streets. She says that she prostitutes herself in exchange for a place to stay. The men who pick her up often offer her drugs or alcohol. She reports she uses drugs to escape shame she feels around her body not "being right" and about the sex work she does to survive.

The transgender population is at high risk for HIV/AIDS, and this is often an important therapeutic issue. Few services are available to transgenders, and those offered are not sensitive to their needs (Clements, Wilkinson, Kitano, and Marx 1999). The same can be said about substance abuse programs, which do not provide groups and programs that are transgender-specific. Seil (2004) points out that substances are used by some in the transgender population to manage internal gender conflict, and clients may become aware of this conflict only after sobriety is attained. He believes that substance abuse problems must be resolved before transition is considered and that, in MTFs, nicotine dependence must be controlled because of the risk of deep vein thrombosis in estrogen therapy. Substance use is quite prevalent in studies of MTFs, and Clements-Nolle, Marx, Guzman, and Katz (2001) reported 34 percent prevalence of lifetime injection drug use. Almost half of these individuals shared syringes and 29 percent shared drug-using equipment with someone else. The MTF individuals in Reback and Lombardi's study (1999) most commonly used alcohol, cocaine/crack, and methamphetamines. Much less is known about the substance use of FTM individuals. Practitioners need to assess whether gender issues are central to, peripheral, or unrelated to substance abuse treatment (Sperber, Landers, and Lawrence 2005).

[6]
Treatment Related to Specific Drugs

In this chapter, the harm reduction perspective and therapeutic issues specific to work with clients who abuse alcohol, opiates, and stimulants are addressed. The use of medications to attain initial abstinence, manage withdrawal, and prevent relapse is also discussed.

Harm Reduction

Most substance abuse treatment in the United States has had the goal of complete abstinence from substances, and clients unmotivated for abstinence have been viewed as resistant and untreatable. Harm reduction is a public health perspective reflecting a paradigm shift that does not view abstinence as the sole measure of success. Instead, the goal is to minimize the harmful effects of substance abuse by meeting clients "where they are" and mutually agreeing upon attainable goals. Abstinence is viewed as an excellent—perhaps ideal—form of harm reduction (Zelvin and Davis 2001), but it is recognized that most clients are not at the action stage of change when they seek services. Harm reduction is not tied to any one treatment theory, so various theoretical approaches can be utilized (Tatarsky 2002). It does, however, recognize the importance of the stages of change model

(Prochaska and DiClemente 1982) and the motivational interviewing techniques that match the individual's current level of change (Miller and Rollnick 2002). As MacMaster (2004) points out, harm reduction strategies have been found to be effective with many clients, but are not necessarily appropriate for clients who are highly motivated for abstinence and already in the action stage of change.

Success in the harm reduction framework refers to any reduction in substance-related harm (Denning 2000). This could mean limiting HIV infection, violence, crime, broken relationships, psychiatric symptoms, incarceration, homelessness, domestic violence, et cetera, without necessarily attaining abstinence from substances (van Wormer and Davis 2003). MacMaster (2004) reviews a variety of programs that have effectively reduced the harmful consequences of substance abuse without requiring abstinence. There are now many examples of harm reduction programs, one of the oldest being methadone maintenance for persons addicted to heroin. There is no longer doubt that methadone maintenance improves health status and reduces crime and drug use (Appel, Joseph, Kott, Nottingham, Tasiny, and Habel 2001). Other examples focus on reducing the spread of HIV infection, and include the following: syringe exchange, free bleach kits for cleaning injection equipment, condom distribution, and education about safe sex and reducing the number of sex partners. Clients can also be supported in using smaller amounts of substances, using less often, and avoiding people and places that increase the opportunity for drug use and unsafe sex. Clients with alcohol abuse problems can attempt to control their drinking through learning to monitor their alcohol intake and rehearsing alcohol refusal skills. Readers who are interested in using moderation approaches with problem drinkers are referred to Rotgers, Kern, and Hoetzel 2002. Finally, smokers utilize harm reduction strategies of nicotine replacement therapies. *

Harm reduction strategies are now being used not only with substance abuse, but also with any self-destructive behavior clients are reluctant to stop (Tatarsky 2002). One such behavior of particular relevance to gay and bisexual men is "barebacking," or unprotected anal intercourse, also known as raw or natural sex. In a New York City study it was found that the use of crystal methamphetamine correlates directly with barebacking among white, black, and Hispanic gay and bisexual men (Halkitis, Shrem, and Martin 2005). Shernoff (2006) notes the recent increase in barebacking

* Margaret is a forty-year-old accountant who self-identifies as bisexual. She states that she is a heavy user of alcohol and cocaine, but that marijuana is her drug of choice. She describes her mother as a depressed alcoholic who had very high expectations of her, but little understanding of her as a unique individual. Father is described as alcoholic, critical, and controlling. Margaret states that she has been aware of her bisexuality since adolescence, and was diagnosed with major depressive disorder at age seventeen. She is currently taking an antidepressant, but continues to suffer from low self-esteem and relationship problems. She has no close friends and, when in an intimate relationship, tends to be conflict avoidant, too needy, and fearful of exposing herself. She does not connect with her coworkers, and admits that her productivity has declined in the past year. She states that she is interested in reducing her use of alcohol and cocaine, but will not stop her daily use of marijuana. Margaret is considered to be a good candidate for a harm reduction approach to her substance abuse.

among MSM, and reviews a variety of reasons for this resurgence. These include complacency about HIV/AIDS, believing that there are cures to AIDS, the ease of finding barebacking partners on the Internet, and an increase in the use of "club drugs." Shernoff proposes that the combination of motivational interviewing, matched to the appropriate stage of change, and harm reduction is useful in working with MSM who bareback. The particular harm reduction strategy he describes is "serosorting," which involves discussing HIV status with potential partners and having condomless sex only with those of a similar serostatus. Another harm reduction strategy involves the negotiation of safety between partners who are HIV-negative; a copy of a sample negotiated safety agreement can be found at http://freedoms.org.uk.

For a detailed case example of the use of harm reduction with a woman who abuses alcohol and cocaine, the reader is referred to Seiger 2004. For case examples of harm reduction treatment with clients who have co-occurring disorders, the reader is referred to the following: (1) problem drinking secondary to depression (Tatarsky 1998); (2) substance use, HIV, and personality disorder (Denning 1998); and 3) ADHD, substance abuse, and PTSD (McCann and Roy-Byrne 1998).

Therapeutic Issues Specific to Alcohol, Opiate,
and Stimulant Dependence

Regardless of the substance involved, the practitioner needs to understand
the client's relevant developmental themes and motivations for use. A
number of recent studies have focused on motivations for substance use
and risky sexual activity, since it is well known that HIV-positive meth-
using MSM have low rates of protected sex (Semple, Zians, Grant, and
Patterson 2006c). Halkitis, Green, Remien, Stirrat, Hoff, and Wolitski et
al. (2005) found that HIV-positive MSM who have unprotected anal intercourse have less concern about reinfection and more hedonistic expectations of sex, and are more likely to inject recreational drugs and use methamphetamine in particular. It was also found that barebackers are more
likely to believe that the responsibility for safer sex resides with their partners and not themselves (Halkitis, Wilton, Wolitski, Parsons, Hoff, and
Bimbi 2005).

A major challenge for the clinician is to help the client establish or rees-
tablish contact with friends and social networks that do not encourage drug
abuse and unsafe sex. As Finnegan and McNally (2002) point out, because
LGBT clients have frequently linked drugs and sex, they may be afraid that
any sexual activity will elicit substance abuse. This needs to be addressed
with clients as they explore how to socialize and have safe sex without
abusing substances. Because some clients have found great comfort in gay
and lesbian bars, the clinician will have to explore with them realistic ways
to make going to these venues safer. Motivational interviewing, based on
the client's stage of change, can address how substances cloud judgment
and contribute to high-risk sexual behaviors and how clients can protect
themselves from HIV and other infections. It is important to keep clients
in treatment and attempt to decrease high-risk behaviors even if abstinence
is not attained. *

Most substance users tend to use a combination of drugs, not just one.
For example, Halkitis, Palamar, and Pandey Mukherjee (2007) found that
the usage patterns of drugs such as methamphetamine, ecstasy, and GHB
among MSM are highly related across time. This suggests that clinicians
should focus on the substance use behaviors themselves and not necessarily the individual drugs that are abused. In spite of this, many treatment
approaches continue to focus on clients who abuse a particular substance.
The next section will address current approaches to clients who abuse al-

* Robert is a twenty-two-year-old gay male whose drug of choice is psilocybin (mushrooms). He states that "shrooms" make him feel good, but also cause him to lose all desire for sex and neglect his physical health and safety. After the effects wear off, he returns to risky sex and his drug-abusing friends in the gay bars. Case managers advised him to try to stay away from these buddies, but he found this quite difficult to do. He was eventually able to cut down on shrooms on week nights (because sales and transactions are slower during the week) and to stay away from the bars on weekends.

cohol, opiates, and stimulants. Particular attention will be given to clients who are LGBT when data are available.

Treatment of Alcohol Abuse and Dependence

During the 1980s most treatment facilities reflected the Minnesota Model, based upon the assumption that alcoholism is a progressive, primary disease. Counselors were typically recovering alcoholics who provided educational lectures and individual and group therapy based on the twelve steps of A.A. Most programs were in residential and inpatient settings where clients remained twenty-eight days or longer. Although similar programs still exist, they are quite expensive and used mainly by those who can afford to pay for their own treatment. Managed care systems have moved most treatment into intensive outpatient (4–6 hours per day for two or more weeks) or traditional outpatient therapy combined with A.A. involvement (once per week for about twelve weeks). Many different therapeutic approaches are offered in these programs, with cognitive-behavioral and motivational approaches receiving strong empirical support. A major national study, Project MATCH, found that cognitive-behavioral, motivational enhancement, and twelve-step facilitation therapy were all effective for clients with alcohol problems (Mattson, Del Boca, Carroll, Cooney, DiClimente, Donovan et al. 1998).

Clients presenting with alcohol abuse and dependence should also be carefully assessed for depressed mood. In a large community-based sample of lesbians, Bostwick, Hughes, and Johnson (2005) found that their rates of depression and alcohol dependence were more than double those for women in general. And unlike studies of women in the general population, lesbians' reports of lifetime depression did not decrease with age.

Treatment of Opiate Dependence

Opiates include opium, morphine, heroin, codeine, and some synthetic drugs, all highly addicting. Treatment for most clients begins with detoxification as either an inpatient or an outpatient under medical supervision. Subsequent treatment occurs in therapeutic communities, outpatient programs, twelve-step programs, and methadone treatment facilities. Newer medications, Subutex (buprenorphine hydrochloride) and Suboxone tablets (buprenorphine hydrochloride and naloxone hydrochloride) are semi-synthetic opiate derivatives that can be prescribed in private offices or substance abuse programs. These drugs reduce heroin use and cravings, have mild withdrawal symptoms, and are less toxic than other medications (Johnson, Chutuape, Strain, Walsh, Stitzer, and Bigelow 2000).

Methadone maintenance programs are quite successful in harm reduction, but continue to be controversial. Many clients attending these programs are also abusing other drugs, requiring separate treatment. For an

---

* Sunny is a thirty-two-year-old lesbian who begs in the street for spare change to buy heroin. Until she left home at age sixteen, she was raised by a single mother who shared marijuana with her and her sibling. By age seventeen she was snorting speed and smoking heroin, and several years later began injecting heroin. She has continued to use marijuana and speed periodically, but they are not her drugs of choice. She states that heroin gives her emotional relief, allows her to dissociate, and keeps her from feeling as isolated. She occasionally has female lovers, but these relationships typically end because of too much drama and competition. She feels more comfortable hanging out with male drug users in their twenties or thirties. Over the years Sunny has been diagnosed with major depressive disorder, borderline personality disorder, and antisocial personality disorder. She is not currently taking any psychotropic medications, but has overdosed several times on heroin. Because her veins have collapsed, she primarily injects in muscles, and seeks agency assistance mainly for treatment of skin abscesses.

extended discussion of the advantages and disadvantages of methadone maintenance programs, gender issues, and the children of methadone clients, the reader is referred to Friedman and Wilson 2004.

Many clients, particularly those with co-occurring disorders, have a very difficult time recovering from heroin addiction. *

Treatment of Stimulant Abuse and Dependence

Stimulants include cocaine and the amphetamines, and are highly addictive. For a review of assessment issues relevant to stimulant abuse, the reader is referred to chapter 4 of this text and to Ockert, Baier, and Coons 2004. In a study of HIV-positive MSM who use methamphetamine, Semple, Patterson, and Grant (2003) found that binge users were significantly more likely than non-binge users to have less education, to have more physical and mental health problems, and to engage in more unprotected sexual activities. Semple, Patterson, and Grant (2004) compared HIV-positive MSM who injected meth to noninjectors, and found that injectors have less education, have more social and health problems, use a greater amount of meth with more frequency, and engage in more sexual risk behaviors. Clearly, these subgroups of MSM are not being reached by prevention or early intervention programs, have low participation in ongoing treatment programs, and are continuing very high-risk behaviors.

Clients who present for methamphetamine dependence frequently suffer from co-occurring psychiatric disorders, and should be routinely evaluated for these disorders. According to Kolodny (2006), heavy meth use is often followed by mood and anxiety symptoms that may persist for weeks. There is sometimes even long-lasting brain damage in the areas associated with depressive and anxiety disorders (London, Simon, Berman, Mandelkern, Lichtman, Bramen et al. 2004), so psychiatric medication may improve treatment outcomes and help clients cope with recovery issues.

Ockert et al. (2004) propose a treatment approach for stimulant dependence based on four phases: initiation of abstinence/crash, the honeymoon phase, the wall phase, and the adjustment phase. Treatment begins with the *initiation of abstinence*, which requires hospitalization only for clients who have repeated failed attempts to abstain, severe depression, paranoid delusional thinking, suicidal ideation, and/or a completely unstructured living environment. Modalities during this phase include individual and

group behavioral therapy, twelve-step support groups, and family education. The client is stabilized emotionally by psychotropic medications ranging from antidepressants to mood stabilizers and neuroleptics.

The *honeymoon phase*, known in twelve-step programs as the "pink
cloud," occurs between 6 and 15 days into abstinence. The client is often
overconfident about remaining drug free, so the treatment focus shifts to
understanding relapse and developing a relapse prevention strategy. Urine
should be tested several times a week, and psychotropic medication is
continued even if mood has improved. Regular aerobic activity should be
encouraged, and family education about the phases of recovery continues.

The *wall phase* occurs about two and a half months after the initiation
of abstinence, and consists of mood swings between agitation and depression. The client expresses frustration and discouragement, which is best
addressed in individual and group therapy by emphasizing the biochemical
causes of the mood swings. Clients need to cognitively rehearse what will
be done if they are confronted with opportunities to use and if use actually
occurs. Relapse, if it does happen, should be dealt with in a nonjudgmental
manner. It is possible that psychotropic medication dosages may need to
be reevaluated and family counseling intensified during this phase.

The *adjustment phase* occurs about 120 to 180 days into abstinence as the
client gradually emerges from depression. Individual and group therapy
can now focus on daily living problems and underlying emotional issues of
anger, guilt, and low self-esteem. Couple and family therapy is helpful, and
psychotropic medication should be continued at least through the sixth
month of abstinence, at which time its continuation is reevaluated.

Guss (2000) notes that some gay men have developed serious problems around compulsive stimulant drug use combined with sex. After
using these drugs, the client's mood is elevated and he feels confident
and invulnerable. He also believes that he is more attractive to other men
and more successful in finding a sexual partner. When stimulant use is
continued during sex, preexisting anxieties disappear, and sex can last for
6–12 hours. If impotence ("crystal dick") does occur, Viagra can be used to
facilitate maintenance of an erection. In their studies of Latino gay men,
Díaz, Heckert, and Sánchez (2005) found that stimulants were used to enhance energy, sex, social connection, and work productivity. Bauermeister
(2007) found that the Latino gay men in his study used drugs to cope with
their sexual identity, to feel like part of the mainstream gay community,
and to reduce sexual inhibitions. Halkitis and Shrem (2006) found that

chronic users of meth were attempting to avoid unpleasant emotions and physical pain. HIV-positive MSM were more likely to use meth to avoid conflict, unpleasant emotions, and social pressures (Halkitis, Green, and Mourgues 2005). Semple, Zians, Grant, and Patterson (2006a) found that the relationship between intensity of meth use and total unprotected sex was strongest among MSM who had higher levels of impulsivity.

In doing individual therapy with these clients during the adjustment phase, Guss (2000) notes "the dynamic importance of the drug/sex addiction in maintaining a fragile or defective sense of self" (p. 110). There is often a sense of shame regarding the body and homoerotic feelings resulting from childhood experiences of being different and invisible. When parents and society do not recognize and support their emerging gay sexuality, these men have difficulty integrating their sexuality into their sense of self and relationships. When using stimulants, the invisible self becomes noticed and desired. When abstinent, they are again invisible and asexual. Ostrow and Shelby (2000) stress the importance of the therapist acting "in such a way that the patient does not feel criticized, attacked or rejected, which would repeat in the treatment the very dynamic that played a role in the formation of distressed feelings about the self" (p. 133). By not retraumatizing the gay client, an idealized transference will gradually unfold and result in the strengthening of the vulnerable self.*

There is an epidemic of crystal use among gay men in some parts of the U.S., and a harm reduction perspective is being utilized effectively with these men. McVinney (2006) discusses a number of ways that harm reduction strategies can be used with MSM who abuse methamphetamine. For example, when the client is injecting crystal, the therapist can discuss safer

---

* Jimmy is a forty-year-old man who self-identifies as gay. He was raised in a fundamentalist Christian household. His family of origin is not supportive of his being gay, and has been praying for God to save Jimmy's soul. Jimmy says that he has had sex with men only when he has been high or drunk. He meets men online on "party and play" Web sites. They meet, use methamphetamine together, and have sex. Jimmy says he feels guilty about having sex with men. He has also heard from the men he meets that sex on meth is much better than sex without meth, and Jimmy is worried that sober sex may be very disappointing.

* Cathy is a thirty-five-year-old Cuban-American lesbian who is employed in telephone sales. She describes her parents as extremely conservative and in denial about her lesbianism. She feels that they have pretty much abandoned her emotionally since she came out to them in her twenties. Cathy has used marijuana and cocaine for fifteen years, but now prefers meth, mostly because it is more affordable. When she initially expressed an interest in just reducing the amount of meth she was using, the therapist told her that she was unaware of anyone being able to control meth use, but that she would be willing to work with her if this is what she wanted. Harm reduction methods were used for over six months, but were unsuccessful. Cathy finally agreed that she needed to abstain entirely from the drug, and entered a residential treatment program.

injection strategies, such as always sterilizing syringes and avoiding needle sharing. The therapist can acknowledge the arousal properties of meth but also remind clients that crystal intoxication ("tweaking") interferes with sexual performance. If the client binges, the therapist can suggest using for just one night instead of over several days. Instead of focusing on abstinence, the therapist can target health concerns such as weight loss, HIV risk, and depression. Specific empirically supported treatment models for stimulant abuse are addressed in chapter 9.

Harm reduction strategies are not always successful. If the therapist starts where the client is and builds trust with harm reduction strategies, some clients will come to the conclusion themselves that abstinence is the best goal for them. *

Pharmacotherapy

Pharmacotherapies for substance abuse are used to attain initial abstinence, manage acute withdrawal, and prevent relapse. Medications are currently being developed or utilized in treating the abuse of alcohol, nicotine, opiates, and stimulants.

Several types of medications are being used with clients who are dependent on alcohol. *Disulfiram* (Antabuse) was approved in the 1940s, and produces nausea, vomiting, facial flushing, and headaches following a drink of alcohol. There are major problems with client compliance, so unless its administration is well supervised, it does not significantly improve abstinence rates compared to placebo (O'Malley and Kosten 2006). *Naltrexone* (Revia or Depade) is an opiate antagonist that was approved in 1994 for the treatment of alcoholism. It blocks some of alcohol's "high effects," increases the percentage of abstinent days, and reduces the risk of relapse to heavy drinking. It is particularly effective for clients with extreme craving at baseline and those with a family history of alcoholism. The most common side effects are nausea and headaches (O'Malley and Kosten 2006). *Acamprosate* (Campral) was approved in 2004 to block both craving and return to alcohol abuse. Although this medication acts on different receptors than naltrexone, both drugs show significantly lower relapse rates than those randomly assigned to placebo (McLellan 2006). It has been suggested that combining some medications could target different components of the addiction. For example, acomprosate might relieve withdrawal and naltrexone might target relapse (O'Malley and Kosten 2006).

Another promising medication for treating alcohol dependence is *ondansetron*, which reduces craving, cuts down consumption, and increases abstinence compared to placebo. This medication has few side effects, and is most effective in reducing drinking in early-onset (dependent before age twenty-five) alcoholics (Hasin, Hatzenbuehler, and Waxman 2006). Finally, some antidepressants (particularly the SSRI Zoloft) appear to reduce drinking in late-onset, but not early-onset, alcoholics. In fact, SSRIs may be counterproductive in early-onset alcoholics (O'Mally and Kosten 2006). Other medications are at earlier stages of investigation for the treatment of alcoholism. For example, *topiramate*, approved for the treatment of epilepsy, appears to reduce drinking amount and increase abstinent days in alcohol-dependent clients compared to those taking a placebo. Other medications being studied include *baclofen, gabapentin*, and *memantine* (Hasin et al. 2006).

Nicotine dependence is treated primarily by pharmacotherapy, with nicotine-replacement therapies (NRT) designed to prevent withdrawal symptoms and improve cessation outcomes. Approved methods include the patch, gum, inhaler, spray, and lozenge. NRTs are intended for short-term use, but a small minority of ex-smokers use them for years. NRTs are significantly more effective than placebos in attaining abstinence from cigarette smoking. *Bupropion* (Zyban), an atypical antidepressant, was the first nonnicotine, antismoking drug approved for sale in the United States. It is also effective compared to placebo in attaining abstinence. *Zyban* is also intended for short-term use, and can be combined with the patch for maximum effect. Side effects include insomnia, headache, and jitteriness, and the drug includes warnings about increased suicidal behaviors. A second drug, *Varenicline* (Chantix) was approved in 2006, and works by binding to nicotine receptors in the brain, reducing the symptoms of withdrawal. Following reports of depression, agitation, and suicidal behavior among clients taking this drug, the FDA announced on February 1, 2008, that Chantix may cause worsening of current psychiatric illness or cause an old psychiatric illness to reoccur. Other medications under investigation for nicotine dependence include *naltrexone, clonidine, nortriptyline* (O'Mally and Kosten 2006), and *methoxsalen* (Zickler 2000).

For clients addicted to opiates, *methadone*-replacement therapy is extremely effective. Once stabilized on methadone, clients do not experience peaks of euphoria or withdrawal symptoms, and can be maintained indefinitely on a fixed dosage (O'Mally and Kosten 2006). *LAAM*, chemically similar to methadone, needs to be taken only once every three days, but the U.S. manufacturer of this drug ceased producing it in 2005. *Buprenorphine* (Suboxone or Subutex) was approved in 2002 for treatment of opioid dependence and is effective in reducing craving for 24–36 hours. It is safer than methadone because there is lower risk of overdose and few or no withdrawal symptoms when discontinued (McLellan 2006). Finally, *naltrexone* (Naltrel) has also been approved for the treatment of opiate addiction. This medication blocks opioid effects for 48–72 hours, providing neither euphoria nor dysphoria to abstinent clients. Unfortunately, compliance has been poor, with retention rates of less than 20 percent (McLellan 2006).

Many medications have been tested for the treatment of cocaine or amphetamine dependence, but to date none have been approved. Those which hold some promise include *disulfiram, desipramine, baclofen, tiagabine, modafinil,* and cocaine vaccines (O'Mally and Kosten 2006).

There is considerable interest in the combination of behavioral and pharmacological approaches, since they target different aspects of substance abuse. Behavioral interventions can increase medication compliance and treatment retention and provide relapse-prevention skills. Pharmacotherapy can also help retain clients in treatment and increase their ability to make use of behavioral interventions (O'Mally and Kosten 2006). This may be particularly relevant to LGBT clients who are HIV-positive, due to the danger of mixing drugs and discontinuing HIV medications if they relapse on illicit drugs.

[7]
Issues Related to Specific Age Groups

In this chapter issues relevant to the assessment and treatment of LGBT children and adolescents with substance use disorders are covered. Assessment and treatment issues relevant to adult, midlife, and old LGBT clients are also discussed.

Children and Adolescents

Substance use is very common among adolescents, and LGBT adolescents are believed to be at even greater risk for use and abuse. Sexual minority adolescents report more alcohol use than their heterosexual peers (Bontempo and D'Augelli 2002), and lesbian/bisexual girls experience higher risk for alcohol problems than gay/bisexual boys relative to their heterosexual peers (Hatzenbueler, Corbin, and Fromme 2008; Ziyadeh, Prokop, Fisher, Rosario, Field, Camargo et al. 2007). The rate of smoking among LGBT youth exceeds that of the general population (Remajedi 2007). Russell, Driscoll, and Truong (2002) and Moon, Fornili, and O'Briant (2007) found that adolescents who were attracted to both sexes were at the highest risk for substance use and abuse. In addition to alcohol abuse, there has been a significant increase in methamphetamine use among adolescents (Meeks and Stevens 2004). Overall, LG youth are more likely to have recently used amphetamines and injected drugs; lesbian and bisexual females are more likely than their heterosexual counterparts to have used amphetamines, injection drugs, LSD, and marijuana (Noell and Ochs 2001). Nonmedical prescription drug use is also increasing, and an overwhelming majority of club-going young adults misuse pain killers, sedatives, and stimulants. Young lesbian/bisexual women are the most likely to abuse these drugs (Kelly and Parsons 2007). A recent meta-analysis of relevant studies found that the odds of substance use for LGB youth were on average 190 percent higher than for heterosexual youth, 340 percent higher for bisexual youth, and 400 percent higher for females (Marshal, Friedman, Stall, King, Miles, and Gold et al. 2008).

There is much less data on transgender adolescents and LGBT clients who are members of racial/ethnic minority groups. Barney (2003) found no significant differences in substance use between gay and heterosexual American Indian or Alaska Native (AIAN) adolescents. He did find that the gay adolescents were twice as likely to have considered or attempted suicide and to have been physically abused and six times more likely to have been sexually abused. Among youth aged twelve to seventeen, the rate of current illicit drug use among AIAN is about twice the overall rate among youth (18.7 vs. 9.8 percent, respectively). The rates are 10.2 percent among blacks, 10 percent among whites, 8.9 percent among Latinos, and 6.7 percent among Asians (Office of Applied Studies 2006). Underage drinking is highest among whites, followed by AIAN, Latinos, blacks, and Asians (Holder 2006). Unfortunately, reliable data are not available for sexual minority members of racial/ethnic minority groups.

LGBT youth experience the same concerns as their heterosexual peers as well as the stress of dealing with external and internalized homo/transphobia. A number of studies have concluded that increased stress and decreased social support cause elevated rates of substance use and abuse (Rosario, Hunter, and Gwadz 1997; Safren and Heimberg 1999). The development of a LGBT identity in adolescence can in itself be a lengthy and stressful process. For example, D'Augelli, Hershberger, and Pilkington (1998) found that the average age of self-awareness of sexual orientation was ten years old, the average age of self-labeling was fourteen years old, the average age of disclosure to a friend was sixteen years old, and the average age of first disclosure to family was seventeen years old. There is evidence that children are disclosing their sexual orientation to parents at younger ages than in earlier generations (Bradford 2005; Savin-Williams 2001). The need to hide sexual orientation or gender identity can lead to anxiety and depression as well as attempts at suicide. Savin-Williams and Ream (2003) note that gay male suicide attempters experience higher levels of stressors than comparable peers who do not attempt suicide. LGBT youth, particularly those who are members of ethnic minority groups, fear rejection from their families and may abuse substances in an attempt to cope with secrecy. Some studies report a higher prevalence of physical abuse by family members among LGB youth compared to their heterosexual peers (Horliss, Cochran, and Mays 2002), and bisexual adolescents appear to be at very high risk for family victimization (Robin, Brener, Donahue, Hack, Hale, and Goodenow 2002). Transgender youth feel different from others at a very young age, and are frequently told by their parents to stop acting like a "sissy" or "tomboy," resulting in their feeling shame about who they are. The more gender nonconforming they are, the more likely they are to be verbally and physically abused by their parents (Grossman, D'Augelli, Howell, and Hubbard 2005).

Homeless LGBT youth have more sexual partners, are victimized more often, and have higher rates of substance use and psychopathology than their heterosexual counterparts (Cochran, Stewart, Ginzler, and Cauce 2002). Young MSM who have been forced to leave their home because of their sexuality and are precariously housed are at significantly greater risk for drug use and involvement in HIV risk–related behaviors (Kipke, Weiss, and Wong 2007). Few of these young MSM had used drugs prior to becoming homeless (Clatts, Goldsamt, Yi, and Gwadz 2005). Consistent with these findings is the fact that LGB youth who leave home at least once are more likely to engage in frequent polysubstance use than those who do not (Wright and Perry 2006). These youth also report more high-risk sexual activity and higher levels of psychological distress. They are much more likely to be physically and sexually victimized when on the streets (Whitbeck, Chen, Hoyt, Tyler, and Johnson 2004). Although the streets are clearly dangerous, staying in school can threaten the safety of LGBT adolescents as well. They are often ostracized and ridiculed by their peers, leading to profound social isolation, anxiety, and depression (Poteat and Espelage 2007).

In addition to exposure to all of these stressors, during adolescence genetic vulnerabilities can begin to interact with psychosocial variables in extremely potent ways. While hormonal changes are in full bloom, the frontal lobes, critical for sound decision-making, will continue to mature into the twenties. This asymmetry explains the adolescent's impulsivity, increased risk taking, and decision-making based on the moment rather than the future. According to Childress (2006):

> The developmental imbalance between the brain's "GO!" and "STOP!" systems in adolescence may represent a critical period of vulnerability for exposure to powerfully rewarding drugs of abuse. The adolescent brain is able to respond to rewards, including powerful drug rewards, but the brain's systems for governing the pursuit of these rewards, and for weighing the potential negative consequences of this pursuit, are often lagging behind . . . this imbalance is a sensitive biological backdrop against which even small additional alterations in the system—by virtue of heredity, environment (including drug exposure), or their interaction—may "tilt the scales" toward addiction.   (p. 49)

Of all adolescents, transgender youth are the most vulnerable. They are subject to extreme harassment and violence from peers and adults, and are the most likely to drop out of school, become homeless, and abuse substances (Sember, Lawrence, and Xavier 2000). Their substance abuse is often accompanied by unsafe sexual practices, exposure to HIV infection, and high rates of depression. MTF transgender youth of color are at significant risk of acquiring HIV. According to Garofalo, Deleon, Osmer, Doll, and Harper (2006), these adolescents report high rates of risky sex with multiple partners, unstable housing, financial and legal problems,

---

* Olivia is an eighteen-year-old MTF who was raised by an abusive father, used drugs and alcohol in the home, and left to live on the streets at age thirteen. She has always felt she was a female, occasionally buys hormones on the black market to attempt to grow breasts, and cannot afford to have surgery. Olivia engages in prostitution for survival, and had a four-year relationship with a young man who did not identify as gay. This relationship involved considerable substance abuse and eventually became very violent. Olivia began her drug use by smoking meth, but soon began to inject it for a better euphoria. She later began to inject heroin to come down from the meth. At present, she rarely uses meth and feels superior to those continuing to do so.

and limited familial support. They can also experience medical problems related to black market self-administered hormones and, in extreme cases, attempts to remove unwanted sex organs (Lev 2004).*

Substance abuse in adolescents affects their judgment, and the resulting risky sexual behaviors put them in danger of contracting HIV (Waldo, McFarland, Katz, MacKellar, and Valleroy 2000). In addition, substance abuse further compromises the immune system, facilitating the progression of HIV. Through 2006, approximately sixteen thousand young people under age twenty in the United States have been diagnosed with AIDS, and a higher proportion of new AIDS diagnoses today are occurring among young MSM, women, and racial/ethnic minorities (CDC 2007). It is now well known that drug abuse treatment is effective HIV prevention. The combination of pharmacological and behavioral treatments affects both HIV risk behaviors and the incidence of infection (Metzger, Navaline, and Woody 1998).

There is considerable debate in the literature about the incidence and prevalence of suicidal ideation and behavior in LGBT youth. Russell and Joyner (2001) found that the overwhelming majority of sexual minority adolescents—85 percent of gay males and 72 percent of lesbian females—report no suicidality. They also found, however, that gay and lesbian youth are twice as likely than their peers to consider and attempt suicide. The evidence now strongly supports the conclusion that sexual minority youth are among those most likely to report suicidal thoughts, plans, and attempts. There is no evidence, however, that LGBT adolescents or adults are at any higher risk of completed suicide (Russell 2003). Havens, Sherman, Sapun, and Strathdee (2006) and Silenzio, Pena, Duberstein, Cerel, and Knox (2007) found that young LGB drug users reported more depressive symptoms and suicidal ideation and attempts than their heterosexual peers, and Roberts, Grindel, Patsdaughter, Reardon, and Tarmina (2004b) found that suicide attempts, especially in lesbian adolescents, continue to be a problem. Sexual minority youths who report methamphetamine use are 3.5 times as likely to have thought about or attempted suicide (Walls, Freedenthal, and Wisneski 2008). Although many have hypothesized that these attempts are related to coming out issues, there has been little research to clarify factors of etiology.†

Given the seriousness of these risk factors, there are still significant protective factors that support the emotional health of LGBT youth. Probably the most important are positive and supportive family relationships

† Frannie was sexually abused throughout childhood by male relatives, placed into numerous foster homes, and eventually ran away from a group home at age thirteen. Since that time she has been on the streets, abusing numerous drugs and engaging in unprotected sex with both males and females. She is quite involved with her street family, is continuously stressed, and has made a number of suicide attempts. Throughout the years, her drugs of choice have been meth, crack, and MDMA. Case management efforts have been unsuccessful with Frannie; she is resentful of advice to address her childhood sexual abuse, pay attention to nutrition, and stop her experimentation with heroin. At age twenty-five, she is still homeless and using meth and ecstasy together to enhance her highs.

(Tharinger and Wells 2000). Parental disapproval of drug use and consistent monitoring of activities and friends are strong protective factors, and counterbalance the influence of peers. Any factor that delays the first use of substances decreases risk. According to Miller and Carroll (2006), "In general, the later a child starts using these substances (if at all), the lower the risk of progression" (p. 300). Religious involvement is also a strong protective factor in the prevention of problematic substance use initiation among children and adolescents (Humphreys and Gifford 2006), although it is not known how religious involvement affects sexual minority youth.

Assessment

When possible, it is desirable to meet first with the adolescent and parents or parental figures, and then with the adolescent alone. The clinician should explain confidentiality issues and how the assessment information will be used, always maintaining a calm and nonconfronting presence. The techniques of motivational interviewing, discussed in chapter 5, are very effective with adolescent substance abusers. In addition, school reports and health/mental health records can aid in the assessment process. If the use of standardized screening and assessment tools is preferred, the reader is referred to CSAT 1999b for a comprehensive list.

As Olson (2000) points out, most substance abuse assessment models do not include evaluation of the adolescent's sexuality and identity formation, and this information is essential in assessing risk factors. Olson recommends including the following elements in a comprehensive substance abuse assessment: substance use history, medical history, psychiatric assessment, and social history. These elements are summarized below.

- The *substance abuse assessment* includes obtaining for each substance information about the age at first use, the pattern of use (amount, frequency, setting, route), the means of acquiring the substance, and the positive and negative effects of the use. It is also important to inquire about tolerance, withdrawal symptoms, and blackouts. What are the triggers to use, the treatment history, and attitude toward treatment?
- The *medical history* involves a physical exam and lab work that includes liver function tests, blood count, breathalyzer, and urine and blood toxicology, as well as a history of physical illnesses.
- The *psychiatric assessment* includes current and past diagnosis of ADHD, mood and anxiety disorders, suicidal thoughts and behaviors, and any other psychological disorder.
- The *social history* includes family of origin relationships, peer and romantic relationships, school performance, work history, hobbies, legal issues, religious beliefs, and trauma history. Olson also includes questions about first sexual activity, sexual orientation, masturbation, anal intercourse, and coerced sexual activities.

LGBT adolescents should be asked about their experiences with heterosexism and homophobia, their coming out experiences, and the reactions of significant others to their disclosures (Jordan 2000). Jordan is also interested in their social support network. Clinicians should specifically inquire about the adolescent's relationships with a "family of choice." In addition to all of these elements, assessment of substance abuse in a transgender client should include questions about their experiences with emergence, external and internalized transphobia, and their thinking about future transition.

Treatment

A comprehensive assessment is the foundation for decisions about the appropriate type and level of care, treatment goals, modalities, and practice

approaches. Just as adolescent substance use behavior can be conceptualized on a continuum of severity (abstinence, use, abuse, dependence),
treatment interventions are on a continuum ranging from minimal outpatient contacts to long-term residential treatment. For specific placement
guidelines for adolescent substance abusers, the reader is referred to CSAT
1998b. In considering the level of care, the clinician needs to keep in mind
the adolescent's developmental level, stage of identity development, stage
of change, and cultural context. Recommendations are given to both the
adolescent and parent figures, always avoiding reactivity and confrontation
by using motivational interviewing techniques matched to the client's current stage of change.

It is critical that the treatment plan be LGBT-affirming. If the assessment indicates a clear link between the substance abuse and the stresses
of being LGBT, individual treatment may be an appropriate initial modality
(Olson 2000). If not, a psychologically safe group should be considered.
It is recommended that groups consist of teens with similar levels of motivation and age, and that teasing and nostalgic stories of substance use
be prohibited. There is limited evidence of the effectiveness of treating
adolescents in groups (CSAT 2006b). Although twelve-step groups may
work for some, they are often not appropriate for younger LGBT teens
because of developmental issues. It is hard for many to relate to the stories of adults and to define themselves as addicts. Adolescent twelve-step
groups designed for LGBT clients would address many of these concerns.
Finally, involvement with the family is almost always appropriate when
working with LGBT adolescents. Family members need to understand how
substances affect the brain and why blaming and shaming are counterproductive. They can be empowered by stopping their enabling behaviors,
adopting a nonreactive stance, and focusing on positive reinforcement of
behaviors that compete with substance abuse.

There are significant advantages of using the harm reduction model
with adolescents. Regardless of the selected modality, the clinician needs
to acknowledge the client's position on the "stages of change" contin-
uum/spiral and formulate motivational questions that match that position. As discussed by van Wormer and Davis (2003), ambivalence is
expected, and resolving it is a major focus of the work. Confrontational
approaches do not work, and the clinician should not prematurely focus on substance abuse or force the adolescent to accept a label such as
"addict." Instead, the practitioner asks reflective open-ended therapeutic

questions, listens, and reframes the client's story in the direction of decision-making. As described in the work of Miller and Rollnick (2002), the clinician is building trust in the *precontemplation* stage by asking the adolescent's definition of the situation, assessing self-efficacy and awareness of risks, and reinforcing discrepancies between the client's and others' perceptions of the problem. In the *contemplation* stage, the clinician presents information in a neutral manner and emphasizes the client's freedom of choice. In the *preparation* and *action* stages, questions continue to slowly move the adolescent forward and roll with the resistance when it occurs. There is collaboration in developing a goal and creating a menu of options. Discussion focuses on possible strategies, potential barriers, and various ways to handle them. Commitment to an action plan is gradually strengthened.

To date, the most effective therapeutic approaches with adolescent substance abusers appear to be cognitive-behavioral therapy (CBT) and family therapy. According to Safren, Hollander, Hart, and Heimberg (2001):

> While there is no reason to believe that cognitive-behavioral therapy would be less effective with bisexual, gay, and lesbian youth than with heterosexual youth, little has been written about how to integrate issues of sexual orientation into therapy with younger individuals.   (p. 215)

The effects of homo/transphobia and chronic related stresses are at the core of the problems that are more prevalent in LGBT adolescents. Safren et al. (2001) note four stressors that are particularly important to LGB youth: harassment and violence, identity development and internalized homophobia, coming out and lack of social support, and development of relationships with LGB peers. These authors suggest that LGB adolescents can be helped by cognitive-behavioral techniques that focus on developing effective coping techniques, social support from peers and family, and more positive events in their lives. Systematic examination of thinking errors/core beliefs and active problem-solving techniques can be quite effective in reducing stressors. Freshman (2004) points out that CBT addresses substance abuse in adolescents by modifying maladaptive coping skills and addressing negative affect through anger management, assertiveness training, and relaxation techniques. Social skills training focuses on initiating social contacts and dealing with criticism. Relapse prevention deals with identifying situations that trigger use and learning alternative responses.

The other effective therapeutic approach with adolescent substance abusers is family therapy. A growing body of evidence indicates that this modality is even more effective in ameliorating substance use than individual or peer group counseling, parent education, or skill-building groups (Liddle, Dakof, Parker, Diamond, Barrett, and Tejada 2001). Family-based approaches are better able to engage and retain clients in treatment as well as reduce substance use at termination and one-year follow-up (Liddle and Dakof 1995). Ideally, then, the family should be involved in all phases of the adolescent's treatment unless this is contraindicated because of abuse or domestic violence.

There are a number of different approaches to family therapy, ranging from behavioral approaches to strategic/structural approaches to integrative approaches that include all of the subsystems with which the adolescent interacts. *Brief strategic family therapy* (Szapocznik and Williams 2000) and *multidimensional family therapy* (Liddle et al. 2001) have been shown to reduce adolescent substance use and improve family functioning.

Adolescents with substance use disorders are much more likely than their peers to have co-occurring psychiatric disorders, particularly affective disorders, anxiety disorders, ADHD, and conduct disorders (Armstrong and Costello 2002; Ciro, Surko, Bandarkar, Helfgott, Peake, and Epstein 2005). If these co-occurring disorders are not treated, the client is more vulnerable to relapse. Adolescents with ADHD, especially when it is accompanied by conduct disorder, are at high risk of developing a substance use disorder. According to Childress (2006):

> A recent study of Colorado twins found that a latent trait represented by symptom counts from ADHD and conduct disorder, along with substance abuse experimentation and novelty seeking, had an extraordinarily high heritability of .84. Even children who fail to meet the full clinical criteria for ADHD or conduct disorder may share a biological vulnerability (e.g., "disinhibition"; poor frontal function) that would increase the risk for managing the pull of rewarding drugs and their associated cues. (p. 57)

Like adults, adolescents with co-occurring disorders have poorer treatment outcomes than those who present with a single disorder. For example, ADHD and conduct disorder are characterized by lack of impulse control, which makes substance abuse treatment more difficult. Since the onset of psychiatric disorders in teens is several years earlier than the onset of substance use disorders, early behavioral interventions could possibly prevent substance abuse (Mueser, Drake, Turner, and McGovern 2006). Unfortunately, this rarely occurs, so the co-occurrence of adolescent substance abuse and mental or behavioral disorders is relatively common.

According to Mueser et al. (2006), "Unlike treatment models for adults with severe mental illness and substance use problems, no specific treatment models for youth with comorbid disorders have been rigorously evaluated" (p. 130). It is known that simultaneous treatment of co-occurring disorders is preferred and sequential treatment is likely contraindicated. Integrated simultaneous treatment means that services are provided by one agency with a single cross-trained staff. At present, two integrated evidence-based approaches hold promise for this adolescent subgroup. *Multisystemic therapy* (MST) is designed for the treatment of youth in the juvenile justice system, and *multidimensional family therapy* (MDFT) is designed for the treatment of youth with substance use disorders. Both are family-centered and deliver services in the family's home, and both report long-term reductions in substance use, delinquent behavior, and family problems (Mueser et al. 2006). It is not known how effective these models would be with LGBT adolescents with co-occurring disorders.

McLellan (2006) points out that programs designed specifically for adolescents comprise only 12 percent of all substance abuse treatment programs. In addition, there is a significant lack of insurance coverage for these programs and many of their counselors are insufficiently trained. The situation is even worse for LGBT adolescents with substance abuse and co-occurring disorders.

Once again, transgender adolescents with substance use disorders are the least likely to find adequate treatment. Treatment agencies do not have policies or programs in place to help them, are not sensitive to their needs, and often evidence clear discrimination (Bockting, Robinson, and Rosser 1998). The development of effective and culturally sensitive programs is particularly critical for transgender youth of color. Lombardi and van Servellen (2000) state that effective programs should incorporate transgender issues into discussions of identity and sexuality, assist clients in completing relevant legal and medical procedures, offer educational support services, and foster supportive peer groups and role models. There should be dedicated shelter space and housing for all LGBT youth, and they should be allowed to receive primary and specialty healthcare services without the consent of a parent or guardian (Ray 2006).

Some trangender clients are fortunate enough to locate appropriate programs.*

* JJ was adopted at age four as a biological female, and by preadolescence was huffing household cleaning products and abusing alcohol and methamphetamines. At age twelve, she was admitted to a residential facility for substance abuse and suicidal ideation, and was able to achieve abstinence. Her depression and suicidal thoughts continued, however, and she was later placed in a group home for homeless youth. JJ states that she always experienced "not feeling right," and in these treatment settings began to clarify her internal struggles. By age fifteen, she had come to identify herself as a male. JJ has been able to access counseling for his depression and support for his gender transition, and feels fully comfortable as a male. He thought in early adolescence that he was lesbian because "dykes want to be men," but today states that he is not attracted to women.

Adult, Midlife, and Old

Substance users today are more likely to be in their mid-thirties to mid-fifties or sixties than anytime in the past, and this rise in use parallels an increase in depression among baby boomers. In 2003 decedents aged 35 to 54 years accounted for more than half of the substance abuse deaths in thirty metropolitan areas (Sherer 2007). In a study of gay males, Stall, Paul, Greenwood, Pollack, Bein, and Crosby (2001) found multiple substance use (three or more illegal drugs in the previous six months) in 22 percent of men in their thirties, 14 percent in their forties, and 7 percent of men aged fifty and over. Comparable data are not available for middle-aged lesbians, bisexual, or transgender individuals.

A dramatic increase in the LGBT population over the age of sixty is expected to occur over the next decade. By 2030 there could be approximately 2–7 million older LGBT people (Shankle, Maxwell, Katzman, and Landers 2003). There are currently approximately one to 2.8 million lesbian and gay older Americans, and relatively little is known about them

(Cahill, South, and Spade 2000). It is known that ageism, loneliness, and health issues are troubling for many in this cohort. The great emphasis on youth, particularly among gay men, results in many feeling undesirable and invisible at a relatively young age. And AIDS has left many with fewer friends and support networks. LGB adults aged 60–91 years who live with domestic partners are less lonely and rate their physical and mental health more positively than those who live alone (Grossman, D'Augelli, and Hershberger 2000). Loneliness may increase significantly after the loss of a partner. Those who are themselves HIV-positive have reduced access to healthcare and social services due to AIDS-related stigma (Heckman, Heckman, Kochman, Sikkema, Suhr, and Goodkin 2002). This is of great concern because the majority of HIV-positive men over age fifty report unprotected sex since diagnosis. African American MSM over age fifty are significantly more likely than white MSM to report unprotected sex and a history of intravenous drug use (Siegel, Schrimshaw, and Karus 2004).

According to Shankle, Maxwell, Katzman, and Landers (2003), "the majority of older LGBT individuals will depend upon Social Security, Medicare and/or Medicaid as their sole means of retirement support" (p. 169), and there is practically no affordable housing designed specifically for older LGBT people. Because lesbians and gay men are denied the federal rights and privileges of marriage, their surviving partners usually suffer greater financial losses than their heterosexual counterparts. They do not have the automatic right to make medical and financial decisions for their partners, and cannot purchase continued healthcare for partners after job loss. They are not entitled to federal medical and bereavement leave, and cannot file joint tax returns or benefit from income and estate taxes. In the event of the partner's death, they cannot receive Social Security survivor benefits, will be heavily taxed on the inheritance of the partner's retirement account, and may have to pay an estate tax on homes they own jointly (Smolinski and Colón 2006). Finally, discrimination is rampant in nursing homes and senior centers, so most older gays and lesbians do not disclose their sexual orientation to healthcare workers.

Among community samples, which generally do not include data on sexual orientation, it is estimated that 6–9 percent of adults over age sixty-five drink more than two drinks per day (Bucholtz, Sheline, and Helzer 1995). They often drink in response to losses, and their alcohol problems are frequently hidden.

Perhaps a larger problem is the use of numerous prescription medications without adequate supervision. Many older adults are addicted to benzodiazepines such as Valium and Xanax. The most commonly prescribed psychoactive medications for older adults are benzodiazepines, antidepressants, and opiate/opioid analgesics, which all interact negatively with alcohol (Barry, Oslin, and Blow 2001). Age-related physical changes increase the impact of alcohol and other medications on the system, resulting in higher blood alcohol levels for longer periods of time. When combined with slower reaction times, there is a greatly increased risk of harm from accidents or falling (Bucholz et al. 1995).

Older LGBT individuals, who grew up during a period in which they were pathologized and societal attitudes toward them were extremely negative, are at higher risk for substance use disorders. In fact, epidemiological studies indicate that alcohol, tobacco, and other drug use are greater among older LGBT people than in comparable heterosexual samples (Satre 2006). One of the few studies of LGBT adults over sixty found that 9 percent could be classified as "problem drinkers," and problems were significantly greater among men than women (D'Augelli, Grossman, Hershberger, and O'Connell 2001). In a study of women over fifty, Valanis, Bowen, Bassford, Whitlock, Charney, and Carter (2000) found that 19 percent of lesbians, 14 percent of bisexual women, and 12 percent of heterosexual women drank seven or more drinks per week. Gruskin, Hart, Gordon, and Ackerson (2001), using stricter criteria for heavier drinking than Valanis et al., did

* Kathryn is a sixty-eight-year-old lesbian whose parents are both deceased. She always idealized her father, in spite of his many infidelities, and viewed her mother as cold and impossible to please. Kathryn was sent to boarding school at age eight and stayed through high school. She has never been comfortable being a lesbian and has always felt unworthy. Kathryn is quite successful professionally, but feels that her lovers use, then abandon, her. She has taken antidepressant medication for many years, and resents society's emphasis on youth and attractiveness. She is lonely, has withdrawn into a small circle of friends, and has regrets about not having children. She has always been a very heavy daily drinker, but her drinking has increased significantly since her retirement two years ago. She states that she doesn't care enough about herself to stop drinking or smoking.

not find differences by sexual orientation or heavy drinking in women over fifty. In regard to tobacco use, Valanis et al. found that 14 percent of lesbians, 10 percent of bisexual women, and 7 percent of heterosexual women used cigarettes. Gruskin et al. found smoking rates of 25 percent in lesbians and bisexual women and 13 percent in heterosexual women. There are no comparable data on older transgender individuals. *

In addition to the common stressors of aging, older LGBT people often deal with internalized homo/transphobia, low self-esteem, depression, isolation, and losses related to the AIDS epidemic. Reliance on bars for socializing is also associated with higher rates of substance use (Stall, Paul, Greenwood, Pollack, Bein, and Crosby 2001). According to Raj (2002), many older transgender individuals are poor, disabled, and without affordable housing and community support. They are thus at high risk for psychiatric problems and alcoholism.

Assessment

Brief screening tools can be used to discriminate between individuals who need thorough assessments for substance use disorders and those who do not. Two tools developed specifically for older adults are the HEAT (Willenbring and Spring 1988) and the MAST-G (Blow, Brower, Schulenberg, Demo-Dananberg, Young, and Beresford 1992), which both screen for alcohol problems. In addition to screening tools, brief nonjudgmental interventions can be very effective with this population. These interventions can last from five minutes to five brief sessions, with the goal of reducing consumption or facilitating entry into treatment. Clients are given individualized feedback regarding medical conditions that can be worsened by drinking and the risks of combining medications with alcohol. They are shown how their level of consumption compares to other older adults and are asked to identify positive and negative aspects of their alcohol use and the benefits of and barriers to change. Clients are then asked to choose a drinking goal (reduction or abstinence), followed by discussion of situational cues that trigger problem drinking. To date there have been two successful trials of brief interventions with older adults, both leading to reduced consumption at twelve months (CSAT 2001b).

When a more thorough assessment is indicated, clinicians should be aware that the criteria for alcohol dependence in the DSM IV-TR are inappropriate for most older clients. While a DSM diagnosis of substance dependence requires tolerance and/or withdrawal symptoms, older adults with late-onset patterns do not develop physiological dependence and withdrawal symptoms are hard to differentiate from symptoms of other medical conditions. More appropriate diagnostic criteria may be poor sleeping and eating habits, depression, and poor cognitive functioning (Farkas 2004).

There are three onset patterns in older adults: early, late, and intermittent (Atkinson, Tolson, and Turner 1990). Those in the *early-onset* group have had substance abuse problems throughout adulthood and often have histories of numerous treatment attempts and serious medical and psychiatric problems. They typically have limited social supports and poor psychosocial skills, often resulting in a poor prognosis. For those still wanting treatment, the focus is on the medical management of withdrawal symptoms and twelve-step involvement. For those who refuse treatment, the best approach is harm reduction, focusing on improved nutrition and medical care and physical safety.

Older adults in the *late-onset* group have developed substance use problems after midlife, following years of social drinking or abstinence. Their substance abuse may result from multiple losses, and they may be successful in hiding it for some time from family and friends. Because of the effect of substances on the older body, problems often develop rapidly, and treatment needs to address relevant loss issues. These clients typically have a support system and do not have significant medical or psychiatric problems, resulting in a very good prognosis.

Finally, older adults in the *intermittent* group have recovered from an earlier substance use problem and are experiencing a reoccurrence of their problem. These clients look similar to the late-onset group, and the reoccurrence may also be related to a significant loss. Their prognosis is very good.

Treatment

At the completion of a thorough assessment, the clinician will need to make decisions about detoxification and various treatment options. Detoxification can be more problematic for older adults due to longer withdrawal and more side effects from sedatives. Treatment options vary from traditional outpatient, intensive outpatient, and day treatment to brief inpatient and residential rehabilitation. Whatever the level of care, the clinician should take a supportive, nonconfrontive stance and involve the client's family if at all possible. Treatment may last longer and proceed at a slower pace, particularly in age-specific programs. It is particularly important to focus on coping with loss, loneliness, and depression, and on strengthening the client's social support network (Richard and Brown 2006).

Effective treatment strategies are ones that are chosen through collaboration with a client and matched to the client's stage of change. Interventions that do not match readiness can lead to an increase in defensiveness, ambivalence, and noncompliance. Therapists may blame clients and label them as resistant when interventions are ineffective, instead of recognizing the lack of match between treatment strategies and readiness. Motivational interviewing and cognitive-behavioral therapy are generally appropriate for older clients who are cognitively intact (Farkas 2004).

Because older LGBT clients with substance use disorders have been neglected by both the geriatrics and addiction fields, relevant clinical literature is very limited (Satre 2006). While there are a number of studies of group treatment with older adults, they do not include data on sexual orientation. It has been suggested that work with older lesbian women should focus on dealing with financial problems, strengthening support systems, and, when appropriate, resolving abuse issues (Finnegan and Mc-Nally 2000). All older LGBT clients in substance abuse treatment should have the opportunity to address their experiences with homo/transphobia, high-risk sexual behaviors, AIDS-related losses, and co-occurring depression and anxiety. Members of ethnic minority groups also deal with racism and heterosexism, and may not identify as gay or seek LGBT treatment resources. Jimenez (2003) found that black and Latino MSM over fifty used drugs in conjunction with unprotected sex, were also sexually active with women, and were very uncomfortable with homosexuality.

Transgender clients deal with the same therapeutic issues as LGB clients as well as lack of access to education, jobs, and healthcare. They are often isolated, discriminated against in the LGB community, and concerned with medical and psychological transition issues.

Because bars have been so central to the social lives of many older LGBT clients, building a clean and sober social network can be a significant challenge. LGBT twelve-step groups can be very helpful in this process, but these groups may not exist in rural areas. Due to the negative attitudes of healthcare providers toward LGBT clients (Claes and Moore 2000), there are advantages to specialized programs that include LGBT staff. These programs are extremely rare, and in fact there are few studies of treatment outcomes for *any* older adults. It does appear, however, that older clients are more likely to complete treatment and attain generally higher rates of abstinence than younger clients (CSAT 2001b).

[8]
Issues Related to Diversity

In this chapter, issues related to the religious, spiritual, and cultural beliefs of clients with substance use disorders are addressed. Issues specific to LGBT clients who are immigrants, have disabilities, are homeless, and/or are members of racial/ethnic minority groups are also discussed.

Religious, Spiritual, and Cultural Beliefs

Cultural, spiritual, and religious beliefs can have a profound impact on LGBT clients with substance use disorders. In discussing this impact, it is important to differentiate between religion and spirituality. According to Humphreys and Gifford (2006):

> A *religion* is an organization that comprises a set of cumulative traditions (e.g., rituals, scriptures, physical structures) and a set of beliefs about some transcendent reality in which its participants have faith. . . . *Spirituality* is an individual's personal sense of the sacred and its relationship to ultimate concerns, namely the meaning of existence, morality, suffering, and death. Spirituality may be tied to or independent from a religious tradition. (p. 258)

Religion-based LGBT prejudices are often entrenched in clients' families of origin, and families with strong convictions frequently support the views of their religion against the client. The more a family relies on religious teachings for guidance, the more negative its response to a gay or lesbian family member (Strommen 1990). Martin and Hetrick (1988) note that no other minority group is rejected from families of origin because of religious dogma.

Organized religion has a long history of perpetrating heterosexism and oppression of LGBT people. Some religions are so homo/transphobic that many clients see church membership as equivalent to staying in an abusive relationship. Haldeman (1996) points out that the foundation for the church's condemnation is the notion that homosexuality is freely chosen behavior. Based on this belief, homosexual behavior is either viewed as a sin or tolerated if the individual is celibate and seeking help for his or her "condition." In both cases, religious groups do not view LGBT families as valid, deny legal marriages to LGBT couples, and deny LGBT people the right to serve in leadership roles (Morrow and Tyson 2006). While religions do vary on the morality of LGBT people, many continue to take strong antigay positions.

Some religions also have very negative views of substance use disorders, compounding the discrimination against affected LGBT clients. According to Finnegan and McNally (2002):

> Religious homophobia does not confine its destructive effects to homosexuality. A number of fundamentalists equate homosexuality with substance abuse and view both states as self-induced, self-inflicted moral sicknesses. These homophobic people contend that all homosexuals and substance abusers have to do is repent, pray, and give up their sinful condition; that perhaps they cannot help becoming substance abusers or homosexuals, but they can (and must) become abstinent.   (p. 77)

Beliefs about substance use vary across and within religions. Christian denominations, for example, vary from Catholic tolerance of moderate drinking to Methodist endorsement of total abstinence. The Jewish religion emphasizes moderation and Islam prohibits all use of intoxicants (Humphreys and Gifford 2006). There are also significant cultural differences in how substance use is viewed. For example, many Native American tribes see drinking alcohol as a way of increasing bonding among family and friends and fear that abstaining may result in being ostracized (Beauvais 1998).

In addition to notions about substance use, some racial and ethnic groups share negative attitudes about being LGBT. Religion plays a major role in the beliefs of many minority cultures, reinforcing homo/transphobic values. LGBT individuals also challenge traditional gender roles and expectations, threatening the very structure of the family. According to Morrow (2006):

> GLB people of color also face the challenges of not being accepted for their GLB identity in their racial or ethnic communities, which are often heterosexist, and of not being fully embraced for their racial identity by the white-dominated GLB communities, where racism persists. (p. 99)

Homo/transphobia in the African American community is thus based on the black church's position that homosexuality is a sin and a purely European phenomenon and that LGBT individuals violate clearly defined gender roles (Jones and Hill 1996).

The attitudes toward LGBT people among Asian Americans derive from their countries of origin. According to Nakajima, Chan, and Lee (1996), the suppression of homosexuality is strong in eastern Asia, but there is more open-mindedness in the Philippines and Thailand. There is greater fluidity among sexual orientation, sexual behavior, and gender identity in many Asian countries, and cross-dressing is more common among lesbians and gay men there than in the West. In Confucian-oriented cultures such as China, Japan, and Korea in East Asia, sons are responsible for continuing the family line and homosexuality is seen as a significant threat to the continuation of the family name. Marriage is often prearranged, but men are free to have sexual relationships with men or women outside the marriage so long as they keep up appearances and produce sons. It is important not to disgrace one's family, so many lesbians and gay men maintain secrecy about their sexual orientation.

The Latino population in the United States is quite diverse, but all subgroups place a high value on close, supportive extended families. The Catholic Church is quite influential, and supports a traditional family structure and condemns homosexuality as a sin. Gender roles in Latino families are relatively rigid, and most families do not discuss sex or sexuality. Men are expected to be virile and hypermasculine, and extramarital relationships are quite common. Traditionally, women are expected to be sexually pure, self-sacrificing, and subservient to men. Latino males have high rates of bisexual behavior, with masculinity associated with the valued penetrator role and a feminine stance associated with the passive, denigrated role of being penetrated (González and Espín 1996). There is little literature on Latina lesbians and practically none on transgenders. According to González and Espín, "Strong familism, rigid sex roles, religiosity, and sexual silence may combine to strongly stigmatize homosexual behavior in Latino culture, because these factors tend to correlate with measures of homophobia" (p. 591).

On a more positive note, many LGBT people respect Native American spirituality, which honors "two-spirit" people as special and powerful because they are able to blend their male and female sides. These individuals do not identify as heterosexual or with traditional Western gender roles (Johnson 2000).

It is difficult to find anything in the literature regarding spiritual or religious beliefs regarding bisexuality. The dichotomization of gender and sexual categories excludes bisexuals, who have historically been a quite invisible minority. Bradford (2004) studied how cultural attitudes toward bisexuality affect bisexual men and women and found many examples of biphobia. Most of the individuals in her sample had experienced invalidation and denial of their orientation, with homophobia from straight people and biphobia from lesbians and gay people. They were rejected for having "heterosexual privilege," for not being able to admit their homosexuality, and for spreading AIDS. In essence, they did not fit into either the mainstream heterosexual culture or the lesbian/gay subculture.

It is extremely important that practitioners evaluate all LGBT clients for religious-based trauma. Many have internalized the hostile treatment and negative messages they have received, resulting in guilt, shame, low self-esteem, depression, and substance abuse (Morrow and Tyson 2006). Clinicians cannot depend upon religious organizations to address substance abuse or refer individuals for treatment. According to Humphreys and Gifford (2006):

> Although churches, temples, and mosques provide naturalistic settings for access to treatment services, clergy seldom receive training in pastoral counseling for substance use. . . . Although 94 percent of clergy report that substance use is a major concern in their congregation, only

12.5 percent ever received any training on the topic, and few clergy report referring congregants to mental health professionals for addiction
treatment.   (p. 268)

When the clinician assesses that religious-based trauma is present in
LGBT clients with substance use disorders, it must be part of the treatment plan. It may require longer-term work to address all of the psychic
wounds around religion and spirituality, but this is usually critical in terms
of lasting recovery. Ultimately, when the pain is resolved, LGBT clients can
decide what role religion and spirituality will play in their lives. Some will
decide that spirituality has little impact on their lives, and others will determine that spirituality is intrinsic to their identity. When organized religion
is important to clients, they can be assisted in finding gay-affirmative religious groups. Haldeman (1996) notes that gay or lesbian therapists, who
are often negative toward religion, should explore this area in a value-neu-
tral manner. For some clients, "the healing journey may lead away from institutional religion toward atheism and humanism, paganism and goddess
worship, witchcraft, New Age metaphysical practice, Buddhism, or some
combination of perspectives" (p. 894). Whatever the client's choice, it is the
clinician's role to consider how the belief system will serve to strengthen
the client's positive sense of self. *

* Janet is a thirty-five-year-old self-identified lesbian who has struggled with
her sexual orientation since early adolescence. She has been married for ten
years and has three young children, who she is certain would be destroyed
if she left her husband. Janet's parents are fundamentalist Christians who
believe without question that homosexuality is a sin that will be punished
by God. They have had very high expectations of Janet, are quite critical of
her, and have controlled all of her major life decisions. Janet is aware of her
internalized homophobia and has considerable shame about her attraction to
women. She feels that her drinking has gotten out of control since she fell in
love with a woman three years ago. She is not in love with her husband, hates
herself for staying with him, but feels she has no right to her own feelings
and will be judged harshly if she goes with the woman she loves. She allows
herself to feel sad only when she is alone, and believes that she will not be
able to fully find her voice until her parents die.

Many LGB clients are involved in spiritually based substance abuse programs, and there is a strong spiritual component in A.A. In fact, spiritual change is viewed as central to recovery in A.A.'s literature, although one-third to four-fifths of members report no significant changes in spirituality (Humphreys and Gifford 2006). For LGBT clients who have been victimized by homo/transphobic religious teachings, it may be impossible to accept A.A.'s emphasis on powerlessness and surrendering to a "Higher Power."

Membership in Multiple Minority Groups

Many LGBT individuals occupy double or even multiple minority–status in society. When multiple oppressions exist, treatment of substance use disorders can be even more complicated. This section will address LGBT clients who are immigrants, who have disabilities, who are homeless, and who are members of racial/ethnic minority groups.

Immigrants

Until 1990 lesbians and gay men were barred from visiting and immigrating to the United States. Currently, foreign same-sex partners of U.S. citizens can enter the country only on a temporary basis, causing considerable concern about deportation and employability (Cahill, Ellen, and Tobias 2002). The consequences of immigration are quite variable, and differ even for those in the same ethnic group. Asian and Latino immigrants, for example, may be suffering from posttraumatic stress resulting from war, living in refugee camps, and separation from their families. When they arrive in the U.S., they often face language problems, inadequate housing, and poverty. As acculturation increases, so do substance use disorders. First-generation youth are particularly vulnerable to substance abuse. Among Latinos, higher levels of acculturation are linked to higher levels of alcohol consumption, especially among women (Randolph, Stroup-Benham, Black, and Markides 1998).

In assessing substance use disorders in clients from a different culture, Amodeo and Jones (1977) suggest that the practitioner explore the cultural attitudes, values, and behaviors regarding substance use, cultural ways of seeking help, the meaning of relapse, and the available support system. The clinician must also understand the client's subgroup identity, degree of acculturation, and the context of migration (trauma history, departure circumstances, legal status). LGBT clients who are immigrants may also be dealing with stress around coming out issues and external and internalized homo/transphobia. These multiple stresses can contribute significantly to the development of a substance use disorder.

Clients with Disabilities

Although several studies indicate that individuals with cognitive or physical disabilities are at higher risk for substance use disorders than the general population, it is not known what percentage are LGBT. CSAT (1998a) estimates that co-occurring disabilities (including psychiatric disorders) affect up to 40 percent of all clients entering substance abuse treatment. While some disabilities, such as mobility impairment, deafness, and visual impairment, are fairly well reported, others, such as traumatic brain injury, learning disability, and ADHD, are probably underreported. CSAT also reports that people with disabilities are less likely to enter or complete substance abuse treatment, undoubtedly because of both architectural and attitudinal barriers.

There is little research on the needs and experiences of LGBT individuals with disabilities. It is known that lesbians and women with disabilities are independently at risk for substance use disorders (Li, Ford, and Moore 2000) and women with disabilities have high rates of stress and depression (Nosek, Howland, and Young 1997). Disability is associated with substance abuse risk factors such as poverty and lower education, and people with disabilities may have the highest rates of substance abuse of any minority population (Olkin 1999). O'Toole and Brown (2003) discuss the barriers to mental health and substance abuse treatment faced by lesbians with disabilities, and Raj (2002) discusses the barriers faced by transgender individuals with disabilities. Raj notes that a large proportion of transpeople experience co-occurring physical and mental disabilities, coupled with a fixed lower income and social isolation. Many of these individuals also suffer from HIV/AIDS. Unlike gay men, lesbians, and others with HIV/AIDS, transgender individuals have few legal protections in the workplace (Hash and Ceperich 2006).

When assessing substance use disorders in clients with disabilities, the clinician needs to be supportive and nonconfrontational, and to find out if any functional adjustments are needed. Integrated, simultaneous treatment of all problems is the most effective strategy. A harm reduction approach with attention to grief and loss issues around the disability and substance abuse may be indicated. The use of motivational interviewing and behavioral therapy is also effective (van Wormer and Davis 2003). In addition, LGBT clients may need to focus on coming out issues and external and internalized homo/transphobia.

Clients Who Are Homeless

Substance use and psychiatric disorders are much higher in homeless populations than in the general population, with prevalence of substance abuse ranging between 30 and 60 percent in the homeless (Toro, Wolfe, Bellavia, Thomas, Rowland, Daescher et al. 1999). It is not known what percentage of these individuals are LGBT. There were few studies of homeless women until the 1980s, when their numbers began to increase significantly (Anderson 1987; Anderson, Boe, and Smith 1988; Corrigan and Anderson 1984; Koroloff and Anderson 1989). Women now comprise one-fifth of the homeless population, and a substantial number have substance use disorders (Deming, McGoff-Yost, and Strozier 2002).

---

* Betty is a homeless eighteen-year-old biological male who identifies and presents as a female. She left home at sixteen and lived on the streets before seeking help at a multiservice agency for homeless youth. Her drug of choice is alcohol, and she has engaged in prostitution to survive on the streets. Her extreme alcohol abuse has resulted in hospitalization, fights, and arrest for public nuisance. After a brief incarceration, she was mandated to substance abuse counseling, and a sensitive case manager was able to arrange inpatient treatment in a women's unit, even though she was pre–hormone/surgical intervention. She benefited from the program, but after several months returned to the streets, alcohol abuse, prostitution, and violence. She eventually found her way to an outpatient program for LGBT clients that has continued to use harm reduction strategies with her. She is sixty days sober at the time of this writing.

Kammerer, Mason, and Connors (1999) discuss the difficulty that home-less transgender people have in gaining access to shelters and appropri-ate counseling. Staff will not accept MTF transgender clients in women's shelters, and most will not permit them in men's shelters unless they wear men's clothes. Like gays and lesbians, transgender individuals are disproportionately represented among street youth, and it is very difficult for them to keep jobs if they do not pass well. Clearly, all of these stressors place them at high risk for substance use disorders. *

Treatment for substance use disorders in the homeless population is most effective when combined with the provision of housing (Oakley and Dennis 1996). Harm reduction strategies include needle exchange programs, provision of supplies of clean needles, and methadone main-tenance programs. Motivational interviewing techniques matched to the client's stage of change can be very effective with this subgroup of LGBT clients (Scheffler 2004). †

† Laura is a twenty-six-year-old lesbian who spent most of her youth alter-nating between her own home and various temporary-care placements. Her mother, also a lesbian, shared marijuana with her throughout her adoles-cence, and Laura sold marijuana to subsidize her evening activities at gay/lesbian clubs. It was at one of these clubs that she did her first line of speed, which she began to combine with alcohol, marijuana, and, eventually, heroin for "relief from stress and anxiety." Heroin became her drug of choice, and she has been through numerous detox and inpatient treatment programs. She has had a few clean periods in the past five years (maximum four months), but relapses due to intense craving. She is currently taking metha-done, which she prefers to buprenorphine, because it gives her a "higher feeling." She has been able to reduce her daily heroin use to two doses, and is now interested in attaining housing and entry into another detox program.

Racial/Ethnic Minority Clients

According to Elze (2006), "Marginalization also occurs within oppressed groups, rendering women, people of color, and bisexual and transgender peo-ple invisible and universalizing the experience of white gay males" (p. 49).

Unfortunately, the same prejudices exist in the LGBT community as in the larger society. Thus, these communities also exhibit racism, Eurocentrism, classism, ageism, and homo/bi/transphobia (Bohan 1996). For example, the gay and lesbian communities marginalize transgender people and often devalue and discriminate against bisexual people. In addition to the prejudices within the LGBT communities, people of color must contend with the homo/bi/transphobia in their own racial and ethnic groups.

There are very few studies exploring the experiences of LGBT adults of color, much less those who have substance use disorders. The *African American* community is dominated by a conservative religious tradition and is less accepting of diversity in sexual orientation and gender expression than the white community (Icard 1996). There may also be resistance to substance abuse treatment due to the stigma attached to being a patient and not being able to solve one's own problems (Jones and Hill 1996).*

* Brianna is a sixteen-year-old African American lesbian who has lived with various members of her extended family since age fourteen, when her single mother was institutionalized. Many of these relatives were involved in illegal money-making activities, and alcohol was always abundant in their homes and used to excess. She initially thought that her lesbianism was a nonissue, but later learned that one relative was concerned that she "might turn another young girl into a dyke," and she was asked to leave. By this time, Brianna was dependent on alcohol, was binge drinking, and believed that her "queer self was being dissed." She has yet to become engaged in any of the substance abuse programs for sexual minority homeless youth.

Asian Americans often equate being LGBT with shaming one's family and rejecting Asian culture, which values traditional sex roles and carrying forward the family line (Chan 1995). Coming out to family members is usually quite difficult, and there is also stigma attached to substance abuse treatment. *Latino* communities tend to value procreation-based heterosexuality and highly defined gender roles, and are typically not accepting of diversity in sexual orientation and gender expression.

Latino MSM are less likely to identify as gay or bisexual than white MSM are. Díaz (1998) explains that Latino gay men have been raised in a culture in which masculinity is expressed through risk taking and sexual prowess with multiple partners. Sexual intercourse is either active (masculine) or passive (feminine), and gay men are perceived as not being "real men." Because homosexuality is shameful, Latino gay men generally separate their sexual/social and family lives. Díaz, Ayala, Bein, Heine, and Marin (2001) found that many Latino gay men report high levels of psychological distress related to racism, homophobia, and poverty. Many use alcohol and other substances to cope with feelings resulting from discrimination (Díaz and Ayala 2001). Since a higher degree of acculturation is associated with more frequent drinking, assessment and intervention need to be sensitive to the degree of acculturation (González and Espín 1996). LGBT people of color may view the coming out process as a white phenomenon that requires them to separate from their culture and family of origin, forcing a choice between the LGBT community and their racial/ethnic community. This issue needs to be explored in the substance abuse treatment of all LGBT clients of color. *

* Maria is a thirty-year-old Mexican-American who came out as lesbian after a ten-year marriage and two children. Her parents are very traditional and her father beat her up when he caught her kissing a girlfriend when she was sixteen. She felt that she never fit in the white schools she attended, and was a heavy user of alcohol, cocaine, and marijuana. She continued to feel like a misfit in her marriage, and her drug use accelerated. An affair with a female coworker led to Maria's divorce, and she reports that she gets drunk and violent when she is feeling hurt or sad. She continues to seek her parents' approval, sabotage herself, and believe that she is undeserving of happiness.

Since the beginning of the AIDS epidemic, members of racial and ethnic minority groups have been disproportionately affected by HIV/AIDS. They now represent the majority of Americans living with AIDS and the majority of new AIDS cases (CDC 2007). Latinos, representing a number of different groups (e.g., Puerto Rican, Spanish, Dominican, Columbian, Cuban, Central American, etc.), are particularly at risk for HIV infection (Shedlin and Deren 2002). Latinos have incidence rates nearly four times those of non-Latino whites (CDC 2007). In a study of HIV-positive Latino gay and bisexual men, nearly half had engaged in unprotected anal intercourse in the past twelve months. Those who had sex under the influence of alcohol or other drugs reported higher numbers of both insertive and receptive partners for unprotected sex. Depressed mood was also associated with a greater number of partners for unprotected anal intercourse (Poppen, Reisen, Zea, Bianchi, and Echeverry 2004).

There have been dramatic increases in HIV-incidence rates for black MSM, with rates almost three times higher than those of Latinos (CDC 2007). The stigma of both homosexuality and HIV in the black community results in attempts to keep both invisible. *

* Tim is a twenty-year-old African American, homeless, gay male described by his case managers as intelligent and attractive. At age seventeen, he began snorting methamphetamine with other gay street youth, liked the euphoria, and enjoyed the sex while high. He eventually began injecting meth, needing higher doses, and losing sleep and weight. As his use increased, he became more isolated and began selling the drug. His depression increased significantly and he had constant thoughts of suicide. In the next few years, Tim was in and out of jail for possession and intent to sell drugs and also contracted HIV. He is unsure of his viral transmission route because he has both engaged in unsafe sex while high and shared injection equipment with other gay men.

In order to engage and maintain LGBT individuals in substance abuse treatment, their racial and ethnic values must be understood and respected. Even though whites and African Americans have the same alcohol dependence rates, the consequences of heavy alcohol use are greater for African Americans. They are more likely to die of cirrhosis of the liver and alcohol-related car crashes and to be incarcerated and reported to child welfare authorities for substance abuse (Henriques and Manatu-Rupert 2001; Jones-Webb 1998; Rhodes and Johnson 1997). In general, national surveys find higher rates of illicit drug use by blacks than by whites or Latinos.

Latino subgroups vary significantly in the prevalence of substance use disorders, with Mexican Americans and Puerto Rican Americans having the highest rates. A recent study by Cochran, Mays, Alegria, Ortega, and Takeuchi (2007) found that Latina and Asian American lesbian/bisexual women were more likely than their heterosexual counterparts to have recent histories of depressive and substance use disorders. Latino gay men report higher rates of heavy alcohol use than their white and black counterparts, and sexual intercourse under the influence of alcohol and other drugs is common (Ramirez-Valles, Garcia, Campbell, Diaz, and Hecka-thorn 2008). In this study, only club drugs were significantly associated with unprotected sexual intercourse. In a study of Asian Pacific Islander MTF transgender individuals, Operario and Nemoto (2005) found that, in the past month, nearly one half had had sex while under the influence of substances and over half had used illicit drugs. Sex under the influence and illicit drug use were both associated with commercial sex work.

American Indian and Alaska Native (AIAN) people identify as lesbian, gay, bisexual, or two-spirit. *Two-spirit* signifies the existence of both femi-nine and masculine spirits within one person, used today to describe gen-der and sexual identities among AIAN and Canadian First Nations people. According to Balsam, Huang, Friedland, Simoni, and Walters (2004):

> Traditional indigenous values often included respect for sexual and gen-der diversity, and many two-spirits had sacred and ceremonial roles in their communities. Colonization and compulsory Christianity let to the suppression of two-spirit roles in many Native communities. Today, most two-spirits face homophobic oppression from both mainstream U.S. so-ciety and their own tribes and communities. (p. 288)

Natives have high rates of poverty, depression, and PTSD. Urban Natives are at particularly high risk for alcohol use disorders; they drink at an earli-er age, drink more frequently and in larger quantities, and experience more negative consequences compared to their non-AIAN peers (May 1996). In their study of LGB/two-spirit and heterosexual AIAN adults, Balsam et al. (2004) found high levels of sustained drinking in the entire sample. Two-spirits were more likely to drink to increase sociability, decrease feelings of inferiority, and manage their mood. Compared with their heterosexual peers, they reported higher rates of childhood physical abuse, higher levels of psychological symptoms, and significantly higher rates of lifetime illicit drug use.

In substance abuse treatment of LGB clients of color, Paz (2002) sug-gests exploring in assessment: (1) the client's cultural beliefs, customs, and practices, (2) the client's language skills, (3) specific strengths and protec-tive factors, and (4) how the treatment can be tailored to fit the client's lan-guage and culture. Clinicians need to be nonconfrontational and involve the extended family in the treatment plan. There is often considerable re-pressed rage toward experiences of racism and homo/transphobia. The use of harm reduction strategies linked to the client's stage of change supports a nonjudgmental attitude toward the user. As Woods (1998) points out, however, many African American communities are opposed to harm reduction practices, which are seen as accepting failure and giving up. Woods believes that for harm reduction to succeed in the African American community, it must be presented as a useful step toward the cessation of use.

There are currently few studies of substance abuse intervention that include sufficiently large numbers of dual (ethnicity/sexual orientation) minority–status individuals. Holder (2006) states that "at this point there have been no substantive outcome evaluations of culturally specific interventions" (p. 159).

[9]
Intervention Models

This chapter covers phases and types of substance abuse treatment, self-help programs, and the strengths perspective. Four empirically supported treatments—motivational enhancement therapy, contingency management, the matrix model, and community reinforcement—are also discussed. Smoking cessation treatment, psychodynamic therapy, relapse management, and ineffective treatment approaches are also addressed.

Phases and Types of Treatment

In the past twenty years the dominant model of substance abuse treatment delivery has become outpatient and intensive day treatment approaches. Inpatient treatment is now much less available and lengths of stay are briefer. McLellan (2006) differentiates three phases of treatment: detoxification/stabilization, rehabilitation, and continuing care. The *detoxification/stabilization* phase is for clients who are experiencing withdrawal symptoms and/or instability following prolonged substance abuse. True physiological withdrawal occurs only from alcohol, opiate, or sedative/tranquilizer dependence, but users of cocaine and amphetamines sometimes require stabilizing treatment. During this phase, clients are given medications to relieve symptoms and reduce craving, usually in a residential or hospital setting. This phase on its own is rarely effective in achieving long-term recovery.

The *rehabilitation* phase can include many different strategies, including counseling, therapy, and mutual support groups, as well as medications for substitution, psychiatric disorders, or drug craving. Outpatient programs may include individual, couple, family, and group therapy, and may last from 30 to 130 days. Intensive outpatient and day hospital programs begin with full or half-days and taper to once per week. Residential programs typically run for 30 to 90 days, and therapeutic community programs range from 90 days to one year. Methadone maintenance programs can last indefinitely.

The *continuing care* phase is designed to provide ongoing support and monitor threats to relapse. This phase is delivered in outpatient settings for approximately one year, and usually includes individual and/or group counseling and self-help groups.

In reviewing outcome research on the various types of settings, McLellan (2006) concludes:

> It has been surprising to many that the great majority of these studies have shown essentially no significant differences in effectiveness between different settings of care, in either alcohol or drug-dependent patient groups. This body of research suggests that across a range of study designs and patient populations, there appears to be no significant advantage provided by inpatient or residential care over traditional outpatient care in the rehabilitation of alcohol or drug dependence—despite the substantial difference in costs (usually 10-fold cost difference). (p. 279)

McLellan's review of randomized studies also revealed that the addition of professional couple counseling, individual psychotherapy, and/or medical care produces significantly better outcomes than substance abuse treatment alone. He concludes that the following variables are associated with better outcomes: (1) longer periods of outpatient treatment, (2) reinforcement contingent upon prosocial behaviors, (3) individual counseling, (4) proper medications, (5) supplemental social services for medical, psychiatric, or family problems, and (6) participation in a mutual self-help group. Although sexual orientation and/or gender identity is not specified in most studies, there is no reason to believe that these conclusions would not pertain to LGBT clients who are substance abusers.

Self-Help Programs

Self-help organizations are peer-led groups of individuals who share a problem and turn to each other for support and guidance (Humphreys and Gifford 2006). They do not have professional leaders and should not be equated with treatment services. Many, but not all, view recovery as a spiritual process. Examples include Alcoholics Anonymous (A.A.), Narcotics Anonymous (N.A.), Cocaine Anonymous (C.A.), Alcoholics Together, Pills Anonymous (P.A.), Methamphetamine Anonymous, and Double Trouble Recovery (D.T.R.) groups for those with co-occurring disorders. Examples of groups without a spiritual orientation include Rational Recovery, Women for Sobriety (W.F.S.), SMART Recovery, and Moderation Management (M.M.). For details about the characteristics of twelve-step programs and the twelve steps, readers are referred to Spiegel and Fewell 2004. Groups such as Al-Anon and Nar-Anon serve the families of those with substance use disorders, and focus on achieving independence from attempts to control the other's substance use and the consequences of the use. Humphreys and Gifford (2006) have reviewed matched comparison group studies of Al-Anon and conclude that "Al-Anon delivers essentially what it promises to members, namely, reduced anger, resentment, depression, and family conflict" (p. 268). Interestingly, they also found that Al-Anon does not usually produce any change in the substance abuser's behavior.

Research studies to date indicate that only about 25 percent of those who try one meeting of A.A. go on to attend ninety meetings and acquire a sponsor. But those who do go on to active participation after treatment have better abstinence rates than those who do not continue after treatment (McLellan 2006). And those who go on to help others recover in A.A. are the most likely to achieve long-term abstinence. While A.A.'s literature maintains that spiritual change is central to recovery, one-third to four-fifths of members report no significant changes in spirituality (Humphreys and Gifford 2006).

It is indisputable that millions of people worldwide have been and continue to be helped by A.A. and other self-help groups. In spite of this, A.A. has been heavily criticized in the professional literature. As noted by van Wormer and Davis (2003):

Common criticisms include: A.A. takes away power from groups that are already disenfranchised (such as women); A.A. adheres to the medical model of disease, not a strength perspective of wellness; the program is just another substitute addiction; A.A. requires total abstinence; A.A. is a religion/cult with a suspiciously white, male, dominant-culture, Christian God; A.A. forces people to constantly degrade themselves by introducing themselves as alcoholics; and A.A. meetings are undependable because they are run by nonprofessionals. (p. 378)

For a detailed discussion of these general criticisms, the reader is referred to chapter 12 in van Wormer and Davis 2003. Many of these concerns are shared by LGBT clients with substance use disorders, and some additional concerns are unique to their situation.

Cabaj (2000) points out that it may be difficult for lesbians and gay men to follow some of the suggestions of twelve-step groups and treatment programs. For example, the suggestion to avoid old friends, especially those who drink or use, may mean staying away from the only comfortable and safe social outlets available. In addition, as noted by Senreich and Vairo (2004), "The emphasis in Alcoholics Anonymous (A.A.) to recognize and surrender to a 'Higher Power' may feel repulsive to someone who has fought for years to free him- or herself from the clutches of homophobic religious teachings" (p. 412). Many LGBT clients have been blatantly denounced and rejected by their religious groups, and fundamentalist religions continue to advocate for the denial of their basic civil rights. According to Staddon (2005):

> For me, A.A. is like an open asylum for people who accept that they can't be cured but do their best to behave in ways society requires alcoholics to behave. In one sense this is the opposite of the lesbian and gay world— out and proud. (p. 75)

Tallen (1990) wonders why the LGBT communities have historically accepted twelve-step programs without questioning their relevance. Kerby, Wilson, Nicholson, and White (2005) note that many lesbians feel that these programs are hypocritical because they are based on the notion of empowerment but are the product of the oppressive white, male, Christian culture. Kasl (1992) points out that twelve-step programs reflect the biases of the white, heterosexual males who founded A.A. Tallen (1990) believes that the ideology of A.A. is inherently Christian, making it inaccessible to Jews and others:

> It is a fundamentally Christian concept to turn oneself over to God (however one understands "Him"). It certainly is a foreign concept to Jew-

ish law and life, as well as many other traditions, where the importance
of individual responsibility and autonomy is stressed. The Fifth Step
("Admitted to God, to ourselves, and to another human being, the exact
nature of our wrongs"), speaks to earthly confession, which again is a
Christian tradition and antithetical to other religions including Judaism.
The Twelfth encourages us to take the message to other alcoholics, in order to proselytize and convert. Many peoples have resisted the Christian
attempt to convert and have seen the Christian missionaries as a crucial
part of imperialism. To act as a missionary, which is clearly the intention
of the step, runs contrary to Jewish belief and law.   (pp. 398–399)

Hall (1994) conducted a feminist ethnographic study of thirty-five lesbians
in recovery, and found that they experienced A.A. as a paternalistic, authoritarian organization that was rife with sexist language and insensitive
to the impact of trauma. Reyes (1998) studied Latina lesbian and bisexual
substance users and found that they experienced A.A. as disempowering.
Many young polydrug-addicted lesbians do not feel like they fit in A.A. and
avoid meetings because the groups are too white, religious, and middle
class for them (Futcher 1995).

While most of the LGBT critique of twelve-step groups and programs
is related to lesbian and feminist issues, Shoptaw and Frosch (2000) note
that many gay men do not feel welcome at traditional A.A. meetings. The
A.A. philosophy of minimizing differences to highlight the shared problem of addiction can alienate gay men who feel "different" because of their
sexuality. In addition, other group members may be uncomfortable with
discussing sexual issues and view homosexuality as pathological. Many gay
men are also troubled by the spiritual components within A.A.

In spite of these criticisms, many LGBT individuals find that their needs
are met by traditional twelve-step meetings. *

LGBT clients who are not comfortable in traditional twelve-step meetings can be referred to specialized LGBT groups when they are available.
Unfortunately, they are often not found in small cities or rural areas. While
transgender clients may feel more comfortable in tolerant gay or lesbian
groups, bisexual clients may prefer mainstream meetings where they can
fit in as heterosexual (Finnegan and McNally 2002). There are no data
available on the level of LGBT participation in twelve-step groups, but specialized groups convene regularly in more than sixty cities in the U.S. and
in twenty countries worldwide (Borden 2007). If LGBT clients refuse to

* Linda is a forty-five-year-old bisexual who has regularly attended A.A. for fifteen years, and has been sober for fourteen years. She states that she was sexually abused by her father between the ages of ten and fifteen, and began drinking during this period. Her mother, still viewed as unsafe, is described as depressed, narcissistic, and promiscuous. When she was drinking, Linda was also quite promiscuous. In therapy since achieving sobriety, she has focused on her depression, anxiety, and feelings of being flawed and invisible. She has experienced considerable shame and fears around intimacy and abandonment. Linda prefers being seen as a lesbian because of the stereotypes of bisexuality. She states that A.A. saved her life, and she has experienced a high level of acceptance and comfort as a member. She believes in the philosophy of A.A. and cannot imagine any other solution to alcoholism. She thinks that you must be willing to look at yourself to benefit, and that you will view others as less judgmental when you become comfortable with yourself. She feels that she will be loved in A.A. no matter what her sexual orientation is. Linda's friends are all in A.A. and she attends 3–5 meetings per week.

even visit a specialized twelve-step group, the clinician needs to help them locate an alternative method of support.

The Strengths Perspective

It is important to remember that many LGBT clients have been strengthened by years of dealing with the stresses of a stigmatized identity. The strengths perspective acknowledges this by applying an empowerment focus to whatever practice theory is being utilized. The strengths perspective is based on the assumption that substance use disorders are chronic, relapsing conditions that exist along a continuum. Practice is collaborative, builds upon the strengths of the client, and respects the client's goal of safer use, moderation, or abstinence. The clinician also looks for resilience in the family of origin and views families as potential resources. Intervention is matched to the client's stage of motivation to change, and motivational interviewing techniques are used in the context of harm reduction. Clinicians roll with any resistance and reframe relapses as important learning experiences.

Again, the strengths perspective can be used with any practice theory or model to increase its effectiveness. Two empirically supported treatments, brief motivational therapy and cognitive-behavioral approaches, were discussed in chapter 5, and effective pharmacotherapy was addressed in chapter 6. The following section will address four additional empirically supported treatments: motivational enhancement therapy, contingency management approaches, the matrix model, and the community reinforcement approach. Couple and family therapy, also empirically supported, will be addressed in chapter 10.

Empirically Supported Treatment

According to Miller and Carroll (2006):

> What is different now from even 20 years ago is that scientific research has revealed a great deal about the nature of drug problems and how they can be prevented and treated. Thousands of new reports appear each year in the scientific literature, so many that it is impossible for any one person to digest them all. That's the good news. The bad news is that very little of this science has found its way into practice.   (p. xi)

Unfortunately, there is a large gap between what research shows to be effective and what is actually practiced in substance abuse treatment settings. What follows is a review of four approaches that currently have significant empirical support.

It is notable that these newer treatment strategies are rarely adapted or evaluated for use with LGBT clients or for use in LGBT-specific treatment programs. There is a great need for the integration and evaluation of newer pharmacotherapy and behavioral therapy options in the substance abuse treatment of LGBT clients (Shoptaw and Frosch 2000).

Motivational Enhancement Therapy (MET)

Motivational interviewing has been adapted to create MET, the treatment of choice for proponents of harm reduction. As discussed previously, these techniques are matched to clients' level of motivation for change with the goal of helping them find their own path to change. The efficacy of MET was first tested in Project MATCH (1997), the largest randomized controlled trial of alcohol treatment ever conducted (with 1,726 clients). This trial compared MET to an A.A.-oriented twelve-step facilitation (TSF) and cognitive-behavioral therapy (CBT). All treatment was individual, and the only group contact was in A.A. meetings. MET was offered only four times and the other two approaches were offered for twelve sessions. There were few differences in results by type of treatment, with all approaches achieving improvements in drinking outcomes one year and three years after treatment. Clients high in religiosity did better with the TSF approach and those low in motivation did better with MET. Less successful outcomes were associated with being male, having psychiatric problems, and having peer group support for drinking. The lack of a no-treatment control group precludes generalizations regarding efficacy, but this project does show that MET, a harm reduction approach, can be as effective in reducing consumption as more intensive approaches. Neither Latino nor African American samples responded differentially to the MET approach. The complete therapy manual for MET techniques can be obtained at no charge from NIAAA, Project MATCH monograph series (Miller, Zweben, DiClemente, and Rychtarik 1995).

In addition to MET, behavioral self-control training (BSCT), a form of CBT, is effective in moderating drinking when compared with abstinence-only or no-treatment control groups (Walters 2000). In an attempt to determine whether the combination of MET and CBT would be more effective than MET alone, Morgenstern, Irwin, Wainberg, Parsons, Muench, Bux et al. (2007) compared a four-session MI intervention, a combined twelve-session MI plus CBT intervention, and a nontreatment-seeking comparison group. The sample consisted of sexually active, HIV-negative MSM diagnosed with an alcohol use disorder. This is an important group since MSM are less likely to accept abstinence as a treatment goal and are at high risk for HIV transmission if they are problem drinkers (Colfax, Vittinghoff, Husnik, McKirnan, Buchbinder, Koblin et al. 2004). In Morgenstern et al's. study, 88 percent of the sample met DSM-IV criteria for alcohol dependence, but few selected abstinence as a treatment goal. At the end of treatment, participants in both treatment groups had significantly reduced their drinking and adding CBT to MI had not resulted in superior drinking outcomes. In explaining this finding, which was contrary to expectations, Morgenstern et al. concluded that "it may be that the content of the CBT sessions was too complicated and distracted the patients from a simple message about reducing drinking" (p. 82).

MET has not been tested as a stand-alone treatment for methamphetamine use disorders. At this time CBT appears to be the most effective treatment for stimulant addiction. The focus is on identifying antecedents (triggers) of use, learning skills to cope with cravings, identifying cognitive distortions, and evaluating the positive and negative consequences of use. MET is helpful in the initial stages of treatment in managing ambivalence and enhancing adherence to treatment (Irwin 2006). The combination of MET and CBT is successful in facilitating behavior change in gay and bisexual club drug users, many of whom are not interested in support groups or being lectured to (Nanin and Parsons 2006).

Motivational interviewing has also been used to attract methamphetamine-dependent MSM into more rigorous treatment programs. In one study, MSM were recruited into groups in which MI was used to discuss party drugs and sexual behavior. After attending the discussion group, 58 percent volunteered for drug addiction counseling, demonstrating that the use of MI in a two-stage strategy can be a very effective way of achieving voluntary acceptance of drug treatment (Kanouse, Bluthenthal, Bogart, Iguchi, Perry, Sand et al. 2005).

In summary, motivational enhancement therapy is effective as a stand-alone treatment for alcohol use disorders and in combination with CBT for stimulant disorders. For a review of the use of MI and CBT in the treatment of crystal methamphetamine abuse/dependence, the reader is referred to Bux and Irwin 2006.

Contingency Management Approaches

Contingency management (CM) approaches decrease substance use by providing an immediate reward to the client for remaining drug free. For example, an individual can be rewarded for a negative urine toxicology result with a voucher that can be exchanged for retail items or services. Vouchers of increasing value can be provided for successive urine samples documenting abstinence. In one randomized controlled trial, methamphetamine-dependent gay and bisexual men were assigned to one of the following treatment conditions for sixteen weeks: (1) CBT; (2) CM; (3) CBT+CM; and (4) a gay-specific CBT. Results indicated that the CM-containing conditions yielded better retention and significantly longer periods of methamphet-amine abstinence compared to CBT. In addition, sexual risk behaviors de-clined substantially (Shoptaw, Reback, Peck, Yang, Rotheram-Fuller, Larkins et al. 2005). Reducing meth use itself also had a concurrent effect on de-pressive symptoms, suggesting that clinicians should evaluate the reduc-tion of co-occurring disorders after meth treatment before beginning more intensive targeted interventions. Those who continue to suffer from depres-sion in the absence of meth use may benefit the most from additional treat-ment (Jaffe, Shoptaw, Stein, Reback, and Rotheram-Fuller 2007).

In another randomized clinical trial, Rawson, McCann, Flammino, Shoptaw, Miotto, Reiber, and Ling (2006) also found that CM was a suc-cessful treatment for reducing cocaine and methamphetamine dependence and was superior during treatment to CBT. At followup, however, CBT also reduced drug use and produced comparable outcomes. The authors con-clude that CM vouchers are useful for engaging and retaining clients in treatment, while CBT provides useful information for relapse prevention.

In summary, although providing incentives to substance abusers for abstinence is controversial, it is clear that even those who are severely de-pendent will stay in treatment and moderate or abstain from substance use when given positive incentives to do so. A recent meta-analysis found that clients receiving contingency management interventions for various types of drug abuse averaged a success rate of 61 percent, compared to 39 percent for clients in the groups to which CM was compared (Prendergast, Podus, Finney, Greenwell, and Roll 2006). Carroll and Rounsaville (2006) note that the principles of contingency management can be applied to a broad range of substance-abusing populations. For example, it could improve compliance with naltrexone treatment of opioid dependence, antiretroviral medications for substance users with HIV, and psychotropic medications for those with co-occurring disorders. It has great appeal to gay and bisex-ual men using stimulants, who are motivated by regular financial rewards but are unwilling to participate in traditional treatment programs (Strona, McCright, Hjord, Ahrens, Tierney, Shoptaw et al. 2006).

The Matrix Model

Rates of methamphetamine dependence have increased significantly in some parts of the U.S. (Winslow, Voorhees, and Pehl 2007). As no consistently effective pharmacological treatment has been developed, behavioral approaches continue to be developed and evaluated. The matrix model of outpatient treatment was originally developed during the 1980s in response to the cocaine epidemic. The model incorporated empirically supported treatment approaches such as education, family involvement, and relapse prevention into a manualized, structured, nonconfrontational cognitive-behavioral program. Early studies showed benefit of the model for cocaine and methamphetamine users (Obert, McCann, Marinelli-Casey, Weiner, Minsky, Brethen et al. 2000; Rawson, McCann, Flammino, Shoptaw, Miotto, Reiber, and Ling 1995; Shoptaw, Rawson, McCann, and Obert 1994).

The largest randomized clinical trial of psychosocial treatments for methamphetamine dependence to date is the CSAT Methamphetamine Project (MTP). This study compared the matrix model with treatment-as-usual (TAU) in eight community outpatient settings in the western U.S. All aspects of TAU varied widely across sites, representing a variety of "real world" psychosocial treatments. There was no attempt to standardize the fidelity of the TAU conditions. The matrix model in this study employed the principles of cognitive-behavioral and motivational interviewing approaches in a multicomponent protocol. Therapists trained in the model were nonconfrontational and made extensive use of positive reinforcement. The treatment package consisted of sixteen weeks of CBT groups (thirty-six sessions), family education groups (twelve sessions), social support groups (four sessions), and individual counseling (four sessions), combined with weekly breath alcohol testing and urine testing for cocaine, methamphetamine, opiates, cannabis, and benzodiazepines. Weekly attendance at twelve-step meetings was also encouraged (Rawson, Marinelli-Casey, Anglin, Dickow, Frazier, Gallagher et al. 2004).

The findings of the MTP indicated that those assigned to matrix treatment attended more sessions, stayed in treatment longer, provided more meth-free urine samples during the treatment period, and had longer periods of in-treatment meth abstinence than those assigned to TAU. Interestingly, the superiority of matrix over TAU was not maintained at one-year postdischarge (Rawson et al. 2004; Shoptaw and Reback 2007). One explanation for the ultimate similarities in outcome could be that all participants in the study were discharged to outpatient treatments that used TAU approaches (GLMA 2006).

A version of the matrix model has been developed specifically for gay and bisexual men suffering from methamphetamine dependence (Shop-

taw, Reback, Freese, and Rawson 1998). This manualized treatment protocol addresses relapse-prevention techniques as well as gay identity, sexual
behaviors, and gay establishments and events (Levounis and Ruggiero
2006). The matrix treatment manuals are available from CSAT (2006a).

Community Reinforcement Approach

The community reinforcement approach (CRA) encompasses the effective
components of many empirically supported therapies, and has a high level
of empirical support itself. The efficacy of CRA was first demonstrated thirty-five years ago with a small inpatient sample and in the early 1980s with
an outpatient trial. CRA is based on the assumption that although environmental contingencies are powerful reinforcers of substance abuse, when
properly managed, they become equally powerful reinforcers of abstinence
(Smith, Meyers, and Delaney 1998; Wolfe and Meyers 1999). The major
goals, then, are to eliminate positive reinforcement for substance abuse and
enhance positive reinforcement for sobriety. Initially, assessment of the current stage of motivation is conducted in a nonconfrontational, motivational
interviewing style. The client's substance use patterns are analyzed and
goals are set. An attempt is then made to increase positive reinforcement
that is unrelated to substance abuse. Positive activities are identified that fill
time previously filled by substance use. There is behavioral rehearsal of assertive communication skills, and significant others become involved in the
therapy (Miller, Meyers, and Hiller-Sturmhofel 1999).

CRA has been ranked in meta-analytic reviews as one of the most successful and cost-effective alcohol treatments available. When used to treat
cocaine dependence, it is typically combined with a contingency management component that provides vouchers for clean urines. The vouchers
are exchanged for material goods and increase in value as the time of con-
tinuous abstinence increases. Several studies have established the efficacy
of these programs in achieving cocaine abstinence, and studies of similar
programs addressing opiate addiction show promising results (Roozen,
Boulogne, van Tulder, van den Brink, De Jong, and Kerkhof 2004). It is
also noteworthy that CRA has been compared to treatment as usual in a
homeless youth drop-in center. Clients assigned to CRA showed statisti-
cally significant greater improvement in substance use, social stability, and
depression (Slesnick, Prestopnik, Meyers, and Glassman 2007).

Recently CRA has been expanded to address individuals who refuse to seek treatment by working through a concerned significant other. Community reinforcement and family training (CRAFT) teaches significant others behavioral techniques that allow them to give nonantagonistic feedback to the substance abuser. Family members learn to increase positive reinforcement for clean and sober behavior and withhold reinforcement for substance-using behavior. In a study of its effectiveness, Miller, Meyers, and Tonigan (1999) found that significant others assigned to CRAFT were much more successful in engaging their loved one into alcohol treatment (64 percent) than were those assigned to the Johnson Institute Intervention (30 percent) or Al-Anon (13 percent). Similarly, with illicit drug–abusing populations, Meyers, Miller, Hill, and Tonigan (1999) found that 74 percent of those trained in CRAFT methods were successful in engaging the resistant individual in treatment. In addition, all concerned significant others showed significant reductions in their own anger, depression, anxiety, and physical symptoms.

In summary, there is strong empirical support for the use of CRA and CRAFT in the treatment of substance use disorders. CRA is a relatively inexpensive outpatient treatment model that is clearly described in a treatment manual (Meyers and Smith 1995), and CRAFT is consistently superior to other approaches in engaging resistant substance-abusing individuals in treatment (Smith, Meyers, and Miller 2001).

There is one other promising approach that merits further evaluation. The ARISE model (A Relational Intervention Sequence for Engagement) is a three-level process that attempts to motivate the addicted person into treatment and the family into recovery. Level I uses motivational techniques to secure a commitment of concerned individuals to attend an initial meeting, and provides scientific information on the neurobiological process of addiction. Level II consists of two to five face-to-face sessions to attain treatment engagement, and Level III, if necessary, involves family and friends setting limits and consequences for the addicted individual (Garrett, Landau, Shea, Stanton, Baciewicz, and Brinkman-Sull 1997; Landau and Garrett 2008). Preliminary outcome data on ARISE indicate that 83 percent of addicted individuals enter treatment after their families' involvement in the model (Landau, Stanton, Brinkman-Sull, Ikle, McCormick, Garrett et al. 2004).

It is important to note that most empirically supported treatments do not differentiate outcomes by sexual orientation or gender identity, although it does appear that neither gender nor racial differences are significant in predicting retention in treatment or outcome. To date, there is a lack of well-designed evaluations of culturally specific interventions (Holder 2006). It is clear, however, that there are now a number of effective treatments for substance use disorders. According to McLellan (2006), the major problem currently is the widening gap between what is known and what is being delivered:

> The substance abuse treatment infrastructure in this country is not capable of delivering these emerging "evidence-based practices." This situation is particularly worrisome within the addiction field because, unlike other areas of health care, there is no primary care for substance use disorders. Only the specialty sector programs provide any care for addiction. The number of these programs is inadequate and many are on the brink of closing. The clinical workforce is turning over at the same rate as that in the fast-food industry. Though very serious within the adult treatment sector, the situation is even worse within the adolescent treatment sector   (p. 290)

Smoking Cessation Intervention

Tobacco dependence is the most common substance use disorder in the U.S. and the primary preventable cause of disease and deaths. Those addicted to alcohol, illicit drugs, or both have smoking rates of about 80 percent (Shoptaw, Rotheram-Fuller, Yang, Frosch, Nahom, and Jarvik 2002), and craving for tobacco appears to increase craving for the illicit drug of choice. Smoking cessation interventions are quite relevant to LGB persons because they have high rates of cigarette smoking.

Clinicians need to integrate assessment questions about nicotine dependence into their initial assessment and treatment plan, and revisit the topic in a nonjudgmental manner throughout treatment. Intervention should be matched to the client's stage of change, and motivational interviewing techniques can assist the client in thinking about quitting in the future. There is strong evidence that psychosocial treatments are effective in treatment of tobacco dependence, but few actually receive counseling as part of their treatment. For detailed information on the assessment and treatment of this disorder, the reader is referred to CSAT 2005a.

Many clients in substance abuse treatment are interested in simultaneous smoking cessation treatment. Of five clinical trials of smoking cessation in clients addicted to other substances, four found that the smoking interventions were not detrimental to other drug treatment outcomes.
One study (Joseph, Willenbring, Nugent, and Nelson 2004) found that the
smoking cessation intervention, when administered concurrently with alcohol treatment, had a significantly negative effect on alcohol outcomes.
While more clinical trials are needed, many substance abuse treatment
facilities are becoming smoke free. Unfortunately, smokers with co-occurring psychiatric disorders and those addicted to other drugs do not achieve
better cessation rates after program intervention than those in control
groups (Doolan and Froelicher 2006).

Only about 3 percent of smoking cessation attempts without formal treatment are successful. The medications approved for nicotine dependence
treatment by the Food and Drug Administration are effective for 25–30
percent of smokers on any one attempt, and this rate increases when combined with psychosocial treatment (CSAT 2005a). The challenge, clearly, is
to motivate smokers to enter and continue participation in programs that
integrate medications with psychosocial treatment.

There is a paucity of research evaluating smoking cessation interventions with LGBT smokers. The tobacco industry has targeted this population, and one study found that smoking rates for lesbians, bisexual women,
gay men, and bisexual men were 25 percent, 27 percent, 33 percent, and 20
percent, respectively (Tang, Greenwood, Cowling, Lloyd, Roesler, and Bal
2004). McKirnan, Tolou-Shams, Turner, Dyslin, and Hope (2006) found
that limited health access and greater vulnerability to depression and alcohol use contributed to the higher smoking rate of MSM. Despite this high
prevalence, Doolan and Froelicher (2006) located only one pilot study related to the LGBT population. This study consisted of a convenience sample
of 98 gay men in England who received a seven-week smoking cessation
intervention combining groupwork, nicotine replacement therapy, and ongoing peer support. At termination, 76 percent had quit smoking (Harding, Bensley, and Corrigan 2004). These are encouraging findings, but
much more research is needed. According to the Gay and Lesbian Medical
Association (2001):

Finally, there are no evaluated model programs for preventing tobacco
use in LGBT populations, no rigorous evaluations of the very few LGBT-

specific smoking cessation programs offered in a handful of localities, and no tracking treatment programs for LGBT people enrolled in managed care organizations. (p. 360)

Psychodynamic Therapy

When the client is no longer using substances or is making serious efforts to moderate use, motivational interviewing and ego-supportive counseling can be quite helpful. Outpatient individual psychodynamic therapy is usually not appropriate until clients are secure in their abstinence, since any anxiety can lead to relapse (Straussner 2004). It is useful for the clinician to have knowledge of psychodynamic theory, however, since, like harm reduction, it can facilitate the understanding of substance abuse without requiring abstinence (Seiger 2004). Khantzian (1997) postulates that substance abusers suffer from fragmented selves and their addiction is an attempt to care for the self and regulate affects. In many instances, when clients are using substances to deal with depression and low self-esteem, clinicians can reduce harm by helping them find alternate ways to handle sad feelings and impulses to use.

Cabaj (2000) agrees that supportive, motivational therapy can be helpful until the client is in recovery, at which time psychodynamic therapy can be used with gay or lesbian clients to integrate their identity and support relapse prevention. Cabaj stresses that substance abuse is not *caused* by any psychodynamic or personality variable alone; genetic and biological factors and the effects of external and internalized heterosexism and homophobia are also contributors. As discussed in an earlier chapter, Cabaj notes that pre–gay and lesbian children learn to dissociate from their true selves and create a false self in order to meet parental expectations. Dissociation and denial then become major defenses, and substance use, which causes dissociation from feelings and anxiety, "mirrors the 'comforting' dissociation developed in childhood" (p. 12). Treatment focuses on recovery from substance abuse and in mourning the loss of the false self.

Guss (2000) also discusses how substance/sex addiction in gay men maintains a fragile, invisible sense of self. Clinicians must appreciate the positive aspects of substance use and its role in self-cohesion and controlling loneliness and rejection. According to Guss:

There are several important processes that significantly contribute to positive outcomes in the treatment of these men. The establishment of a stable, containing treatment setting in which to examine the relationship with stimulant drugs and sex can lead to the reduction in defenses against awareness of the negative consequences of the addiction. This stabilizes recovery. Clarification and explication of the defenses of denial, minimization, projection, splitting, *as applied to the relationship with the drug itself,* can lead to greater persistence of the experienced need for abstinence and thus the patient is able to withstand greater storms of craving and longing (p. 121).

Many of these same points are made by Goldstein (2004) in discussing work with clients who have both substance use and borderline disorders. Goldstein stresses the importance of seeing beyond clients' self-destructive behavior to their underlying anxiety, low self-esteem, fears of abandonment, and feelings of being unlovable. These clients need to be helped to develop adaptive coping mechanisms and to understand the relationship between their feelings and their substance use. Goldstein warns that it is inadvisable to divert the treatment focus away from feelings or help clients manage their emotional states only through cognitive-behavioral methods. The validation of their feelings and needs is both soothing and ego-strengthening.

Ostrow and Shelby (2000) acknowledge that when gay men are substance *dependent,* the focus must initially be on the addiction. Even in cases of severe addiction, however, they believe that understanding the motivations for substance use is crucial to treatment. Their psychodynamically based therapy does not focus on the behavioral "symptoms" of substance abuse, but rather on the vulnerabilities of the self. In addressing the role of particular behaviors in maintaining the self, an idealized transference unfolds and enables a strengthening of the self. In essence, attending to the needs of the self allows the client to become more comfortable with himself and have less need to manage anxiety through substance use.

Relapse Management

Relapse prevention helps clients learn how to cope with craving, refuse substances, solve problems, and avoid a full-blown relapse if an episode of use occurs. Guss (2000) notes that relapse fantasies are common in the long-term treatment of substance use disorders and, in the case of gay men, "the problem usually lies not so much with *how* to maintain abstinence, as it does with the question of *why*" (p. 119). The client often wonders if a sober life can ever be an exciting or fulfilling one.

Friends and partners can affect relapse, since the risk is lower when the client's social network supports abstinence and there are fewer substance users in the network. When friends and peers do use substances, the risk for relapse is heightened (Moos 2006). Living with a substance abuser after treatment is particularly risky, significantly increasing the odds of relapse (McCrady 2006).

Relapse is commonly referred to as a "lapse" by harm reduction proponents, and is viewed as a warning signal and valuable learning opportunity. Clients are helped to avoid feelings of self-blame, review the situation leading up to the lapse, make an immediate plan for recovery, and draw on their support network (Weingardt and Marlatt 1999). Relapse-prevention therapy occurs in an outpatient setting, utilizes cognitive-behavioral techniques, and typically lasts from six weeks to six months. Lapses can be prevented if the clinician is familiar with the warning signs of relapse, which cluster under the general factor of "demoralization/depression" (Miller and Harris 2000). When clients have a depressed mood and sense of hopelessness, they should also be evaluated for the appropriateness of psychotropic medications (O'Dwyer 2004). The clinician should be cognizant at all times of the association between unresolved grief and depression and substance abuse. The relapse-prevention plan should stress getting adequate nutrition and sleep, attending a self-help support group, securing family involvement, finding healthy hobbies and new friends, and, when appropriate, random toxicology screening and medications (Gray and Gibson 2004).

Relapses are quite common among substance abusers, particularly when the treatment goal is total abstinence. When a lapse does occur, Berg and Shafer (2004) recommend five steps to help clients continue the recovery process:

1. Ask clients how they were able to stay substance-free since the last lapse and obtain the details of what has worked in the past.

2. Ask the details of how clients *stopped* the substance use during the lapse—what they did successfully even in the midst of failure.

3. Ask what clients have done since they stopped the substance abuse, so they can repeat these useful strategies earlier next time.

4. Ask how the current lapse is different from the last one, pointing out their ability to do things differently.

5. Discuss what lessons clients have learned from this lapse and what changes they need to implement immediately.

Most of the literature on relapse and prevention strategies does not deal specifically with LGBT clients. Clearly, there are the additional risk factors of homo/transphobia, both external and internalized, which must always be taken into consideration by clinicians when working with these clients.

Ineffective Practices

Miller (2006) discusses three broad approaches for which there is strong evidence of ineffectiveness in treating substance use disorders: enlightenment, confrontation, and punishment. *Enlightenment* assumes that substance abuse occurs because people lack information or insight, so programs include films and educational lectures to increase clients' knowledge base. While education does increase knowledge, "its effects on attitudes are marginal and on behavior negligible. Insight-oriented (e.g., psychoanalytic) psychotherapies similarly yield little or no change in addictions" (p. 144). *Confrontation* is the second ineffective strategy, usually provided in the form of anecdotes or victim-impact panels such as those promoted by Mothers Against Drunk Driving. While offenders attending these events often leave feeling remorseful, well-designed studies find no beneficial effect on recidivism. In some instances there can even be a paradoxical detrimental effect. Finally, a third ineffective strategy is *punishment*. Criminal sanctions for substance use are ineffective in decreasing abuse and dependence, since "punishment suppresses behavior while aversive contingencies are in effect, but does nothing to shape and reinforce alternative behavior" (p. 145).

Carlson (2006) discusses other variables that can compromise outcome in the treatment of substance use disorders. He notes that there is often a mismatch between the goals of the client and the treatment program. For example, a crack cocaine smoker may be motivated to stop using crack, but have no intention of stopping alcohol or marijuana use. In addition, waiting lists can result in the loss of a "teachable moment," and rigid admissions criteria can force clients to threaten suicide or become acutely intoxicated in order to gain entry. A major obstacle to problem recognition is the notion that a person must "hit bottom" or "be ready" in order to receive help, which is just not so. Finally, the bivariate outcome of abstinence or failure overlooks the potential benefits of reducing use or the harm of use. These ineffective strategies and barriers to effective treatment are just as relevant to LGBT clients as they are to heterosexual ones.

Practice with Couples, Families, and Small Groups

The focus of this chapter is on empirically supported substance abuse treatment with couples, families, and small groups. It will also address therapeutic issues unique to LGBT clients treated in these modalities.

There is relatively little research on LGBT couples and their relationships with their children. It is known that lesbian couples do not differ significantly from other couples in the quality of their relationships (Laird and Green 1996) but are more likely than heterosexual couples to share equally in child-rearing and household tasks (Matthews, Tartaro, and Hughes 2003). When compared to heterosexual couples, same-sex couples are less religious, more likely to share finances, and less close to their families of origin (Solomon, Rothblum, and Balsam 2004, 2005). A number of studies suggest that support from "families of choice" buffers the negative effects of low family of origin support for lesbian couples. Lesbian couples are more likely than gay couples to be monogamous when in a committed relationship. La Sala (2001) found that, as the length of gay relationships increases, so does the likelihood of establishing open relationships. In these gay nonmonogamous relationships, external sexual activities are not viewed as betrayals or indicative of failure of the primary couple relationship. In her study of bisexual men and women, McLean (2004) found that many chose to be in mutually agreeable open relationships. Contrary to stereotypes, these individuals were committed to honesty and good communication in their relationships, which were sometimes, but not always, monogamous.

Raising children is important to many LGBT individuals, and their sexual orientation is less of an issue for children than the quality of the parent-child relationship (Patterson 2000). In a comprehensive review of studies, Stacey and Biblarz (2001) found no differences in psychosocial development between children of LGB parents and children in heterosexual families. The children did not differ in self-esteem, psychological well-being, or quality of parent-child relationships. The children of transgender parents also develop normally; the majority do not suffer any mental health problems or gender-identity disturbances as a result of their parent's gender transitions (Ettner and White 2000; Green 1998).

When the LGBT parent also has a substance use disorder, he or she is usually distracted by the drug and emotionally unavailable to the child. These parents are also anxious, depressed, and irritable, typically arousing anxiety and anger in their children. While most of the research in this area focuses on the children of alcoholic parents, it is thought that similar dynamics occur with the children of stimulant and opiate abusers. Markowitz (2004) has reviewed the coping mechanisms and treatment of these children. She notes that they frequently are the parent's confidante and become overly sensitive to the needs, wishes, and unconscious signals of others. While this role provides many secondary gains, it also leaves them feeling empty and alone. Their isolation can be reduced by involvement in a therapy group, Alateen, or Narateen. Whatever the modality used, they need education about substance abuse and the normality of feeling angry. They also need to understand that they are not responsible for their parent's substance abuse and cannot control it.

Substance Abuse Treatment with Couples

Family predictors of positive treatment outcome include the presence of an intimate relationship and a partner who is clear and direct about drinking (McCrady 2006). Predictors of poorer treatment response include high levels of expressed emotion and a partner who withdraws, tolerates, or is passive about substance use. McLellan (2006) notes that the addition of professional couple therapy, individual therapy, and/or medical care produces significantly better outcomes than substance abuse treatment alone. More than twenty-five years ago, Zweben and Pearlman (1983) noticed that problem drinkers were more likely to remain in treatment and have more favorable treatment outcomes when their spouses were involved in sessions. This awareness led to his further research on the role of the spouse in motivational counseling. Since that time, behavioral couples therapy (BCT) has emerged as the most effective couple therapy method of treating substance abuse among adults. According to O'Farrell and Fals-Stewart (2006):

> With by far the largest number of studies supporting its effectiveness . . . BCT is well known among substance abuse researchers. Unfortunately, BCT is virtually unknown and unused by practitioners.   (p. vii)

These authors note that the family disease approach has been and continues to be the most widely used approach in substance abuse treatment programs. This approach uses separate, parallel programs for the patient and family member, offering the partner educational groups, individual or group therapy, and referral to Al-Anon or Nar-Anon. Partners are urged to give up attempts to influence the patients' substance use, but relationship issues are not directly addressed. BCT, on the other hand, focuses on both substance use and relationship issues in order to break up the destructive cycle in which each induces the other. BCT emphasizes abstinence as a primary goal and consists of 12–20 weekly one-hour couple sessions. The first few sessions focus on the recovery contract, which specifies behaviors that each can practice to reduce conflict around substance abuse and to reward abstinence, and relationship-focused interventions are added when abstinence is stabilized. Outcome studies indicate that clients who receive BCT have more abstinence, fewer substance-related problems, happier relationships, and lower risk of divorce than those receiving only individual therapy. BCT also reduces partner violence, improves children's functioning, and increases compliance with recovery-related medications. In addition, BCT clients are less likely to relapse than clients who get only individual substance abuse counseling.

O'Farrell and Fals-Stewart state that this outcome research has included diverse client populations, including gay and lesbian clients and their same-sex partners. For a comprehensive guidebook and session-by-session BCT treatment manual, the reader is referred to O'Farrell and Fals-Stewart 2006.*

* Jeri and Grethe, both in their forties, have been together for eight years and handle their differences by violent outbursts or withdrawal and long silent periods. Jeri is dependent on marijuana and Vicodin, and Grethe is dependent on alcohol. They are interested in reducing, but not stopping, the use of these substances. Jeri states that she grew up in a poor, neglectful family, and was sexually abused by her stepfather for many years. Both parents were Christian and very homophobic; after being abandoned on several occasions, Jeri was placed in foster care at age twelve. She is currently cut off from both parents. She self-identifies as bisexual, and was married for eight years before divorcing to be with Grethe. She states that she uses the marijuana and Vicodin to deal with depression and chronic pain, both physical and emotional. Grethe has self-identified as lesbian since preadolescence, and this is her second long-term relationship. Her father physically abused her, her younger sister, and her mother. Her family was extremely chaotic, and she views her mother as controlling, manipulative, and cold. Grethe has been cut off from both parents for many years. In her relationship with Jeri, she feels disrespected and vulnerable, and is frequently reactive and defensive. She appears to trigger in Jeri a sense of powerlessness that increases her depression, and Jeri relives her parental abandonment issues by provoking Grethe to leave her. The therapist will use motivational strategies to help the couple acknowledge the impact of their substance abuse, then move to the integration of behavioral and family systems therapies.

Substance Abuse Treatment with Families

Family therapy can be invaluable in helping members of the current family, family of origin, and family of choice understand and support the client's recovery. Unfortunately, the families of LGBT clients are often rendered invisible by clinicians, and "the full integration of family therapy into standard substance abuse treatment is still relatively rare" (CSAT 2004: xvii). In spite of this, substance abuse treatment and family therapy can be integrated to increase effectiveness, and a growing body of data is demonstrating the cost benefits of doing so. This requires an integrated model, and a large number of these have been discussed in the literature. For example, some models have been developed to help families motivate the user to seek help. Generally called "unilateral family therapies," these models focus on teaching assertive communication skills, giving feedback about the consequences of use, and making specific requests for change. These models have been shown to be effective in motivating substance abusers to seek treatment, although they have not been tailored specifically for use with LGBT clients (McCrady 2006).

Another model for motivating users to enter treatment is a formal "intervention," developed more than twenty years ago by Dr. Vernon Johnson (1986). This model requires a great deal of preparation with family members, who are coached to develop for a group meeting a script about how substances have eroded their relationship with the user. As many people as possible are present for the actual intervention, at which time the user is given the choice of two treatment facilities or continuing to use and suffer the consequences determined by the family. For a detailed discussion of the intervention process, the reader is referred to McIntyre 2004. The major difficulty with this model, as pointed out by Miller (2006), is that up to 80 percent of families refuse to go through with the intervention. For those who do complete it, however, a high percentage of the substance-abusing family members enter treatment. It is not known how effective this model is with LGBT substance abusers.

The stages of change model (Prochaska and DiClemente 1992) can be used to assess the family's readiness to change and used as a framework for treatment. Not every family member will necessarily be at the same stage of change, however, so this needs to be carefully evaluated. Van Wormer and Davis (2003) have reviewed these stages as they apply to families, but again this is not specific to LGBT families.

There are now convincing data that family therapy is effective for both adults and adolescents with substance use disorders, and family intervention is associated with higher rates of treatment retention than is treatment without family involvement (Rowe and Liddle 2003; Szapocznik and Williams 2000; Waldron and Slesnick 1998). When family members understand their role in the substance abuse and are willing to support recovery, the likelihood of long-term recovery improves (CSAT 2004). According to McCrady (2006), successful family treatment can be predicted by the absence of substance problems in other family members, a more severe substance abuse problem in the identified client, some degree of social and relationship stability, and coming to treatment after a crisis. Mc-Crady notes that there is strong empirical support for focusing on improving daily family interactions, increasing positive exchanges, and teaching constructive communication and problem solving.

In adolescents, as with adults, family therapy is strongly associated with better retention and treatment outcomes. Burkstein (2000) found family interventions empirically well-supported for youth with a substance use disorder. And for adolescents with co-occurring disorders (substance use and conduct disorder), family therapy is among the most effective interventions (Waldron 1997).

As mentioned, a number of integrated models of family therapy have been described in the literature. Unfortunately there are still many unanswered questions about their utility. As summarized by CSAT (2004):

> At present, research cannot guide treatment providers about the best specific matches between family therapy and particular family systems or substances of abuse. Research to date suggests that certain family therapy approaches can be effective, but no one approach has been shown to be more effective than others. In addition, even through the right model is an important determinant of appropriate treatment, the exact types of family therapy models that work best with specific addictions have not been determined.   (p. 16)

It follows that research is also insufficient to suggest the efficacy of any one model of family therapy over another for use with LGBT families. Lev (2004) has discussed the emergence stages of family members of gender-variant people, but notes that "clinically, little guidance is available on how to work with partners, spouses, children, and other family members" (p. 271).

It is clear, however, that many LGBT clients have unresolved issues with their families of origin, often related to their sexual orientation or gender identity. It is important to explore these unresolved issues, since they can act as emotional triggers to relapse. In some cases, clients may be hiding their sexual orientation, and treatment may or may not involve coming out to the family of origin. In other cases, the family may experience guilt about the client's homosexuality and/or substance abuse or blame each for the other's existence (Senreich and Vairo 2004). Many clients may be reluctant to include family of origin members in therapy because they fear rejection and an increase in their own anxiety.

When LGB clients do agree to engage in family of origin therapy, it can be a very powerful experience for them. As Juhnke and Hagedorn (2006) point out, "even minute insights from one's family of origin can create major self-perception shifts" (p. 280). Murray Bowen (1978), the originator of family systems theory, posited that substance abuse is one way that individuals and families attempt to manage anxiety. Bowen noted that emotional responses are passed down from one generation to another, and that clients can be helped to become more differentiated and less enmeshed in the family emotional system. A detailed case example of the use of Bowen Family Systems Theory with a lesbian couple is included in chapter 12.

There are a few instances in which family therapy is contraindicated, the major one being a history of significant domestic violence. McCrady (2006) also notes that some family interactions are so "toxic" that family therapy is inappropriate. In her view, toxic families may:

(1) Communicate in such cruel and destructive ways that involving them in therapy will increase the user's negative experience; (2) be unable to harness their hostility enough to be able to support the user's efforts to change; (3) be largely unresponsive to the therapist's interventions to teach constructive communication skills; or (4) have significant alcohol or drug problems themselves that they do not want to change.   (pp. 178–179)

For a review of the variety of family therapy approaches used in substance abuse treatment, the reader is referred to CSAT 2004. Again, it should be noted that it is not yet known which approach is most effective with LGBT clients.

Group Therapy for Substance Use Disorders

Substance abuse treatment has been intricately associated with group therapy since alcoholism was first recognized as a diagnostic entity, and group therapy has never had to fight to prove its efficacy as a modality in this field (Reading and Weegmann 2004). Straussner (2004) notes that group counseling is the treatment of choice for many substance abusers. The numerous advantages of groups include the following: providing positive peer support and pressure to abstain from substances, reducing a sense of isolation, witnessing the recovery of others, providing useful information, offering family-like experiences, learning or relearning essential social skills, providing needed structure and discipline to clients' lives, and instilling hope (CSAT 2005b).

As in individual therapy, the client's stage of change will dictate which group models and methods are appropriate at a particular time. Van Wormer and Davis (2003) point out that group progression is typically from a focus on highly structured educational issues to longer-term, more psychologically difficult issues. The principles of motivational interviewing continue to be important in group therapy, and there are now a number of group therapy manuals based on motivational interviewing. Because the highest dropout rates are seen in the first few sessions, MI groups can be used to engage and retain people in treatment. A group for new clients prior to or as part of the assessment process could shorten waiting lists and engage clients in planning the next steps in their treatment. Ingersoll and Wagner (1997) developed a manual for polysubstance-dependent clients that covers single-session, four-session, and eight-session formats. Velasquez, Mauer, Crouch, and DiClemente (2001) produced a manual describing how key aspects of motivational interviewing can be delivered within a group setting. Fields (2004) developed a manual for a five-week motivational group for clients at various stages of change. To date, effectiveness studies of MI/MET in group settings have yielded mixed results. Several studies in the 1990s showed positive outcomes, but others found that their use in a group setting was less effective than in individual counseling, and in one case group clients fared slightly worse than those in the no-treatment control group (Walters, Bennett, and Miller 2000).

More recently, three studies have supported the efficacy of motivationally enhanced group counseling. Rosenblum, Magura, Kayman, and Fong (2005) studied soup kitchen guests with substance use problems who were randomly assigned to a twelve-session motivational group. At follow-up, those in motivationally enhanced group counseling were significantly more likely than controls to participate in formal treatment and twelve-step groups and to reduce substance abuse, particularly if they started with high severity of use. In a study of college students adjudicated for violation of alcohol policy, LaBrie, Lamb, Pedersen, and Quinlan (2006) found significant reductions in drinking following a single-session group motivational enhancement intervention. Finally, Santa Ana, Wulfert, and Nietert (2007) studied the impact of adding MI in a group format to the standard treatment program of an inpatient psychiatric hospital for male and female individuals with co-occurring psychiatric and substance use disorders. The group MI protocol consisted of two 120-minute sessions. At the twelve-month followup, participants who received the MI protocol attended significantly more aftercare treatment sessions, consumed less alcohol, and engaged in less binge drinking. The treatment effect on other drug use was evident only at the one-month followup.

In some cases group therapy is clearly more helpful than individual therapy (Scheidlinger 2000). Carroll (1996) found that relapse prevention groups were more effective than other approaches for clients with more severe substance abuse and fewer coping skills. These groups normalize relapse and view it as a normal and common part of change. Clients in the group are helped to figure out what led to the lapse and develop new strategies to more effectively handle future vulnerabilities. Schmitz, Oswald, Jacks, Rustin, Rhoades, and Grabowski (1997) found that clients treated in relapse-prevention groups reported fewer cocaine-related problems than those treated in individual sessions. McKay, Alterman, Cacciola, Rutherford, O'Brien, and Koppenhaver (1997) found that cocaine abusers treated in a group setting displayed higher rates of sustained abstinence than those treated individually.

There is far less literature on group therapy for substance abuse with LGBT clients. McDowell (2002) argues in favor of creating separate gay and lesbian groups to deal with substance abuse, and values these groups for countering feelings of loneliness and alienation. Once early sobriety has been obtained, the main goals of the group are learning to cope without substances and avoiding relapse. McDowell believes the most effective groups provide a mixture of cognitive education, relapse-prevention techniques, and insights about self issues. Developmental and family of origin issues are explored when sobriety is more solid. Many clinicians have noted the value of separate groups for substance-abusing women (Beyer and Carnabucci 2002), and intimacy may be more easily attained in same-sex groups for LGBT clients as well. Although traditional therapy groups usually prohibit contact among members outside of the group, McDowell states that in gay and lesbian groups telephone or social contact may be useful, as long as the contact is discussed in the next group meeting.

Lev (2004) believes that group therapy is often a useful modality for working with transgender clients, particularly youth who are living without the support of their families. In addition to addressing their substance abuse, transgender clients in a group can "try on new identities and explore their abilities to pass in their chosen gender" (p. 224).

There are some instances in which group therapy is contraindicated. Groups may not be appropriate for LGBT clients who refuse to participate, cannot honor group agreements, are in the middle of a life crisis, cannot control their impulses, cannot tolerate strong emotions, or experience severe internal discomfort in groups (CSAT 2005b).

For a review of various group models, specialized groups in substance abuse treatment, matching clients with groups, phase-specific group tasks, and the stages of treatment, the reader is referred to CSAT 2005b. As is the case with family therapy, it is not yet known which group model is most effective with LGBT clients.

Therapeutic Issues in Couples and Family Therapy

Therapeutic issues relevant to practice with individuals were addressed in chapter 5. These included coming out, managing violence, dealing with internalized homo/transphobia, managing co-occurring disorders and HIV disease, addressing family of origin issues, and dealing with parenting issues. Issues unique to transgender clients were also discussed in chapter 5. Couples and families deal with all of these therapeutic issues as well as some that are more specific to relationships. These issues must be addressed in treating LGBT clients with substance use disorders because they often act as triggers for substance abuse. Clinicians need to assess how relationships with families of origin, partners, and families of choice contribute to substance abuse problems and/or serve as resources in supporting recovery.

Clinicians may become involved with couples as a spouse comes out as lesbian, gay, bisexual, or transgender. This often, but not always, leads to the dissolution of the marriage. In some cases, these clients knew they were LGB before entering the marriage, and in others they considered themselves heterosexual before marriage. The straight spouse is usually shocked and angry about the disclosure, feeling confused and betrayed. When the partner is coming out as transsexual, the nontranssexual partner must reexamine his or her own sexuality and make decisions about continuing as an intimate or nonintimate partner or dissolving the relationship (Brown and Rounsley 1996). These situations are even more difficult to resolve when substance abuse is involved.

When working with lesbian and gay couples, it is important that the clinician not use heterosexual relationship models. There is much more role flexibility in gay and lesbian relationships, and monogamy is not always the norm in gay relationships (Senreich and Vairo 2004). The majority of lesbian couples prefer monogamy, and an affair is often the crisis event that brings lesbian couples into therapy. Lesbian and gay couples also differ from heterosexual ones in that they must deal with homophobia and heterosexism, issues around coming out, and complicated family of origin and family of choice issues. Partners may differ on how "out" they are to their families of origin and are frequently conflicted around loyalty to their partners and families. This can result in distancing from partners or cutting off from families of origin. Finally, it is not unusual for gay and lesbian couples to include former lovers in their current social networks. These differences from heterosexual couples should not be viewed as pathological (Bepko and Johnson 2000).

In working with gay male couples, the clinician must appreciate their lack of legal recognition and role models as well as their male gender acculturation, which can make male-to-male intimacy difficult (Tunnell and Greenan 2004). Because of their male socialization, gay men may have more trouble showing emotional vulnerability to other men and may attempt to avoid direct conflict. Tunnell and Greenan suggest that substance abuse "can be reframed by the therapist as [a way] of disengaging from the partner in order to avoid open conflict through power struggles" (p. 19). In spite of these dynamics, seen in some clinical couples, Green, Bettinger, and Zacks (1996) found that the gay couples in their sample had higher ratings of couple cohesion than did the heterosexual couples. Other studies have found no significant differences between lesbian, gay, and heterosexual couples in relationship closeness and satisfaction (Peplau 1991).

In working with lesbian couples, it is important to recognize that problems with closeness are much greater when there is a history of trauma or addiction (Bepko and Johnson 2000). And many lesbian partners are at different life-cycle stages, have different racial/ethnic identifications, and vary greatly in financial status. These imbalances in professional status and power often lead to affairs. In spite of these potential difficulties, high levels of intimacy are found in many lesbian relationships (Green, Bettinger, and Zacks 1996), and parental disapproval does not appear to negatively affect these relationships (La Sala 2005).

In both gay and lesbian couples, the term *enabler* has been used to describe the ways nonaddicted partners perpetuate substance abuse by removing consequences of the abuse or attempting to control the addicted person's behavior. As Zelvin (2004) points out, nonaddicted partners may also deny their partner's substance abuse, minimize its extent, and deny their own problems. As a result, these nonaddicted partners gradually develop an unnaturally high tolerance for unacceptable behavior.

Initially, this *enabling* behavior of partners was labeled by those in the chemical dependency field as *codependency*, a concept that has since been applied to all kinds of families. Codependency is described as a primary disease present in every member of an addictive family, often worse than the disease itself. Although men can theoretically be codependent, the literature refers almost exclusively to women as having the disease. The origins are thought to be found in early childhood, at which time the individual learns a tendency to enter into addictive relationships. The codependency movement does, in fact, pathologize behaviors associated with female qualities and overlook the significance of oppressive social and political structures in shaping the personalities of women. Females are trained in excessive caretaking of others and to deny their own well-being to feel connected with others. Van Wormer and Davis (2003) suggest that instead of using the pejorative term *codependent*, "the more positive term *survivor* be applied to women (and men) who have done whatever is necessary to protect themselves and their families from the consequences of their partners' drinking and drug use" (pp. 293–294). For a more extensive critique of the concept of codependency, the reader is referred to Anderson 1994.

Clients who are in bisexual relationships (those in which at least one of the individuals is bisexual) deal with all of the therapeutic issues of gay and lesbian couples as well as some unique ones. While there is no one model for a successful bisexual relationship, there must be agreement between partners about what will be exclusive to the primary relationship and what, if anything, will occur with other relationships. Because many bisexual men engage in unprotected sex with both men and women, the threat of HIV/AIDS is a major issue. Substance use is often involved in this unprotected sex, so it needs to be openly acknowledged in therapy. When the bisexual couple has negotiated some degree of sexual "openness," issues of jealousy, boundaries, and communicating needs to partners often arise in therapy (McLean 2004). While it can be assumed that many of these therapeutic issues are experienced by transgender couples who are lesbian, gay, or bisexual, there are no empirical data to confirm this.

In summary, LGBT couples and families present an array of therapeutic issues in addition to those presented by individuals. The clinician always needs to assess the degree of internalized homo/transphobia in each partner, since a poor sense of self can be related to problems with intimacy (La Sala 2001). Gay and bisexual men in particular sometimes need help developing nonsexual intimacy and learning how to talk with other gay and bisexual men. According to Tunnell and Greenan (2004):

> The therapist's role in treatment is to create the conditions that are conducive for the men to experiment with new ways of interacting. To do that the therapist must be comfortable with encouraging two men to reveal greater emotional vulnerability, which creates greater intimacy, and be willing to access and model his or her own inherent "feminine" qualities. (p. 21)

It is possible that the presenting couple and family problems result from the projection onto partners of unresolved family of origin issues. Differentiation is increased by achieving autonomy from the family of origin while also maintaining connections with family members (Bowen 1978). La Sala (2005) found that a lesbian's partner can be an important resource in the resolution of family of origin issues, so this potential should be assessed by the clinician. Bepko and Johnson (2000) note that the Bowen approach with gay and lesbian couples involves handling conflicts around distance regulation, linking couple and family of origin functioning, and encouraging extended family work. There is a focus on power, differentiation, and triangles in addition to all of the issues unique to LGBT couples and families. Again, these issues are most productively addressed after the attainment of sobriety.

[11]
Conclusions About Practice

In this chapter specialized programs for LGBT clients and the challenges facing these programs are addressed. The use of scientific research in practice is also discussed.

Specialized Programs for LGBT Clients

Specialized treatment programs for lesbians and gay men did not exist until 1986, with the formation of the Pride Institute (Ratner 1988). Although the outcome data on these programs are limited, there is agreement that programs that are free of homophobic bias are the most beneficial to LGBT clients. This is relevant to outcome since "openly LGBT clients enter treatment with greater severity of substance abuse and other psychological problems and face greater psychosocial challenges than heterosexual clients" (Cochran and Cauce 2006:145). Because it is possible that LGBT substance abusers fare better when programs are tailored to address their unique needs (Hicks 2000), it is fair to assume that these programs might reduce treatment dropout and relapse. Unfortunately, access to LGBT-specific treatment services is quite limited. Although 11.8 percent of substance abuse treatment programs in the United States and Puerto Rico report that they offer specialized LGBT services, 70.8 percent of these programs were no different in 2004 from those offered to the general population (Cochran, Peavy, and Robohm 2007). In fact, only 7.4 percent of these programs could identify a service specifically tailored to LGBT clients.

The specialized programs in existence offer both outpatient and residential substance abuse treatment to LGBT clients. For example, Center CARE, part of the LGBT Community Center in New York City, provides assessment, referral, and individual, couples, and group counseling. Group services include recovery groups for men and women and support groups for those living with HIV/AIDS. Innovative substance abuse programs can be very helpful to LGBT clients. *

* Benito is a twenty-four-year-old gay male who came to the U.S. from Mexico with his family as a young child. Soon after arrival, he was left in the care of a relative due to the parents' inability to care for him. At eighteen, he was told to leave this home and earn his own living, beginning a five-year period of existing on the streets, occasional employment, and alcohol abuse. At age twenty-three, he was recruited by an evening-only pilot outreach program designed for homeless individuals over twenty years of age who have not been case managed. This outreach team roams the streets in the evenings identifying appropriate young people and referring willing ones to a building where a meal is served, a movie is showing, and case managers and medical services are available. Benito has utilized the gay-affirming case management and drug-abuse counseling services in this program, and now has stable employment and a comfortable level of control over his alcohol consumption.

Within programs there is also a need to develop gender-specific treatment protocols, since there are significant gender differences. A greater proportion of women receive services, enter treatment with more psychosocial problems, receive more services, and experience a greater reduction in substance use posttreatment (Marsh, Cao, and D'Aunno 2004). In her summary of treatment recommendations for women with alcohol use disorders, Staddon (2005) concludes that these clients do best in women-only groups, with individual counseling, and when they are allowed to have their children with them in residential treatment.

There are far too few specialized, affordable residential programs to meet the needs of LGBT clients. For example, the New Seasons Clinic in

Port Hueneme, California, is a tailor-made treatment center for meth addicts that includes neurocognitive rehabilitation and costs $28,000 for the one-month primary program. The nation's oldest and largest substance abuse treatment provider for LGBT individuals is the Pride Institute, offering inpatient addiction and mental health treatment in six facilities across the United States. The Lambda Center in Washington, D.C., is a dual-diagnosis treatment program offering inpatient and partial hospitalization for LGBT clients with psychiatric and/or substance abuse problems. These programs, and others like them, are able to address issues usually overlooked in mainstream programs, such as coming out, internalized homophobia, intimacy for sexual minorities, and the use of certain recreational drugs (Hicks 2000).

Programs specializing in the unique needs of transgender clients with substance use disorders remain in particularly short supply. One such program is the Transgender Recovery Program, a residential substance abuse and mental health treatment program for MTF transgender women in San Francisco. This program reported an 81 percent success rate in retaining clients in its first nine months, which was attributed to affirming clients' identities as women, providing transgender staff, and developing peer support and community ties (Oggins and Eichenbaum 2002).

To date, there are not enough controlled studies to demonstrate the effectiveness of specialized treatment settings compared to mainstream programs. Though not a controlled study, Pride Institute commissioned an outcome analysis of their clients compared to those from five inpatient programs in three eastern U.S. cities. Pride Institute clients showed similar improvements in substance use problems at long-term followup, as well as favorable reductions in psychiatric problems (McLellan 1991). Cochran, Peavy, and Robohm (2007) point out that future research needs to clarify what exactly a specialized LGBT program should look like:

> For example, what kinds of training and experience should the treatment provider(s) and support staff have? What issues and concerns should be addressed in the treatment? What resources and referral information should be available? Does the sexual orientation or gender identity of the treatment provider(s) matter? (p. 170)

In reviewing evaluations of substance abuse treatment specifically for MSM, Shoptaw and Frosch (2000) note that these settings rarely adapt or evaluate new treatment strategies. For example, gay-specific settings have not reported on the use of pharmacotherapy in treating MSM with substance use disorders. Shoptaw and Frosch conclude that these specialized programs

> often integrate general recovery strategies with interventions that address issues specific to the concerns of MSM in recovery. Still, when such services exist, they typically feature a 12-step or recovery model, implying needs for integration of these new pharmacotherapy and behavioral therapy options in settings specific to treating MSM.   (p. 198)

In summary, there are compelling reasons LGBT clients should receive specialized substance abuse treatment. This type of treatment may be required to attract these clients to treatment and retain them long enough for them to benefit from services. But the content of these specialized programs must be defined more explicitly, they must include empirically supported treatments, and they must be subjected to controlled outcome research.

Use of Scientific Research in Practice

In New Mexico in 2004 a "think tank" conference was convened to bring together leading addiction scientists to share their research and discuss implications for practice. In summarizing the findings from this conference, Miller and Carroll (2006) conclude:

> We do have available an impressive range and depth of science regarding the nature, causes, course, and resolution of drug problems. That breadth of information is not often gathered together and synthesized, and certainly society has not adequately applied even a fraction of this science in practice.   (p. 293)

Miller and Carroll go on to note that funding cutbacks are dismantling the treatment infrastructure, specialist programs are competing for survival, and "interventions are rarely even nominally based on scientific knowledge" (p. 294).

Miller and Carroll make a number of recommendations for intervention, based on the current scientific knowledge base. They acknowledge that change begins with motivation and that brief motivational interventions often trigger change. These can be followed by other effective strategies, such as positive reinforcement and substitute agonist medications. Families can also be helped to learn to reinforce behavior incompatible with drug use. Better outcomes are associated with clinicians who are competent in expressing accurate empathy and delivering a range of evidence-based interventions. Finally, effective supervision can occur only when supervisors observe (via audio or videotape) what clinicians are actually *doing* with clients.

In addition to the "think tank" conference in 2004, the National Quality Forum (NQF) convened a workshop of experts to discuss evidence-based treatment for substance use disorders (National Quality Forum 2005). Consistent with the conclusions of the "think tank" experts, this group identified empirically supported practices as motivational interviewing and enhancement therapy, contingency management, pharmacotherapy, and couples/family therapy. They also identified cognitive-behavioral therapy and community reinforcement therapy as effective practices. They identified as *ineffective* any of the following as a standalone treatment for substance use disorders: acupuncture, relaxation therapy, didactic group education, biological monitoring of substance use, and detoxification. In addition, ineffective practices include individual psychodynamic therapy, unstructured group therapy, confrontation as a principal treatment approach, and discharge from a treatment program in response to relapse.

It is quite unfortunate that the findings of these two groups of addiction experts have not been consistently integrated into practice. It is critical that clinicians become proficient in these recommended practices and implement and evaluate them in all treatment modalities utilized with LGBT clients with substance use disorders.

Case Study

A Lesbian Couple with a Substance Use Disorder

The following case reflects a model of couples therapy used by the author (Anderson 1995) that integrates knowledge of substance use disorders with family-centered therapy and focuses on both family of origin and family of creation issues. The model is strengths-based and utilizes techniques from motivational interviewing, cognitive-behavioral therapy, and family systems therapy.

Assessment

Fusion in Lesbian Couples

Much of the clinical literature on lesbian couples focuses on the concepts of fusion, merging, or enmeshment (Burch 1982, 1986, 1987; Decker 1984;

The material presented in this chapter has been adapted from "Addressing heterosexist bias in the treatment of lesbian couples with chemical dependency," *Journal of Feminist Family Therapy* 7.3/4 (1995): 87–113. This material is used with the permission of the Haworth Press. Article copies are available from the Haworth Document Delivery Service: docdelivery@haworthpress.com.

Krestan and Bepko 1980). Mencher (1990) notes how patterns of intimacy in lesbian couples have been pathologized as fusion, and concludes that the relationship characteristics most valued by lesbian couples are those that would be labeled as "fusion." Bowen (1978) has been unfairly criticized for devaluing the "feminine" relationship orientation and overvaluing separateness and autonomy. In fact, he repeatedly emphasized the importance of balance, viewing a fused and reactive emotional position, not a relationship orientation, as problematic. As Walsh and Scheinkman (1989) point out, poorly differentiated people are dominated by their emotions and are overdependent on others, either too closely fused, reactively distanced, or cut off from their families. Differentiation always involves the maintenance of self *in relation to* one's family, being *both* separate and connected. Autonomy and intimacy are equally valued and not mutually exclusive (Nelson 1989).

Pearlman (1989) believes that intense emotional bonding occurs in most relationships to varying degrees. In some, it is present mainly during sexual or emotional closeness. In others, "it is a normative preference for intense connection which can include some loss of individuality" (p. 78). In still others, it is more permanent and includes excessive dependency and loss of self. Intense bonding may appear more easily in lesbian relationships because of similar socialization, joining forces against a hostile world, or many other reasons. When it is excessive, couples complain of feeling trapped, bored, or overwhelmed by conflict, or become involved in outside affairs. But extreme closeness is not in itself pathological (Falco 1991), and it is even possible that what is normative for lesbian couples may be healthy for all couples (Brown 1989). In my experience the intense emotional connection experienced by lesbian couples is indeed the most valued aspect of their relationship.

When this pattern of intimacy evolves into excessive dependency and loss of self, the couple may seek treatment. One such couple, Arlene and Carol, came into therapy because their initially intense and close relationship had become distant and conflictual. Carol was feeling lonely and rejected, and Arlene was feeling trapped and considering having an affair. Arlene had learned in childhood to keep her feelings to herself, stay in control, and avoid self-pity. Trusting, expressing affection, and becoming vulnerable were unsafe; one could stay safe by withdrawing. Carol described herself as a shy, only child who was lonely, dependent, and terrified of conflict and rejection. Both had distanced themselves from their families of origin and had turned to the other to compensate for earlier losses. Carol, under extreme stress from employment problems, became increasingly demanding of emotional support. Arlene reacted by becoming more distant and withdrawn. Carol was depressed and drinking heavily by the time of their first appointment. They both yearned for their initial intimacy without the anxiety associated with being too close or too distant.

Codependency

As discussed previously, adherents of codependency define it as a primary disease present in every member of an addictive family, involving dependence on approval from others for one's self-worth and identity. Work focusing on codependency often requires clients to view themselves as having a disease stemming from a dysfunctional family of origin, not as members of an oppressed group who have been socialized to be dependent.

The concept of codependency is not useful in dealing with women with relationship difficulties. Instead of demanding that lesbian couples separate, the challenge is to help them define a separate sense of self within the relationship (Bushway 1991; Sloven 1991). The concept of codependency lacks validity, pathologizes characteristics associated with women, involves generalizations about alcoholic families that focus on pathology, and encourages separation rather than connection with the family of origin (Anderson 1994).

Treatment

The significant others of lesbian couples may include the family of origin and the extended family of lesbian friends. Lesbian couples are much more likely than heterosexual couples to rate friends rather than family members as providers of social support (Morris, Waldo, and Rothblum 2001), but they frequently want and need strong connections with their families of origin and bring unfinished business from those relationships into their current ones. For this reason I believe that adequate treatment of lesbians with substance use disorders must take a family perspective that includes both the families of origin and created family systems. The next section of this chapter will discuss such a model.

A Proposed Model

There are a number of models of couples therapy that can be used when one partner is still drinking; these focus either on active methods of motivating the alcohol abuser to change or on detachment and self-care of the nonalcoholic partner. This chapter will not address this situation but will focus instead on those cases in which the lesbian couple is voluntarily seeking help for problems related to alcohol abuse or dependence in one or both partners.

Pasick and White (1991) note that few clinicians are trained to reconcile traditional alcohol treatment with family-centered therapy. While addiction treatment typically addresses alcohol abuse before any other problem and focuses on denial in the alcoholic client, family-centered therapists work toward changing the family instead of the identified client and do not impose their opinions on the family. In interpreting these two models, Pasick and White propose that

> the goals of treatment are to support the addicted client while challenging the chemical use, and to support the family's recovery while challenging the underresponsible and overresponsible behavior of its members. The centerpiece is a therapeutic stance founded in part on feminist ideals, one of which is collaborative, respectful, non-hierarchical, and appropriately responsible.   (p. 89)

Traditional alcohol treatment counselors and family therapists typically disagree about the etiology of alcoholism in women. Although alcohol dependency is heavily controlled by genetic vulnerability in lesbian women, internalized homophobia can result in tremendous anxiety and self-hatred, sometimes assuaged by alcohol. The ultimate etiological model will consider both genetic vulnerability and environmental reactivity.

The specific treatment model proposed here reflects the integration of my own experience and the adapted models of Wetchler, McCollum, Nelson, Trepper, and Lewis (1993) and Bepko (1989). The model assumes that relationship patterns are repeated multigenerationally and that current relationships play a role in maintaining alcohol abuse. Thus, both historical and present family processes become part of the treatment focus (Wetchler et al.).

Stage 1: Developing a Collaborative Therapeutic Alliance

The initial interview is framed as a consultation during which I discuss with the couple their concerns, and we make a decision about working together. I assume an active questioning role in this session, taking a thorough substance use history, inquiring about relationship issues, and determining whether substance abuse is central to the couple's problems or concurrent with or secondary to an underlying psychiatric disorder. In the latter case, when appropriate, the client is encouraged to obtain an evaluation for psychotropic medication after abstinence is established.

I ask what solutions have been attempted by the couple. In most cases, ongoing drinking has resulted in clear and painful imbalances in underresponsible and overresponsible behavior. There is discussion of how standard responses to drinking, usually controlling or protective behaviors, can contribute to the maintenance of the problem. Feelings of anger, depression, and anxiety are normalized. Education about alcohol abuse and dependency is provided if appropriate. The focus is on coping skills that are working. Severe relationship problems are not addressed until sobriety is well established.

When sufficient trust has been established, typically by the second or third interview, a multigenerational family genogram is completed for each partner. In this process the clients tell their stories about family emotional relationships, substance abuse, physical and sexual abuse, family rituals, family strengths, family heroines and heroes, and other important relationships and social supports. Clients are routinely asked about other gay or lesbian family members. Although it is typical to focus almost exclusively on alcohol abuse early in treatment, some lesbian clients may need to deal initially with issues around their sexual orientation. It is critical to explore both internalized heterosexism and sexism and to recognize the multiple sources of stress under which lesbians function. A deliberate lesbian affirmative approach validates the couple's lifestyle, recognizes the oppression they face, and actively helps them deal with it (Fassinger 1991).

When clients are alcohol-dependent (i.e., evidence tolerance, withdrawal symptoms, or a pattern of compulsive use), abstinence is the most appropriate goal. Although it is optimal that they stop drinking immediately, many alcohol-dependent clients are not capable of this and need ongoing therapeutic support for their attempts to achieve sobriety. I do not refuse to work with couples when one or both are having trouble abstaining, but if a client has numerous relapses without increasing intervals of sobriety between episodes, I encourage her to seriously consider an intensive out-patient or residential treatment program.

In the first phase of treatment clients are encouraged to avoid situations that trigger drinking and to develop resources and activities that reinforce abstinence and take the place of time spent drinking. Clients are encouraged to create supportive environments by meeting more lesbian couples, becoming involved in lesbian groups, and shopping around for an appropriate self-help group. Involvement in some type of sobriety support group is enormously helpful in achieving and maintaining abstinence. I discuss with all clients the philosophy and format of Alcoholics Anonymous, Rational Recovery, Women for Sobriety, and Secular Organizations for Sobriety. After visiting several groups, most clients are able to find one consistent with their particular needs and values. As they begin this shift to a sober lifestyle, their defenses are supported and redirected instead of interpreted and confronted, in order to keep anxiety and the subsequent risk of drinking to a minimum.

Although Bepko (1989) states that in the beginning phase of treatment it may be more effective to work with the alcoholic woman alone, she makes this point while discussing heterosexual couples. My own experience indicates that working with the lesbian couple from the beginning and throughout treatment is the most honoring of their relationship and the most supportive of long-term recovery.*

* CASE EXAMPLE
Rewriting and Reclaiming Histories of Loss

Sarah, a thirty-six-year-old attorney, and Cate, a thirty-four-year-old medical illustrator, were referred by their internist because of Cate's alcohol problem and couple communication problems, both of which had worsened over the course of their two-year relationship. In the initial interview I established the norm of having them talk through me to the other, allowing me to hear both of their stories and blocking them from defending their own position. All of my questions were about the self rather than the other or the relationship. A genogram of each woman began the process of understanding how current problems were related to past losses.

Sarah stated that she no longer felt close to Cate, that Cate drank excessively and was rarely there for her. She periodically tried to control Cate's drinking, but typically just withdrew. She described a distant relationship with her older sister and a very uncomfortable, tense relationship with her sixty-eight-year-old mother, whom she described as extremely quiet, never initiating conversations or expressing feelings. She described her father as having been uninvolved with the family. He had died unexpectedly six years earlier, and his death had never been discussed. Sarah stated that she was angry about having always been invisible to both parents, and acknowledged that she would like to be closer to her mother. She would like them to be able to talk about her father's death and Sarah's adult relationships. She had come out to her mother ten years earlier, with little response, but had never told her father she was a lesbian. Sarah knew very little about her grandparents and nothing about her great-grandparents.

Cate described a pattern of alcohol use that had become of increasing concern to her over the past ten years. In the past two years she had noticed increased tolerance and mild withdrawal symptoms on Mondays. She had made several unsuccessful attempts to control her drinking, avoided social activities that were alcohol-free, and recognized that her drinking was destroying her relationship with Sarah. Although she was still functioning adequately in her profession, her productivity had declined significantly in the past few years. Cate viewed her mother as an angry, anxious, cold woman with whom she had never connected, while she described her father as an alcoholic, violent, and physically abusive to her mother. She had a distant relationship with two older brothers, both alcoholic. She had little knowledge of her extended family. Cate had come out to her mother eight years earlier. Her mother begged her not to tell her father, and she never had. Cate's alcohol dependence appeared to have connections to both unresolved family of origin issues and internalized homophobia, and perhaps with genetic predisposition. She acknowledged that her drinking increased dramatically when she felt anxiety around contacts with her family, or when she was exposed to sexist or homophobic attitudes in the workplace.

At the end of her first interview, I shared with the couple my thinking about Cate's alcohol problem, namely, that she was psychologically and physically dependent and that abstinence was the appropriate goal. She adamantly refused referrals for intensive outpatient treatment and outpatient detoxification, but did agree to start shopping around for an appropriate self-help group. I ended the first interview by asking the couple to think about how alcohol was used to "make it safe" in the relationship, and what the loss would be to them if the problem did not exist.

The first stage of our work together focused on developing activities that would substitute for the time Cate spent drinking, and on respectfully challenging her denial about the consequences of her drinking. Cate was supported in her attempts to avoid going to bars to drink with friends, and in her participation in positive activities such as yoga, piano lessons, political activism to defeat an antigay ballot measure, and joining a lesbian self-help group. She was able to follow through to some extent with all of these activities. The couple was advised to avoid all anxiety-provoking situations. They also were encouraged to discuss their concerns about reactions to their lesbianism. Both talked at length about the hurt they experienced from not having their relationship taken seriously by relatives. There was enormous joy and celebration over the siblings' marriages, whereas their commitment to each other was ignored. I asked questions about what these events triggered for each of them, and what they did to cope with these injustices.

Stage II: Challenging Behaviors and Expanding Alternatives

This stage usually begins when the alcohol-dependent client has less conscious conflict about abstinence, is taking responsibility for her own drinking behavior, and is beginning to resolve grief around losses due to alcohol and the loss of alcohol itself. Some couples have unrealistic expectations around sobriety, and may be destabilized by abstinence. The therapist should always be aware of this possibility, and normalize this phenomenon for the couple.

This phase focuses on the improvement of communication and conflict-resolution skills and making explicit the connection between present and past family patterns (Wetchler, McCollum, Nelson, Trepper, and Lewis 1993). Zacks, Green, and Marrow (1988) stress the importance of building on each woman's strengths and viewing high cohesiveness as a positive sign of satisfaction rather than a negative sign of enmeshment or fusion. As mentioned, therapists need to help lesbian clients find a sense of self within healthy connections rather than focusing on autonomy, separation, or codependency (Bushway 1991). Clients may need to grieve the loss of "heterosexual privilege" in the family of origin and learn ways to challenge parental homophobia (Murphy 1989).

If couples are struggling with alcohol abuse and lack of differentiation, each can be helped to (1) develop her own friends and activities, (2) define her own boundaries, set limits, and be assertive, and (3) voice disagreement in nonreactive ways (Zacks et al. 1988). As Bepko (1989) points out, an important goal is to change patterns of underfunctioning and overfunctioning that serve to maintain drinking problems. The therapist needs to assess the adaptive consequences of the alcohol abuse for the relationship, with the objective of attaining relationship goals without the use of alcohol. It is a mistake, however, to assume that shifting the system will eliminate the need for alcohol. As noted by Bepko (1989), "The relationship between the addict and the drug needs to be disrupted as well. Systemic change is a necessary, but not sufficient, response to an addiction" (p. 407). Bepko also notes that A.A. and Al-Anon tend to reinforce gender stereotypes and do not encourage women to take differentiated positions. Although some lesbian clients find support in lesbian A.A. groups and alternative twelve-step programs, therapists need to be ready to counteract unhelpful sexist and homophobic messages espoused by some of these groups.*

* SARAH AND CATE IN STAGE II

As our work continued it became clearer that Sarah and Cate had similar types of unfinished business with their original families. Both had reactively distanced from their families and looked to the relationship to make up for earlier losses and provide feelings of being safe and special. Although both complained of too much distance in the relationship, their tendency to alternate pursuing and distancing behaviors indicated that they both needed the distance to stay safe. Their anxiety about feeling abandoned by their parents seeped into their relationship, further intensifying each partner's feelings of loss. Cate once stated, "Her coldness makes me so anxious . . . she's like a critical parent . . . I'm so afraid that she'll leave."

In the first few months of treatment, Cate had two brief relapses, which were framed as opportunities to learn more about herself and her grief around the loss of alcohol. As she began to take more responsibility for her drinking behavior, our work began to focus more on the connections between the current relationship, alcohol problems, and families of origin. Both identified multigenerational family themes of loss, lack of safety, and distancing though alcohol abuse and emotional cutoffs. I began to talk about how the distance they felt in their relationship was more about the sadness and anxiety each brought into the relationship than about what the other was doing. As we moved toward exploring the impact of unfinished business on their current needs for distance and on Cate's use of alcohol, I continued to focus my questions on self issues (Freeman 1992). I asked, for example: What do you want from your partner that you feel you did not get from your original family? What gets stirred up in you (how do you explain it to yourself) when your partner is not there for you? What losses does this remind you of? How do you take care of yourself when you feel you are not good enough? What is different about you when your needs *are* met? How do you teach your partner what you need when you feel sad and alone? What is going on with you when you need your partner to be different? If you changed the way you perceived your partner, how would you have to be different in the relationship?

Stage III: Consolidating Change

In this phase of treatment clients become more aware of the early warnings of relapse and of methods of coping with potential problems (Wetchler, McCollum, Nelson, Trepper, and Lewis 1993). Because the need for abstinence has been internalized, more difficult relationship problems, which often elicit anxiety, may now be addressed. This phase of treatment continues to focus on the needs of women as individuals as well as on the needs of the relationship. I agree with Bepko (1989) that longer-term Bowen-based family of origin interventions will maximize sustained change.*

* SARAH AND CATE IN STAGE III

As we moved into our next stage of work Cate had been abstinent for four months and had a sound understanding of early warning signs of relapse. She had very effective ways of dealing with anxiety and craving and was an active member of her lesbian A.A. group. In this stage she spent a great deal of time discussing chronic feelings of self-hatred and shame about being a lesbian. Both she and Sarah had ongoing concerns about being "out" in the workplace. I continued to validate their lifestyle as well as their legitimate concerns around coming out issues. As alcohol was removed as a distancing issue, anxiety in the relationship temporarily increased and both expressed new concerns about the future of their relationship. It was at this point that I began to question and gently challenge their stories about their original families. I asked each what the loss would be to them of changing their story about their mother or father. What would each lose by giving up their old issues with their parents? How would they go about discovering new stories about their families? What would it stir up in them if they were less anxious and reactive when with their families?

Stage IV: Family of Origin Work

Although some couples with alcohol problems choose to terminate therapy at the end of stage III, most wish to strengthen their relationship by now focusing on unresolved family of origin issues. Lesbians who are alcohol-dependent may have problematic relationships with their families of origin whether or not they have told them about their sexual orientation (Holleran and Novak 1989). As Freeman (1992) notes, unresolved loss issues with the family of origin often lead to relationship problems in adulthood since it is hard to give to a partner what has not been received from one's original family. Clients' stories about their unfinished needs in their families of origin are replicated in some form in their current relationships. In order to rewrite their own stories, they must hear their parents' stories and observe their parents' anxiety without needing to fix, control, or distance from them. When this is mastered, they will be less anxious and needy in their current relationships and much less likely to relapse into drinking in times of stress.

The difficulty of coming out to parents and siblings is compounded by coming out as an alcoholic, which often results in profound feelings of failure in the parents (Nardi 1982). Questions about disclosure to parents may permeate all phases of therapy with lesbian couples. For those who have not come out to their family, the last phase of therapy often involves continued discussion of the implications of secrecy and disclosure, the recognition of different timetables for coming out, and preparation for disclosure. The risks involved in coming out should never be underestimated, and the dynamics of the process vary by age, race, ethnicity, social class, and geography. Some well-differentiated clients will choose not to come out to their families, and their wisdom in this decision needs to be respected. Even in these cases, however, the therapist should avoid comments that could serve to solidify distance from family and preclude connections that could be important to long-term recovery. Lesbians, if storied at all, are storied in very negative and oppressive ways. As Laird (1994) notes, clients who are lesbians need to recognize the sources and contexts of their stories, construct new stories, and develop new interpretations of old self and social stories.

When clients are out to their parents and less reactive to them, it is my preference to invite parents in for at least one session during the last stage of treatment. The purpose of such sessions is to challenge the family mythology by asking the parents to tell stories about their lives. As Freeman (1992) notes, these stories inform adult children about how events shaped their parents' responses to them and can be used as positive legacies. The daughter observes but does not participate, and the session is videotaped for future viewing and as a gift to subsequent generations. The rationale for the daughter's silence in the interview is based on Freeman's observations that adult children often have emotional reactions to their parents' sad stories, and the parents worry about these reactions. The therapist is more likely to be able to ask less reactive questions, stay calm, and find aspects of the story that emphasize survival, connections, and competence. In telling their stories, parents are encouraged to talk about their personal losses and loss of expectations for their daughter. In some instances parents can be helped to revise their self-blaming stories into more empowering ones. Such sessions are usually preceded and followed by Bowen-based visits home by each client to reposition with the family and begin to broaden the story about parents and siblings. Attention is given to the grieving of family of origin losses and finding a way, even if imperfect, to stay connected to family.*

---

* SARAH AND CATE IN STAGE IV

The final stage of work with this couple, which began six months after Cate achieved sobriety, focused on active repositioning with the families of origin. I continued to ask questions that introduced doubt into their theories about their parents and wondered how their parents' losses, what *they* didn't get, affected their parenting. As they developed more curiosity about their own histories, we began to discuss the implications of secrecy and Cate's disclosure of her lesbianism to her father and siblings. Each woman decided on different methods of repositioning with her parents. Two examples of their initial efforts will be described.

Sarah's mother was planning a visit from the East Coast and was invited for an interview. Sarah agreed to observe without participating, and the session was videotaped. Her mother's story was one of profound loss and sadness. She was quite young when her family lost everything in the Depression, and her father subsequently developed a serious drinking problem. As an only child, she felt responsible for taking care of her mother's fairly constant sadness. She described herself as a quiet, good child who tried to stay out of the way of her parents' conflicts. She idolized her own mother, was very dependent on her, and was devastated by her "horrible death" from cancer the year before Sarah was born. Her father died six years later. I asked questions about what she had learned from these experiences and what she had learned about survival. I asked what lessons she had learned from her parents and grandparents, who her role models were, and with whom she felt safest. She said that she had only wanted Sarah and her sister to have everything she did not have, like independence and education. She did not want to interfere with their lives or burden them in any way. She viewed her distancing from them as protecting them from her sadness. Sarah commented in the next session that she had reviewed the videotape and it was a great relief to realize that her mother's parenting of her was about her mother's losses and not about lack of love for her.

Cate chose to initiate repositioning with her father through letters and phone calls. She worked several weeks on a letter in which she came out to him and expressed curiosity about his family. Over the course of several letters, her father acknowledged her lesbianism (although he disapproved), noting that he had known for some time and felt, as always, left out of important information. He thanked her for telling him. For the first time he began to tell her his own story. He carried a great deal of shame throughout his life for being born out of wedlock to an alcoholic mother in Germany. As a small child he was abandoned a number of times and abused by his stepfather. He left Nazi Germany and came to New York alone at age twelve, surviving but struggling his whole life with loneliness, depression, and alcoholism. As Cate began to let her father back into her life, she shared with him her memories of how he made her feel special when she was young, and her sadness about not having a relationship with him for so many years. She also began to make phone calls to her brothers, came out to them, and had the first visit from her mother without her father. The visit went well, and she began to gradually change her story about her mother as well.

As Sarah and Cate made peace with their original family losses, they were able to change their stories about themselves and each other. They no longer needed to use distance and alcohol to stay safe with each other or to deal with the stresses related to being lesbian in this society.

[13]
Ethical and Legal Issues

In this chapter ethical challenges commonly encountered in working with LGBT clients with substance use disorders are covered. Relevant legal issues, including state and federal laws, are also discussed.

Ethical Challenges

Most professional associations have taken affirmative positions with regard to sexual minority populations. For example, NASW has issued policy statements in support of full civil rights of LGBT people with regard to nondiscrimination in employment, housing, health care, parental rights, inheritance rights, and insurance benefits (National Association of Social Workers 2003). And it is clear that ethical practice with sexual minority clients requires constant attention to the effects of homo/transphobia and heterosexism. As stated by Brown (1996):

> The mental health professional who feels strongly that, despite the evidence, sexual minority individuals have a form of psychopathology or the mental health professional whose religious convictions generate a belief that being a sexual minority is a sin in need of psychotherapeutic in-

tervention would be ethically well advised to abstain from working with any sexual minority patient because such beliefs are likely to harm the patient. (p. 905)

The ethical issues covered in this chapter include the use of conversion (reparative) therapies, the unique dilemmas of sexual minority therapists, and the handling of confidentiality.

NASW (2003) has issued a policy statement in opposition to conversion (reparative) therapy with LGBT people, and it is considered unethical by most national associations of mental health professionals. These therapies clearly violate the professional ethic of doing no harm and are, according to Brown (1996),

> ethically problematic because they are known to be patently ineffica-
> cious. Few other groups of people, aside from sexual minorities, have
> been consistently offered clearly inefficacious and often harmful treat-
> ments. Consequently, for a psychotherapist to persist with this approach
> to treatment, given the strong data regarding lack of successful outcome
> for the so-called conversion therapies, would constitute ethically prob-
> lematic action. (p. 904)

Practitioners working with LGBT clients with substance use disorders should be aware that the referral of clients to reparative therapies consti-tutes unethical practice.

Some unique ethical dilemmas are faced by sexual minority clinicians who live and work within the same community as their clients. Because it is common in these communities to encounter clients accidentally in social situations, the clinician must pay constant attention to boundary is-sues. Ethical problems can be avoided if practitioners talk with clients about these unintentional encounters, discuss them in consultation groups, and have their own social network of friends who have no relationships with their clients (Brown 1996).

In addition to principles about competent practice and professional boundaries, all professions providing mental health and substance abuse treatment embrace confidentiality as a core ethical principle. Unfortunate-ly, relatively few jurisdictions have laws that specifically protect the rights of LGBT individuals, so practitioners must show extra sensitivity regarding confidentiality about sexual orientation, gender identity, and HIV status.

The potential loss of civil rights for some clients is even greater if they are also struggling with a substance use disorder. Clients need to know, however, that regardless of the importance of confidentiality, it is not an absolute value. The law has created many circumstances in which confidentiality may or must be breached, and clients have a right to know of these exceptions.

One ethical issue that predominates in the substance abuse and HIV treatment fields, and often involves LGBT clients, is the duty to warn sexual partners of the risk of acquiring HIV infection. In the twenty-two research studies reviewed by Kalichman (2000), approximately one-third of HIV-positive persons reported continued unprotected intercourse following knowledge of their HIV status. Whether the duty to protect applies to HIV/AIDS is a complex issue requiring a case-by-case analysis. Practitioners need to consult with an attorney familiar with state law to learn whether their state imposes a duty to warn, as well as whether state law prescribes the ways a provider can notify the person at risk. The American Psychological Association takes the position that the duty to protect should not be imposed on clinicians but that if legislation were written, it would support disclosure only when the identifiable potential victim is known by the clinician, there is compelling reason to believe this person is at significant risk for infection, and the clinician has made attempts to have their client inform the potential victim (Melchert and Patterson 1999; Yarhouse 2003). For sample codes of ethics for programs and therapists treating persons with HIV/AIDS and substance abuse disorders, the reader is referred to appendix E in Center for Substance Abuse Treatment 2000.

Legal Issues

Confidentiality is both an ethical and a legal concern. Both state and federal laws protect the confidentiality of healthcare information, but these laws have many exceptions and are inconsistent from state to state. In addition, advances in technology have increased dramatically the number of people with access to personal information. As each state law creates exceptions to confidentiality, many permit a variety of disclosures without client consent.

In contrast to state laws, a federal law and a set of regulations guarantee strict confidentiality of information about all persons who seek or receive substance abuse assessment and treatment. The legal citations for these laws and regulations are 42 U.S.C. and 42 CFR Part 2 (hereafter referred to as Part 2). This law is designed to protect privacy rights in order to attract people into treatment, and prohibits practitioners from disclosing even the client's name. The law applies to any program receiving federal assistance that specializes, *in whole or in part*, in providing treatment, counseling, or assessment and referral services for people with substance problems. Restrictions on disclosure apply to any information that would identify a former, deceased, or current client as a substance abuser, either directly or by implication.

Separate state standards for mental health information and federal standards for substance use information can create difficulties for practitioners treating clients with co-occurring mental illness and substance use disorders. In this case practitioners may be operating under two quite different legal standards in handling requests for information on the same client. This raises the question of whether there should continue to be separate legal standards for mental health and substance use confidentiality.

The federal confidentiality regulations (Part 2) have now been in effect for three decades. They were followed by the Health Insurance Portability and Accountability Act of 1996 (HIPAA) and the HIPAA Privacy Rule of 2002. Substance abuse treatment programs that are subject to HIPAA must now comply with the Privacy Rule, which parallels the requirements of Part 2 in many areas. The Privacy Rule applies to treatment programs, health plans, healthcare clearinghouses, and providers who transmit "protected health information" (PHI) in electronic form. Programs subject to both Part 2 and HIPAA rules must comply with both. In many instances the Privacy Rule does not change the rules in Part 2. For example, in both, a minor must always sign the consent form for a program to release information even to his or her parent or guardian. Some states require programs to obtain parental permission before providing treatment to a minor. In these states only, programs must get the signatures of both the minor and a parent, guardian, or other person legally responsible for the minor.

In other instances there are major differences between the regulations of Part 2 and the Privacy Rule. They differ in the definition of protected information, the uses and disclosures of health information, the content of consent forms, the revocation of consent, and a number of other regulations. For detailed information on the differences between Part 2 and the HIPAA Privacy Rule, the reader is referred to http://www.hipaa.samhsa.gov.

All of these ethical and legal issues apply, of course, to LGBT clients with substance use disorders. That said, the legal system does not grant equal civil rights to LGBT individuals or protect them from discrimination and violence. The lack of legal recognition of same-sex relationships is a glaring example of unequal rights under the law. There are more than one thousand legal rights accorded to legally married couples that are unavailable to same-sex couples. According to Cahill, Ellen, and Tobias (2002), these include the right to access coverage of partners under Medicare and Social Security, file joint tax returns, obtain death benefits when a partner dies, obtain health and retirement benefits from an employer, take sick or bereavement leave to care for a partner or partner's child, make medical decisions for an ill partner, access stepparent adoption of partner's children, use the courts for divorce, and sue for wrongful death. In addition, same-sex couples cannot assume that children born to a marriage are the children of both partners, regardless of biological relationship. The children of same-sex parents do not automatically have the right to live with a nonbiological parent after a biological parent dies, access health benefits and inherit death benefits from either parent, receive Social Security benefits if either parent dies, or receive financial support and a continued relationship with both parents if their parents separate. Practitioners working with same-sex couples need to help them maximize their rights by obtaining the appropriate written documents. They might also recommend *A Legal Guide for Lesbian and Gay Couples* by Curry, Clifford, and Hertz (2002).

Transgender individuals have few legal protections. According to Lombardi and Davis (2006), current legislation does not allow for gender transition or legal protection for those who do transition. There is no federal antidiscrimination legislation and state laws are inconsistent and vary widely. Unlike lesbians, gay men, and persons with HIV/AIDS, transgender employees have few legal workplace protections.

Practitioners working with LGBT clients need to understand how the lack of basic civil rights affects the inner experience of these individuals. They must assess the role of these realities in the etiology and/or maintenance of the clients' substance use disorder and do everything in their power to address these injustices.

Policy and Legislative Issues

In this chapter existing and proposed social policies and legislation that affect LGBT clients with substance use disorders are addressed. Social workers and other healthcare professionals have the skills to challenge the policies and practices that oppress these clients, and need to advocate for policies that acknowledge and provide rights to a variety of family forms. These oppressive policies include nondiscrimination laws, civil recognition of same-sex couples and transgender relationships, discriminating adoption and fostercare policies, hate crimes laws, and laws affecting sex education in schools. In addition, LGBT individuals are oppressed by policies regarding public assistance, housing, employment, health and mental health, aging services, criminal justice, military service and benefits, and immigration (Messinger 2006a). In the case of transgender clients, Lev (2004) notes that insurance companies refuse to cover services that are not "medically necessary," even if this means obtaining a psychiatric diagnosis that interferes with other civil liberties.

Policy recommendations on the state and national levels have been clearly explicated by the Policy Institute of the National Gay and Lesbian Task Force. The reader is referred to *Family Policy* by Cahill, Ellen, and Tobias (2002) and *Transgender Equality* by Currah, Green, and Minter (2000). Much of the energy of the gay rights movement has recently been devoted to obtaining legally recognized same-sex marriage. As this fight proceeds, La Sala (2007) notes that

> it is important to question why such privileges are bestowed on marriage and why social work, with its commitment to social justice, has not challenged this privileging. (p. 181)

He asks if it is fair or legitimate to link legal and social benefits to one's willingness or ability to commit to a legally sanctioned relationship. Why aren't social workers and LGBT activists investing their energy in obtaining economic and legal equity for everyone, regardless of sexual orientation or marital status?

These oppressive social policies are even more burdensome for LGBT clients struggling with substance use disorders. Current drug policies range from imprisonment to drug courts to harm reduction strategies aimed at facilitating entry into treatment. There is considerable agreement that "the current federal policy for combating drug use, endorsed by most state and local governments, has not only failed, but has exacerbated the problem" (McNeece 2003:193). As McNeece points out, the U.S. currently spends over $40 billion on the "War on Drugs" while prisons are overwhelmed by the numbers of drug offenders and relatively few of those in need of treatment are receiving it. McNeece recommends a switch from the "zero tolerance" to a harm reduction philosophy as well as the legalization of some currently illicit drugs. This shift would define substance use problems as public health rather than criminal justice concerns, allowing the police to focus on more serious crimes. In the U.S., needle-exchange and methadone maintenance programs are the best-known harm reduction strategies, both effective in reducing substance abuse, HIV infection, and drug-related crimes (Des Jarlais, Marmor, Paone, Titus, Shi, Perlis et al. 1996). A disproportionate representation of ethnic minority groups and women are in prison for drug violations. Social workers need to advocate for these individuals by opposing mandatory minimum sentences, random urine testing of those charged with non-drug-related offenses, and preventive detention (Brocato and Wagner 2003).

The establishment of drug courts reflects the failure of public and private substance abuse treatment systems to address the needs of the criminal justice population. Drug courts mandate treatment and close probationary supervision in lieu of incarceration for nonviolent drug offenders. They allow clients a way around classist and racist antidrug laws that impose mandatory minimum sentencing, and attempt to demonstrate the cost-effectiveness of treatment over imprisonment (van Wormer 2004). Most of the studies evaluating the effectiveness of drug courts have methodological weaknesses, rendering it hard to determine at present whether drug courts actually reduce recidivism and prevent relapse. It is clear, however, that they provide an incentive to substance abusers to stay in treatment and reduce the costs associated with incarceration. It is not known how many LGBT individuals have been affected by the drug court movement.

In addition to supporting social policies that reduce harm to clients and society, practitioners need to consider the overall design of substance abuse treatment programs and systems. On the program level, according to Ryan and Gruskin (2006), all agencies should have a policy on serving LGBT clients. Agencies need to provide regular staff training, recruit openly LGBT staff, use appropriate wording on forms, include materials on LGBT issues in waiting rooms, include families of choice in treatment, and help clients with important legal documents. On the systems level, Miller and Carroll (2006) point out that the treatment of substance use disorders has historically been segregated into specialist programs that are distanced from mainstream health services. They view the consequences of this phenomenon, although unintended, as quite negative. For example, compared to other health professionals, drug treatment counselors have less education and much lower status and pay. Because the treatment is specialized and separate, mainstream professionals are dissuaded from dealing with these clients and feel no responsibility to do so. Miller and Carroll make the case that

> screening, prevention, and intervention for substance use disorders should be integrated within mainstream health and social services, and more generally should be a shared responsibility among social institutions including schools, sports, employers, religions, and the judicial and correctional systems. This is not a problem to be understood or addressed in isolation. . . . Given the high rates of concomitant health, social, and psychological problems among drug-dependent people, treatment should be integrated as much as possible in one-stop health and social service settings that connect people with other services that they need. . . . As with other chronic health problems, the successful resolution of drug problems depends heavily on long-term behavioral self-management. (pp. 302–303)

Miller and Carroll recognize the possibility that drug problems could be given low priority in such a merger, and they do not address how LGBT clients might fare. Although many make the case for specialized treatment for LGBT clients, it has not been definitely proven that the benefits of these programs surpass those of mainstream programs. It is probable that successful treatment for LGBT clients would ultimately require significant reductions in homo/bi/transphobia in both mainstream and integrated programs.

Whether or not drug services merge with mainstream healthcare, there is a need for family therapy to merge with substance abuse treatment. This will require policy changes around insurance reimbursement as well as a considerable investment in staff training and supervision. There are currently a number of obstacles to the integration of family and substance abuse treatment, as well as other obstacles to adequate treatment. For example, waiting lists, geographic inaccessibility, cost, restricted hours, and limited program goals are also problematic (Miller and Carroll 2006). The National Quality Forum (2005) identified a number of additional policy barriers to the adoption of evidence-based substance abuse treatment. They recommended increased funding to improve access to evidence-based treatment, payment mechanisms and incentives to promote evidence-based practice, and improved identification and retention of qualified staff. It is problematic that clients with substance use disorders are subject to irrational insurance policies that cover only brief outpatient or inpatient programs in a hospital setting. Insurance seldom covers the long-term outpatient care that is often needed to effectively treat meth and other substance dependence (GLMA 2006). All of these recommendations are relevant to the treatment of LGBT clients with substance use disorders.

Join Together (2004), a project of Boston University School of Public Health, has developed a list of substance abuse policy measures that have been proven to be effective. In addition to those already mentioned, they include the following:

- Increase alcohol prices through taxes, particularly on beer. Youth drink less when beer costs more, leading to fewer auto accidents, fights, and suicide attempts.
- Limit alcohol advertising and promotional activities that target young people.
- Require and enforce equal insurance coverage for drug and alcohol treatment.

- Support the development and use of effective medications for addiction treatment.
- Make unobtrusive screening for alcohol and drug problems a routine part of every primary care and emergency room visit.
- Repeal policies that prevent ex-offenders from returning to full participation in society. Federal and state laws that impose lengthy bans on federal student aid, cash assistance, food stamps, public housing, and many types of employment do not prevent drug use, but do impede recovery.

Finally, it is now clear that substance abuse treatment has significant value as an HIV-prevention method. Reback, Larkins, and Shoptaw (2004) found that gay and bisexual meth abusers reduced sexual risk behaviors and sustained these reductions over one year following substance abuse treatment. These clients reported fewer anonymous sexual partners, reductions in episodes of receptive and insertive anal intercourse, and an increased sense of responsibility to disclose their HIV status. Mausbach, Semple, Strathdee, Zians, and Patterson (2007) demonstrated the efficacy of a behavioral skills intervention for increasing safer sex behaviors in the context of ongoing meth use in a sample of HIV-positive, meth-using MSM. Based on their review of relevant research on MSM, Shoptaw and Frosch (2000) made the following policy recommendations:

- Develop treatment strategies that target substance use and high-risk sexual behavior simultaneously.
- Recognize treatment as HIV prevention in this population.
- Educate counselors on cultural and sexual risk issues specific to substance-abusing MSM.   (p. 193)

Oppressive social policies and practices are extremely deleterious to LGBT clients struggling with substance use disorders. The clear failure of federal "War on Drugs" policies calls for a shift in paradigm to a harm reduction perspective on substance abuse. Treatment programs need clear and affirmative policies on serving LGBT clients, and specialized programs must offer evidence-based treatment. It is critical that LGBT clients with substance use disorders have access to services that are empirically supported.

The Future of the Field

This chapter addresses clinical education and supervision related to LGBT issues and substance use disorders. The challenges of conducting research in this area, gaps in the knowledge base, and the importance of refining empirically supported practices are also discussed.

Although "homosexuality" was removed as a diagnostic category from the American Psychiatric Association's *Diagnostic and Statistical Manual of Mental Disorders* in 1973, it was not until 1991 that the Council on Social Work Education (CSWE) required content on sexual orientation in social work programs. The National Association of Social Workers' (NASW) *Code of Ethics* (1996) clearly states that practitioners cannot discriminate against clients or refuse to provide services because of a client's sexual orientation.

In spite of the stated positions of most professional associations, heterosexist bias is common among mental health and substance abuse practitioners, and it is clear that they are being inadequately prepared for practice with LGBT populations. CSWE requirements notwithstanding, lesbian and gay subject matter not related to HIV/AIDS constitutes only about one percent of the social work literature. Most of these articles focus on helping lesbian clients adapt to their heterosexist environments; few address changing heterosexist attitudes, behaviors, or policies (Van Voorhis and Wagner 2002). These authors add that "social work journals must increase the number of articles on homosexuality and, moreover, those articles must address practice interventions with the heterosexist conditions that oppress gay and lesbian clients" (p. 353). Articles and books addressing bisexual and transgender clients are even rarer than those dealing with clients who are gay or lesbian.

Professional Education

As discussed previously, clinical education and supervision related to LGBT issues and substance use disorders are substandard in social work, psychology, and medicine. CSWE, for example, has no standard on substance abuse content for MSW programs, and whatever education is provided is marginal to core courses. In a detailed analysis of the substance abuse content in MSW courses, Saarela (2005) notes the overwhelming focus on the disease model and the twelve-step approach. Of particular concern is the lack of coverage of harm reduction strategies, motivational interviewing, club drugs, and alternatives to the twelve-step approach. Women for Sobriety, Rational Recovery, SMART Recovery, and Secular Organizations for Sobriety received minimal attention, and Moderation Management, the only self-help program that is not abstinence-based, received the least attention. Although not noted by Saarela, these neglected content areas are ones that are particularly relevant to substance abuse treatment of LGBT clients.

In an effort to increase the substance abuse content in social work curricula, the NIAAA has developed a curriculum guide for classroom use in MSW programs. Continually updated and accessible via the World Wide Web, modules include PowerPoint presentations, handouts, classroom activities, and case examples. Module 10G of this curriculum focuses on sexual orientation and alcohol use disorders (http://pubs.niaaa.nih.gov/publications/Social/Module10GSexualOrientation/Module10G.html).

In addition to insufficient substance abuse content, the majority of graduate programs lack specialized coursework or formal training in working with LGBT clients (Carroll and Gilroy 2002; Cole, Denny, Eyler, and Samons 2000). With the goals of increasing awareness of attitudes, knowledge, and skills in counseling LGB clients across the lifespan, Lidderdale (2002) describes an elective graduate-level course with the class structure similar to a psychoeducational group. Recognizing that students have somewhat different needs, the "Transtheoretical Model of Change" is used to assess student readiness to change heterosexist beliefs and/or attitudes. Session topics and experiential activities are available from the author.

In summary, in the last thirty years there have been many calls by experts to increase educational exposure to LGBT issues and substance use disorders, and little has changed. Sexual orientation and gender identity are interrelated with substance use disorders in complex ways, resulting in the unique needs of LGBT clients. The professionals who treat these clients must have access to the latest empirically supported knowledge in both chemical dependency and the specific challenges and strengths of LGBT clients.

Research

As Cochran (2001) points out, there are significant methodological barriers to research with the LGBT population. They are relatively more hidden than other minority populations, so most research has had to rely on convenience-based sampling. Sample sizes tend to be small and there are usually no comparable heterosexual groups. Only since the onset of the HIV epidemic have population-based surveys added questions that assessed markers of homosexuality. Even when this information is obtained, there is often a lack of statistical power due to the low base rate of homosexuality in the population.

In the future, it will be critical that valid measures of sexual orientation and gender identity are included in national and local substance abuse studies. While there is some research on risk factors, little is known about resilience and protective factors among LGBT individuals. Hughes and Eliason (2002) call for well-designed studies of the impact of minority stress on substance abuse. It still is not understood *how* internalized homo/transphobia, stress, and depression are associated with substance abuse.

It does appear that LGBT clients have increased risk for some disorders. Cochran (2001) notes that lesbians and gay men have greater risk for depression and suicide attempts, and lesbians are more at risk for developing alcohol dependency than other women. Most hypothesize that the causation of higher risk is social, but much more research is needed to confirm this. Hughes and Eliason (2002) conclude after their literature review that heavy alcohol and other drug use is prevalent among young lesbians and gay males, but much less is known about bisexual and transgender individuals. Because these latter groups are marginalized by both heterosexual and gay/lesbian communities, they may be at even greater risk for substance abuse.

There is very little research on substance abuse in LGBT clients who are midlife and older, live in nonurban areas, and/or belong to a racial or ethnic minority group. Clinical differences between lesbians, gay men, bisexual, and transgender clients need to be clarified (Satre 2006), and there needs to be much more attention to various subgroups within the LGBT population. Because there is so little research on members of racial or ethnic minority groups, it is not known whether (or if) the effects of multiple marginalized statuses are additive or synergistic (Cochran 2001).

Although there is now more research on drugs other than alcohol, most of this focuses only on gay or bisexual men. Hughes and Eliason (2002) stress the importance of understanding which drugs are abused by which segments of LGBT populations:

> Prevention strategies can then target the groups at greatest risk. For example, poppers and methamphetamines are common drugs of abuse among gay and bisexual men; methamphetamines and nonprescribed hormones are commonly used by some transgender individuals, especially MTFs. Among lesbians, alcohol use appears to be among the greatest risks for substance abuse, though methamphetamine use is becoming more common among some groups of lesbians.   (p. 290)

With the increased research focus on drug use by MSM comes a biased media portrayal that demonizes gay and bisexual men and reinforces negative views of them. Their use of meth is associated with "reckless" sexual behavior with no recognition of the role of external and internalized homophobia, low self-esteem, and rejection by families of origin (GLMA 2006).

One area of research that will continue to develop is the use of medications to treat substance dependence. A number of medications are currently being investigated, and genetic differences between individuals will probably affect their responses to these medications. If genetic tests could yield valid information about the risk of dependence, there would be a more solid base for individual decision-making about use. According to Hasin, Hatzenbuehler, and Waxman (2006):

In the field of alcohol, we remain without guidelines concerning who really must stop drinking in order to recover from DSM-IV alcohol dependence, and who can recover stably from dependence even while drinking moderately. . . . The field of genetics research has much to contribute to understanding the etiology and treatment of alcohol and drug use disorders. (pp. 75–76)

There is also much to be learned about the relationship between pharmacological and behavioral therapies. It has been pointed out that many behavioral approaches are effective, but they are far from perfect (GLMA 2006). Future pharmacological approaches could be particularly useful in helping clients get beyond initial craving, depression, and anxiety.

Research must continue on the effectiveness of empirically supported practices and the understanding of how to implement them. At present, brief motivational therapy, contingency management, cognitive-behavioral approaches, and couple/family therapy have the most empirical support, but they are rarely available in the current treatment system (Carroll and Rounsaville 2006). Despite an increased need for treatment, there are fewer programs and fewer clients in treatment today than there were in 1990. And the gap is widening between what we know is effective and what we can deliver (McLellan 2006). This situation creates huge challenges for both researchers and clinicians.

The most significant question related to LGBT clients with substance use disorders is whether treatment strategies that have demonstrated effectiveness with heterosexual populations will be as effective with LGBT individuals. These empirically supported strategies have been addressed in this book in the hope that they will be implemented and evaluated with LGBT clients. To date, the field has not developed adequate LGBT-specific standards or evidence-based practice guidelines for substance abuse treatment services. It remains to be determined whether LGBT-specific treatment is more effective than mainstream treatment for these clients.

Social workers and other healthcare professionals have an ethical obligation to develop and continuously evaluate empirically supported treatments for LGBT clients with substance use disorders. For most, this will require ongoing continuing education about these populations as well as the screening, assessment, and treatment of substance abuse dependence. As advocates, we need to work for the dismantling of discriminatory federal, state, and agency policies and to educate others about the insidious effects of homo/bi/transphobia and heterosexism. LGBT individuals do not have higher rates of substance use disorders as a natural function of their gender identity or sexual orientation, but rather as a consequence of living in a society that stigmatizes and oppresses them. Changing society's attitudes and values will significantly reduce the substance abuse of LGBT individuals and will improve their ability to recover with treatment.

References

Alessi, E. J. 2008. Staying put in the closet: Examining clinical practice and counter-transference issues in work with gay men married to heterosexual women. *Clinical Social Work Journal* 36:195–201.

Amadio, D. M. 2006. Internalized heterosexism, alcohol use, and alcohol-related problems among lesbians and gay men. *Addictive Behaviors* 31:1153–1162.

American Psychiatric Association. 1952. *Diagnostic and Statistical Manual of Mental Disorders* (DSM-1). 1st ed. Washington, DC: Author.

——. 1980. *Diagnostic and Statistical Manual of Mental Disorders* (DSM-III). 3rd ed. Washington, DC: Author.

——. 1987. *Diagnostic and Statistical Manual of Mental Disorders* (DSM-III-R). 3rd ed., rev. Washington, DC: Author.

——. 2000. *Diagnostic and Statistical Manual of Mental Disorders* (DSM-IV-TR). 4th ed., rev. Washington, DC: Author.

American Psychological Association. 2008. Answers to your questions: For a better understanding of sexual orientation and homosexuality. Washington, DC: Author. Retrieved from www.apa.org/topics/sorientation.pdf.

Amodeo, M., and L. Jones. 1997. Viewing alcohol and other drug use cross-culturally: A cultural framework for clinical practice. *Families in Society: Journal of Contemporary Human Services* 78.3:3–14.

Anderson, R. N., and B. L. Smith. 2002. Deaths: Leading causes for 2001. *National Vital Statistics Report* 52.9:27–33.

Anderson, S. C. 1987. Alcoholic women on skid row. *Social Work* 32.4:362–365.

——. 1994. A critical analysis of the concept of codependency. *Social Work* 39.6:677–685.

——. 1995. Addressing heterosexist bias in the treatment of lesbian couples with chemical dependency. *Journal of Feminist Family Therapy* 7.3/4:87–113.

——. 1996. Substance abuse and dependency in gay men and lesbians. *Journal of Gay and Lesbian Social Services* 5.1:59–76.

——. 2001. Lesbian and bisexual women: Relevant policy and practice issues. In K. J. Peterson and A. Lieberman, eds., *Building On Women's Strengths: A Social Work Agenda for the Twenty-First Century*, 219–252. New York: Haworth Press.

Anderson, S. C., T. Boe, and S. Smith. 1988. Homeless women. *Affilia: Journal of Women and Social Work* 3.2:62–70.

Anderson, S. C., and M. Holliday. 2004. Normative passing in the lesbian community: An exploratory study. *Journal of Gay and Lesbian Social Services* 17.3:25–38.

——. 2007. How heterosexism plagues practitioners in services for lesbians and their families: An exploratory study. *Journal of Gay and Lesbian Social Services* 19.2:81–100.

Anderson, S. C., and D. Mandell. 1989. The use of self-disclosure by professional social workers. *Social Casework* 70.5:259–267.

Anderson, S. C., and B. Sussex. 1999. Resilience in lesbians: An exploratory study. In J. Laird, ed., *Lesbians and Lesbian Families: Reflections on Theory and Practice*, 307–329. New York: Columbia University Press.

Anderson, S. C., and L. E. Wiemer. 1992. Administrators' beliefs about the relative competence of recovering and nonrecovering chemical dependency counselors. *Families in Society: Journal of Contemporary Human Services* 73.10:596–603.

Angelino, A. F., and G. J. Treisman. 2001. Management of psychiatric disorders in patients infected with HIV. *Clinical Infectious Diseases* 33:847–856.

Appel, P. W., H. Joseph, A. Kott, W. Nottingham, E. Tasiny, and E. Habel. 2001. Selected in-treatment outcomes of long-term methadone maintenance treatment patients in New York State. *Mount Sinai Journal of Medicine* 68.1:55–61.

Appleby, G. A., and J. W. Anastas, eds. 1998. *Not Just a Passing Phase: Social Work with Gay, Lesbian, and Bisexual People*. New York: Columbia University Press.

Appleby, P. R., L. C. Miller, and S. Rothspan. 1999. The paradox of trust for male couples: When risking is part of loving. *Personal Relationships* 6.81–93.

Arend, E. D. 2005. The politics of invisibility: Homophobia and low-income HIV-positive women who have sex with women. *Journal of Homosexuality* 49.1: 97–122.

Armstrong, T. D., and E. J. Costello. 2002. Community studies on adolescent substance use, abuse, or dependence on psychiatric comorbidity. *Journal of Consulting and Clinical Psychology* 70:1224–1239.

Arreola, S. G., T. B. Neilands, L. M. Pollack, J. P. Paul, and J. A. Catania. 2005. Higher prevalence of childhood sexual abuse among Latino men who have sex with men than non-Latino men who have sex with men: Data from the Urban Men's Health Study. *Child Abuse and Neglect* 29.3:285–290.

Atkinson, R. M., R. L. Tolson, and J. A. Turner. 1990. Late versus early onset problem drinking in older men. *Alcoholism: Clinical and Experimental Research* 14:574–579.

Avants, S. K., L. A. Warburton, K. A. Hawkins, and A. Margolin. 2000. Continuation of high-risk behavior by HIV-positive drug users: Treatment implications. *Journal of Substance Abuse Treatment* 19:15–22.

Badgett, M. V. L. 1998. *Income Inflation: The Myth of Affluence Among Gay, Lesbian, and Bisexual Americans*. New York: National Gay and Lesbian Task Force Policy Institute and the Institute for Gay and Lesbian Strategic Studies.

Bailey, J. M., and D. S. Benishay. 1993. Familial aggregation of female sexual orientation. *American Journal of Psychiatry* 150.2:272–277.

Bailey, J. M., and R. C. Pillard. 1991. A genetic study of male sexual orientation. *Archives of General Psychiatry* 50:217–223.

Baldwin, A., C. Baldwin, T. Kasser, M. Zax, A. Sameroff, and R. Seifer. 1993. Contextual risk and resiliency during late adolescence. *Development and Psychopathology* 5:741–761.

Balsam, K. F., T. P. Beauchaine, and E. D. Rothblum. 2005. Victimization over the life span: A comparison of lesbian, gay, bisexual, and heterosexual siblings. *Journal of Consulting and Clinical Psychology* 73.3:477–487.

Balsam, K. F., B. Huang, K. C. Friedland, J. M. Simoni, and K. L. Walters. 2004. Culture, trauma, and wellness: A comparison of heterosexual and lesbian, gay, bisexual, and two-spirit Native Americans. *Cultural Diversity and Ethnic Minority Psychology* 10.3:287–301.

Barney, D. D. 2003. Health risk-factors for gay American Indian and Alaska Native adolescent males. *Journal of Homosexuality* 46.1/2:137–157.

Barret, R. L., and C. Logan. 2002. *Counseling Gay Men and Lesbians.* Pacific Grove, CA: Brooks/Cole.

Barry, K. L., D. W. Oslin, and F. Blow. 2001. *Alcohol Problems in Older Adults: Prevention and Management.* New York: Springer.

Bartholow, B. N., L. S. Doll, D. Joy, J. M. Douglas, G. Bolan, J. S. Harrison et al. 1994. Emotional, behavioral, and HIV risks associated with sexual abuse among adult homosexual and bisexual men. *Child Abuse and Neglect* 18:747–761.

Bartlett, N. H., P. L. Vasey, and W. M. Bukowski. 2000. Is gender identity disorder in children a mental disorder? *Sex Roles* 43:753–785.

Bauermeister, J. A. 2007. It's all about "connecting": Reasons for drug use among Latino gay men living in the San Francisco bay area. *Journal of Ethnicity in Substance Abuse* 6.1:109–129.

Baumeister, R. F. 2000. Gender differences in erotic plasticity: The female sex drive as socially flexible and responsive. *Psychological Bulletin* 126:347–374.

Beauvais, F. 1998. American Indians and alcohol. *Alcohol Health and Research World* 22.4:253–260.

Bem, D. J. 1998. Is EBE theory supported by evidence? Is it androcentric? *Psychological Review* 105:395–398.

Benotsch, E. G., S. C. Kalichman, and M. Cage. 2002. Men who have met sex partners via the Internet: Prevalence, predictors, and implications for HIV prevention. *Archives of Sexual Behavior* 31.2:177–183.

Benotsch, E. G., S. C. Kalichman, and J. A. Kelly. 1999. Sexual compulsivity and substance use in HIV-seropositive men who have sex with men: Prevalence and predictors of high-risk behaviors. *Addictive Behaviors* 24:857–868.

Bepko, C. 1989. Disorders of power: Women and addiction in the family. In M. McGoldrick, C. M. Anderson, and F. Walsh, eds., *Women in Families,* 406–426. New York: Norton.

Bepko, C., and T. Johnson. 2000. Gay and lesbian couples in therapy: Perspectives for the contemporary family therapist. *Journal of Marital and Family Therapy* 26.4:409–419.

Berg, I. K., and K. C. Shafer. 2004. Working with mandated substance abusers. In S. L. A. Straussner, ed., *Clinical Work with Substance-Abusing Clients,* 82–102. New York: Guilford Press.

Bernhard, L. A. 2000. Physical and sexual violence experienced by lesbian and heterosexual women. *Violence Against Women* 6.1:68–79.

Beyer, E. P., and K. Carnabucci. 2002. Group treatment of substance-abusing women. In S. L. A. Straussner and S. Brown, eds., *The Handbook of Addiction Treatment for Women*, 515–538. San Francisco: Jossey-Bass.

Bien, T. H., W. R. Miller, and J. S. Tonigan. 1993. Brief interventions for alcohol problems: A review. *Addiction* 88:315–336.

Bing, E. G., M. A. Burman, D. Longshore, J. A. Fleishman, C. D. Sherbourne, A. S. London et al. 2001. Psychiatric disorders and drug use among human immunodeficiency virus–infected adults in the United States. *Archives of General Psychiatry* 58:721–728.

Binson, D., W. J. Woods, L. Pollack, J. Paul, R. Stall, and J. A. Catania. 2001. Differential HIV risk in bathhouses and public cruising areas. *American Journal of Public Health* 91.9:1482–1486.

Black, B., T. P. Oles, and L. Moore. 1998. The relationship between attitudes: Homophobia and sexism among social work students. *Affilia: Journal of Women and Social Work* 13:166–189.

Blank, S. 2006. Crystal methamphetamine use and sexually transmitted infection: The importance of sexual history taking. *Journal of Gay and Lesbian Psychotherapy* 10.3/4:73–84.

Blow, F. C., K. J. Brower, J. E. Schulenberg, L. M. Demo-Dananberg, J. P. Young, and T. P. Beresford. 1992. The Michigan Alcoholism Screening Test—Geriatric version (MAST-G): A new elderly-specific screening instrument. *Alcoholism: Clinical and Experimental Research* 16:372.

Bocklandt, S., S. Horvath, E. Vilain, and D. H. Hamer. 2006. Extreme skewing of X chromosome inactivation in mothers of homosexual men. *Human Genetics* 118.6:691–694.

Bockting, W., C. Huang, H. Ding, B. Robinson, and B. R. S. Rosser. 2005. Are transgender persons at higher risk for HIV prevalence and risks? *International Journal of Transgenderism* 8.2/3:123–131.

Bockting, W. O., B. E. Robinson, and B. R. S. Rosser. 1998. Transgender HIV prevention: A qualitative needs assessment. *AIDS Care* 10.4:505–526.

Bohan, J. S. 1996. *Psychology and Sexual Orientation: Coming to Terms.* New York: Routledge.

Bontempo, D. E., and A. R. D'Augelli. 2002. Effects of at-school victimization and sexual orientation on lesbian, gay, or bisexual youths' health risk behavior. *Journal of Adolescent Health* 30:364–374.

Borden, A. 2007. *The History of Gay People in Alcoholics Anonymous: From the Beginning.* New York: Haworth Press.

Bostwick, W. B., T. L. Hughes, and T. Johnson. 2005. The co-occurrence of depression and alcohol dependence symptoms in a community sample of lesbians. *Journal of Lesbian Studies* 9.3:7–18.

Bowen, M. 1978. *Family Therapy in Clinical Practice.* New York: Aronson.

Boylan, J. F. 2003. *She's Not There: A Life in Two Genders.* New York: Broadway Books.

Bradford, J. 2005. Lesbian health in the U.S.: Our foundation and our future. Paper presented at the Annual Conference of the Gay and Lesbian Medical Association, September 22–24, Montreal, Quebec.

Bradford, M. 2004. The bisexual experience: Living in a dichotomous culture. *Journal of Bisexuality* 4.1/2:7–23.

Breban, R., I. McGowan, C. Topaz, E. J. Schwartz, P. Anton, and S. Blower. 2006. Modeling the potential impact of rectal microbicides to reduce HIV transmission in bathhouses. *Mathematical Biosciences and Engineering* 3.3:459–466.

Brennan, D. J., W. L. Hellerstedt, M. W. Ross, and S. L. Welles. 2007. History of childhood sexual abuse and HIV risk behaviors in homosexual and bisexual men. *American Journal of Public Health* 97.6:1107–1112.

Brocato, J., and E. F. Wagner. 2003. Harm reduction: A social work practice model and social justice agenda. *Health and Social Work* 28.2:117–125.

Brooks, D., and S. Goldberg. 2001. Gay and lesbian adoptive and foster care placements: Can they meet the needs of waiting children? *Social Work* 46.2:147–157.

Brown, L. S. 1989. New voices, new visions: Toward a lesbian/gay paradigm for psychology. *Psychology of Women Quarterly* 13:445–456.

——. 1996. Ethical concerns with sexual minority patients. In R. P. Cabaj and T. S. Stein, eds., *Textbook of Homosexuality and Mental Health*, 897–916. Washington, DC: American Psychiatric Press.

Brown, M. L., and C. A. Rounsley. 1996. *True Selves: Understanding Transsexualism for Families, Friends, Coworkers, and Helping Professionals.* San Francisco: Jossey-Bass.

Bucholtz, K. K., Y. Sheline, and J. E. Helzer. 1995. The epidemiology of substance use, problems, and dependence in elders: A review. In T. Beresford and E. Gomberg, eds., *Alcohol and Aging*, 19–41. New York: Oxford University Press.

Bull, S. S., P. Piper, and C. Rietmeijer. 2002. Men who have sex with men and also inject drugs. *Journal of Homosexuality* 42.3:31–51.

Buloff, B., and M. Osterman. 1995. Queer reflections: Mirroring and the lesbian experience of self. In J. M. Glasgold and S. Jasenza, eds., *Lesbians and Psychoanalysis: Revolutions in Theory*, 93–106. New York: Free Press.

Burch, B. 1982. Psychological merger in lesbian couples: A joint ego psychological and systems approach. *Family Therapy* 9:201–208.

——. 1986. Psychotherapy and the dynamics of merger in lesbian couples. In T. S. Stein and C. J. Cohen, eds., *Contemporary Perspectives on Psychotherapy with Lesbians and Gay Men*, 57–71. New York: Plenum.

——. 1987. Barriers to intimacy: Conflicts over power, dependence, and nurturing. In Boston Lesbian Psychologies Collective, ed., *Lesbian Psychologies: Explorations and Challenges*, 126–141. Urbana: University of Illinois Press.

Burgard, S. A., S. D. Cochran, and V. M. Mays. 2005. Alcohol and tobacco use patterns among heterosexually and homosexually experienced California women. *Drug and Alcohol Dependence* 77.1:61–70.

Burkstein, O. G. 2000. Disruptive behavior disorders and substance use disorders in adolescents. *Journal of Psychoactive Drugs* 32.1:67–79.

Bushway, D. J. 1991. Chemical dependency treatment for lesbians and their families: The feminist challenge. *Journal of Feminist Family Therapy* 3:161–172.

Bux, D. A., and T. W. Irwin. 2006. Combining motivational interviewing and cognitive-behavioral skills training for the treatment of crystal methamphetamine abuse/dependence. *Journal of Gay and Lesbian Psychotherapy* 10.3/4:143–152.

Cabaj, R. P. 1988. Homosexuality and neurosis: Considerations for psychotherapy. *Journal of Homosexuality* 15:13–23.

——. 1995. Sexual orientation and the addictions. *Journal of Gay and Lesbian Psychotherapy* 2:97–117.

——. 1997. Gays, lesbians, and bisexuals. In J. Lowenson, P. Ruiz, R. Millman, and J. Langrod, eds., *Substance Abuse: A Comprehensive Textbook*, 3rd ed., 725–733. Baltimore: Williams and Wilkins.

——. 2000. Substance abuse, internalized homophobia, and gay men and lesbians: Psychodynamic issues and clinical implications. *Journal of Gay and Lesbian Psychotherapy* 3.3/4:5–24.

Cadwell, S. A. 1994. Over-identification with HIV clients. *Journal of Gay and Lesbian Psychotherapy* 2.2:77–99.

Cahill, S., M. Ellen, and S. Tobias. 2002. *Family Policy: Issues Affecting Gay, Lesbian, Bisexual, and Transgendered Families*. New York: Policy Institute for the National Gay and Lesbian Task Force.

Cahill, S., K. South, and J. Spade. 2000. *Outing Age: Public Policy Issues Affecting Gay, Lesbian, Bisexual, and Transgender Elders*. New York: Policy Institute of the Gay and Lesbian Task Force.

Campos-Outcalt, D., and S. Hurwitz. 2002. Female-to-female transmission of syphilis. *Sexually Transmitted Diseases* 29.2:119–120.

Carey, K. B., D. M. Purine, S. A. Maisto, and M. P. Carey. 2001. Enhancing readiness-to-change substance abuse in persons with schizophrenia: A four-session motivation-based intervention. *Behavior Modification* 25.3:331–384.

Carlson, R. G. 2006. Ethnography and applied substance misuse research. In W. R. Miller and K. M. Carroll, ed., *Rethinking Substance Abuse*, 201–219. New York: Guilford Press.

Carroll, K. M. 1996. Relapse prevention as a psychosocial treatment: A review of controlled clinical trials. *Experimental and Clinical Psychopharmacology* 4.1:46–54.

——. 1998. *A Cognitive-Behavioral Approach: Treating Cocaine Addiction*. Therapy Manuals for Drug Addiction: Manual 1. Rockville, MD: National Institute on Drug Abuse.

Carroll, K. M., and B. J. Rounsaville. 2006. Behavioral therapies. In W. R. Miller and K. M. Carroll, eds., *Rethinking Substance Abuse*, 223–239. New York: Guilford Press.

Carroll, L., and P. J. Gilroy. 2002. Transgender issues in counselor preparation. *Counselor Education and Supervision* 41:233–242.

Carroll, L., P. J. Gilroy, and J. Ryan. 2002. Counseling transgendered, transsexual, and gender-variant clients. *Journal of Counseling and Development* 80:131–139.

Carroll, R. 1999. Outcomes of treatment for gender dysphoria. *Journal of Sex Education and Therapy* 24:128–136.

Cass, V. C. 1979. Homosexual identity formation: A theoretical model. *Journal of Homosexuality* 4.3:219–235.

——. 1984. Homosexual identity formation: Testing a theoretical model. *Journal of Sex Research* 20.2:143–167.

Celentano, D. D., L. A. Valleroy, F. Sifakis, D. A. MacKellar, J. Hylton, H. Thiede et al. 2006. Associations between substance use and sexual risk among very young men who have sex with men. *Sexually Transmitted Diseases* 33.4:265–271.

Center for Substance Abuse Treatment (CSAT). 1998a. *Substance Use Disorder Treatment for People with Physical and Cognitive Disabilities*. Treatment Improvement Protocol (TIP) 29. DHHS Pub. No. (SMA) 98-3249. Rockville, MD: Substance Abuse and Mental Health Services Administration.

——. 1998b. *Treatment of Adolescents with Substance Use Disorders.* Treatment Improvement Protocol (TIP) 32. DHHS Pub. No. (SMA) 07-4080. Rockville, MD: Substance Abuse and Mental Health Services Administration.

——. 1999a. *Enhancing Motivation for Change in Substance Abuse Treatment.* Treatment Improvement Protocol (TIP) 35. DHHS Pub. No. (SMA) 07-4212. Rockville, MD: Substance Abuse and Mental Health Services Administration.

——. 1999b. *Screening and Assessing Adolescents for Substance Use Disorders.* Treatment Improvement Protocol (TIP) 31. DHHS Pub. No. (SMA) 99-3282. Rockville, MD: Substance Abuse and Mental Health Services Administration.

——. 2000. *Substance Abuse Treatment for Persons with HIV/AIDS.* Treatment Improvement Protocol (TIP) 37. DHHS Pub. No. (SMA) 06-4137. Rockville, MD: Substance Abuse and Mental Health Services Administration.

——. 2001a. *A Provider's Introductionto Substance Abuse Treatment for Lesbian, Gay, Bisexual, and Transgender Individuals.* DHHS Pub. No. (SMA) 03-3819. Rockville, MD: Substance Abuse and Mental Health Services Administration.

——. 2001b. *The Hidden Epidemic: Prevention and Intervention of Alcohol and Medication Misuse and Abuse Among Older Adults Meeting Summary.* Rockville, MD: Substance Abuse and Mental Health Services Administration.

——. 2004. *Substance Abuse Treatment and Family Therapy.* Treatment Improvement Protocol (TIP) 39. DHHS Pub. No. (SMA) 06-4219. Rockville, MD: Substance Abuse and Mental Health Services Administration.

——. 2005a. *Substance Abuse Treatment for Persons with Co-Occurring Disorders.* Treatment Improvement Protocol (TIP) 42. DHHS Pub. No. (SMA) 05-3922. Rockville, MD: Substance Abuse and Mental Health Services Administration.

——. 2005b. *Substance Abuse Treatment: Group Therapy.* Treatment Improvement Protocol (TIP) 41. DHHS Pub. No. (SMA) 05-3991. Rockville, MD: Substance Abuse and Mental Health Services Administration.

——. 2006a. *Counselor's Treatment Manual: Matrix Intensive Outpatient Treatment for People with Stimulant Use Disorders.* DHHS Pub. No. (SMA) 06-4152. Rockville, MD: Substance Abuse and Mental Health Services Administration.

——. 2006b. *Substance Abuse: Clinical Issues in Intensive Outpatient Treatment.* Treatment Improvement Protocol (TIP) 47. DHHS Pub. No. (SMA) 06-4182. Rockville, MD: Substance Abuse and Mental Health Services Administration.

Centers for Disease Control and Prevention (CDC). 1999. *HIV/AIDS and U.S. Women Who Have Sex with Women (WSW).* Rockville, MD: Author.

——. 2007. *HIV/AIDS Surveillance Report* 17. Atlanta, GA: Author.

Chan, C. S. 1995. Issues of sexual identity in an ethnic minority: The case of Chinese American lesbians, gay men, and bisexual people. In A. R. D'Augelli and C. J. Patterson, eds., *Lesbian, Gay, and Bisexual Identities Over the Lifespan,* 87–101. New York: Oxford University Press.

Chase, C. 2005. Intersex 101: A human rights perspective. Workshop presented at the National Conference for the Lesbian, Gay, Bisexual and Transgender Movement, Nov. 12. Oakland, CA.

Childress, A. R. 2006. What can human brain imaging tell us about vulnerability to addiction and to relapse? In W. R. Miller and K. M. Carroll, eds., *Rethinking Substance Abuse,* 46–60. New York: Guilford Press.

Chu, S. Y., T. A. Peterman, L. S. Doll, J. W. Buehler, and J. W. Curran. 1992. AIDS in bisexual men in the United States: Epidemiology and transmission outcome. *American Journal of Public Health* 82.2:220–224.

Ciesielski, C., R. H. Kahn, M. Taylor, K. Gallagher, L. J. Prescott, and S. Arrowsmith. 2005. Control of syphilis outbreaks in men who have sex with men: The role of screening in nonmedical settings. *Sexually Transmitted Diseases* 32.10:S37–S42.

Ciro, D., M. Surko, K. Bandarkar, N. Helfgott, K. Peake, and I. Epstein. 2005. Lesbian, gay, bisexual, sexual-orientation questioning adolescents seeking mental health services: Risk factors, worries, and desire to talk about them. *Social Work in Mental Health* 3.3:213–234.

Claes, J. A., and W. Moore. 2000. Issues confronting lesbian and gay elders: The challenge for health and human service providers. *Journal of the Health and Human Services Administration* 23:181–202.

Clatts, M. C., L. A. Goldsamt, and H. Yi. 2005. Club drug use among young men who have sex with men in NYC: A preliminary epidemiological profile. *Substance Use and Misuse* 40.9/10:1317–1330.

Clatts, M. C., L. A. Goldsamt, H. Yi, and M. V. Gwadz. 2005. Homelessness and drug abuse among young men who have sex with men in New York City: A preliminary epidemiological trajectory. *Journal of Adolescence* 28.2:201–214.

Clements, K., R. Marx, R. Guzman, S. Ikeda, and M. Katz. 1998. Prevalence of HIV infection in transgendered individuals in San Francisco. International Conference on AIDS; 12:449 (abstract no. 23536).

Clements, K., W. Wilkinson, K. Kitano, and R. Marx. 1999. HIV prevention and health service needs of the transgender community in San Francisco. *International Journal of Transgenderism* 3.1/2 (serial online).

Clements-Nolle, K., R. Marx, R. Guzman, and M. Katz. 2001. HIV prevalence, risk behaviors, health care use, and mental health status of transgender persons: Implications for public health intervention. *American Journal of Public Health* 91.6: 915–921.

Clements-Nolle, K., R. Marx, and M. Katz. 2006. Attempted suicide among transgender persons: The influence of gender-based discrimination and victimization. *Journal of Homosexuality* 51.3:53–69.

Cochran, B. N., and A. M. Cauce. 2006. Characteristics of lesbian, gay, bisexual, and transgender individuals entering substance abuse treatment. *Journal of Substance Abuse Treatment* 30.2:135–146.

Cochran, B. N., K. M. Peavy, and A. M. Cauce. 2007. Substance abuse treatment providers' explicit and implicit attitudes regarding sexual minorities. *Journal of Homosexuality* 52.3:181–207.

Cochran, B. N., K. M. Peavy, and J. S. Robohm. 2007. Do specialized services exist for LGBT individuals seeking treatment for substance misuse? A study of available treatment programs. *Substance Use and Misuse* 42:161–176.

Cochran, B. N., A. J. Stewart, J. A. Ginzler, and A. M. Cauce. 2002. Challenges faced by homeless sexual minorities: Comparison of gay, lesbian, bisexual, and transgender homeless adolescents with their heterosexual counterparts. *American Journal of Public Health* 92.5:773–777.

Cochran, S. D. 2001. Emerging issues in research on lesbians' and gay mens' mental health: Does sexual orientation really matter? *American Psychologist* 56.11:932–947.

Cochran, S. D., and V. M. Mays. 2000. Lifetime prevalence of suicide symptoms and affective disorders among men reporting same-sex sexual partners: Results from NHANES III. *American Journal of Public Health* 90.4:573–578.

Cochran, S. D., J. Sullivan, and V. M. Mays. 2003. Prevalence of mental disorders, psychological distress, and mental services use among lesbian, gay, and bisexual adults in the United States. *Journal of Consulting and Clinical Psychology* 71.1:53–61.

Cochran, S. D., D. Ackerman, V. M. Mays, and, M. W. Ross. 2004. Prevalence of nonmedical drug use and dependence among homosexually active men and women in the U.S. population. *Addiction* 99.8:989–998.

Cochran, S. D., C. Keenan, C. Schober, and V. M. Mays. 2000. Estimates of alcohol use and clinical treatment needs among homosexually active men and women in the U.S. population. *Journal of Consulting Clinical Psychology* 68.6:1062–1071.

Cochran, S. D., V. M. Mays, M. Alegria, A. N. Ortega, and D. Takeuchi. 2007. Mental health and substance use disorders among Latino and Asian American lesbian, gay, and bisexual adults. *Journal of Consulting and Clinical Psychology* 75.5:785–794.

Coffey, R., L. Graver, D. Schroeder, J. Busch, J. Dilonardo, M. Chalk et al. 2001. *Mental Health and Substance Abuse Treatment: Results from a Study Integrating Data from State Mental Health, Substance Abuse, and Medicaid Agencies.* DHHS Pub. No. (SMA) 01-3528. Rockville, MD: Substance Abuse and Mental Health Services Administration.

Cohler, B. J. 1999. The gay therapist's response to a gay client practicing unsafe sex: A dilemma in brief psychotherapy. *Psychoanalytic Social Work* 6.3/4:161–201.

Cole, C., M. O'Boyle, L. Emory, and W. Meyer. 1997. Comorbidity of gender dysphoria and other major psychiatric disorders. *Archives of Sexual Behavior* 26:13–26.

Cole, S. S., D. Denny, A. E. Eyler, and S. L. Samons. 2000. Issues of transgender. In T. Szuchman and F. Muscarella, eds., *Psychological Perspectives in Human Sexuality*, 149–195. New York: Wiley.

Coleman, E. 1982. Developmental stages of the coming out process. *Journal of Homosexuality* 7.7:31–43.

Colfax, G., T. J. Coates, M. J. Husnik, Y. Huang, S. Buchbinder, B. Koblin et al. 2005. Longitudinal patterns of methamphetamine, popper (amyl nitrite) and cocaine use and high-risk sexual behavior among a cohort of San Francisco men who have sex with men. *Journal of Urban Health* 82.1:62–70.

Colfax, G. N., G. Mansergh, R. Guzman, E. Vittinghoff, G. Marks, M. Rader et al. 2001. Drug use and sexual behavior among gay and bisexual men who attend circuit parties: A value-based comparison. *Journal of Acquired Immune Deficiency Syndromes* 28.4:373–379.

Colfax, G. N., E. Vittinghoff, M. J. Husnik, D. McKirnan, S. Buchbinder, B. Koblin et al. 2004. Substance use and sexual risk: A participant- and episode-level analysis among a cohort of men who have sex with men. *American Journal of Epidemiology* 159:1002–1012.

Comacho, A., S. C. Matthews, and J. E. Dimsdale. 2004. Use of GHB compounds by HIV-positive individuals. *American Journal on Addictions* 13.2:120–127.

Comacho, A., S. C. Matthews, B. Murray, and J. E. Dimsdale. 2005. Use of GHB compounds among college students, *American Journal of Drug and Alcohol Abuse* 31.4:601–607.

Conway, L. 2002. How frequently does transsexualism occur? Retrieved from www.intersexualite.org/frequency_of_TS.html.

Copeland, J., and P. Dillon. 2005. The health and psychosocial consequences of ketamine use. *International Journal of Drug Policy* 16.2:122–131.

Corliss, H. L., C. E. Grella, V. M. Mays, and S. D. Cochran. 2006. Drug use, drug severity, and help-seeking behaviors of lesbian and bisexual women. *Journal of Women's
Health* 15.5:556–568.

Corliss, H. L., M. D. Shankle, and M. B. Moyer. 2007. Research, curricula, and resources
related to lesbian, gay, bisexual, and transgender health in U.S. schools of public
health. *American Journal of Public Health* 97.6:1023–1027.

Corrigan, E. M., and S. C. Anderson. 1984. Homeless alcoholic women on skid row.
American Journal of Drug and Alcohol Abuse 10.4:535–549.

Crisp, C. 2006. The gay affirmative practice scale (GAP): A new measure for assessing
cultural competence with gay and lesbian clients. *Social Work* 51.2:115–126.

Crosbie-Burnett, M., T. L. Foster, C. I. Murray, and G. L. Bowen. 1996. Gay and lesbians'
families of origin: A social-cognitive-behavioral model of adjustment. *Family Relations* 45.4:397–403.

Crosby, R. A., and N. L. Pitts. 2007. Caught between different worlds: How transgendered women may be "forced" into risky sex. *Journal of Sex Research* 44.1:43.

Currah, P., J. Green, and S. Minter. 2000. *Transgender Equality.* New York: Policy Institute of the National Gay and Lesbian Task Force.

Curry, H., D. Clifford, and F. Hertz. 2002. *A Legal Guide for Lesbian and Gay Couples.*
11th ed. Berkeley, CA: Nolo Press.

D'Augelli, A. R., A. H. Grossman, S. L. Hershberger, and T. S. O'Connell. 2001. Aspects
of mental health among older lesbian, gay, and bisexual adults. *Aging and Mental
Health* 5:149–158.

D'Augelli, R. R., S. L. Hershberger, and N. W. Pilkington. 1998. Lesbian, gay, and bisexual youth and their families: Disclosure of sexual orientation and its consequences.
American Journal of Orthopsychiatry 68:361–371.

Decker, B. 1984. Counseling gay and lesbian couples. *Journal of Social Work and Human
Sexuality* 2:39–52.

DeCrescenzo, T. A. 1984. Homophobia: A study of the attitudes of mental health professionals toward homosexuality. *Journal of Social Work and Human Sexuality* 2:
115–136.

Deming, A. M., K. McGoff-Yost, and A. Strozier. 2002. Homeless addicted women.
In S. L. A. Straussner and S. Brown, eds., *The Handbook of Addiction Treatment for
Women,* 451–469. San Francisco: Jossey-Bass.

Denning, P. 1998. Therapeutic interventions for individuals with substance use, HIV,
and personality disorders: Harm reduction as a unifying approach. *In Session: Psychotherapy in Practice* 4.1:37–52.

——. 2000. *Practicing Harm Reduction Psychotherapy.* New York: Guilford Press.

DeSandre, P. L. 2006. Methamphetamine emergencies. *Journal of Gay and Lesbian Psychotherapy* 10.3/4:57–65.

Descamps, M. J., E. Rothblum, J. Bradford, and C. Ryan. 2000. Mental health impact of
child sexual abuse, rape, intimate partner violence and hate crimes in the National
Lesbian Health Care Survey. *Journal of Gay and Lesbian Social Services* 11.1:27–55.

Des Jarlais, D., M. Marmor, D. Paone, S. Titus, Q. Shi, T. Perlis et al. 1996. HIV incidence among injecting drug users in New York City syringe exchange programs. *The
Lancet* 348:987–971.

Devor, A. H. 2004. Witnessing and mirroring: A fourteen-stage model of transsexual identity formation. *Journal of Gay and Lesbian Psychotherapy* 8.1/2:41–67.

Díaz, R. 1998. *Latino Gay Men and HIV: Culture, Sexuality, and Risk Behavior*. New York: Routledge.

Díaz, R. M., and G. Ayala. 2001. *Social Discrimination and Health: The Case of Latino Gay Men and HIV Risk*. New York: Policy Institute, National Gay and Lesbian Task Force.

Díaz, R. M., G. Ayala, E. Bein, J. Heine, and B. V. Marin. 2001. The impact of homophobia, poverty, and racism on the mental health of gay and bisexual Latino men: Findings from three U.S. cities. *American Journal of Public Health* 91:927–932.

Díaz, R. M., A. L. Heckert, and J. Sánchez. 2005. Reasons for stimulant use among Latino gay men in San Francisco: A comparison between methamphetamine and cocaine users. *Journal of Urban Health* 82.1:71–78.

DiClemente, C. C. 1991. Motivational interviewing and the stages of change. In W. R. Miller and S. Rollnick, eds., *Motivational Interviewing*, 191–202. New York : Guilford Press.

——. 2006. Natural change and the troublesome use of substances: A life-course perspective. In W. R. Miller and K. M. Carroll, eds., *Rethinking Substance Abuse*, 81–96. New York: Guilford Press.

Doolan, D. M., and E. S. Froelicher. 2006. Efficacy of smoking cessation intervention among special populations. *Nursing Research* 55.4:29–37.

Drabble, L., L. T. Midanik, and K. Trocki. 2005. Reports of alcohol consumption and alcohol-related problems among homosexual, bisexual and heterosexual respondents: Results from the 2000 National Alcohol Survey. *Journal of Studies on Alcohol* 66.1:111–120.

Drabble, L., and K. Trocki. 2005. Alcohol consumption, alcohol-related problems, and other substance use among lesbian and bisexual women. *Journal of Lesbian Studies* 9.3:19–30.

Dworkin, S. H. 2001. Treating the bisexual client. *In Session: Psychotherapy in Practice* 57.5:671–680.

——. 2006. The aging bisexual: The invisible of the invisible minority. In D. Kimmel, T. Rose, and S. David, eds., *Lesbian, Gay, Bisexual, and Transgender Aging: Research and Clinical Perspectives*, 36–52. New York: Columbia University Press.

Elford, J., G. Bolding, M. Maguire, and L. Sherr. 1999. Sexual risk behavior among gay men in a relationship. *AIDS* 13:1407–1411.

Eliason, M. J. 2000. Substance abuse counselors' attitudes regarding lesbian, gay, bisexual, and transgender clients. *Journal of Substance Abuse* 12:311–328.

Eliason, M. J., and T. Hughes. 2004. Treatment counselor's attitudes about lesbian, gay, bisexual, and transgendered clients: Urban vs. rural settings. *Substance Use and Misuse* 39.4:625–644.

Ellis, K. M., and K. Eriksen. 2002. Transsexual and transgenderist experiences and treatment options. *Family Journal: Counseling and Therapy for Couples and Families* 10.3:289–299.

Elze, D. E. 2006. Oppression, prejudice, and discrimination. In D. F. Morrow and L. Messinger, eds., *Sexual Orientation and Gender Expression in Social Work Practice*, 43–77. New York: Columbia University Press.

Ettner, R. I., and T. J. H. White. 2000. Children of a parent undergoing a gender transition: Disclosure, risk, and protective factors. *International Journal of Transgenderism* 4.3 (serial online).

Falco, K. L. 1991. *Psychotherapy with Lesbian Clients: Theory Into Practice.* New York: Brunner/Mazel.

Farkas, K. J. 2004. Substance abuse problems among older adults. In S. L. A. Straussner, ed., *Clinical Work with Substance-Abusing Clients,* 330–346. New York: Guilford Press.

Fassinger, R. E. 1991. The hidden minority: Issues and challenges in working with lesbian and gay men. *Counseling Psychologist* 19:157–176.

Fausto-Sterling, A. 2000. *Sexing the body: Gender politics and the construction of sexuality.* New York: Basic Books.

Fergus, S., M. A. Lewis, L. A. Darbes, and R. M. Butterfield. 2005. HIV risk and protection among gay male couples: The role of gay community integration. *Health Education and Behavior* 32.2:151–171.

Fernandez, M. I., G. S. Bowen, L. M. Varga, J. B. Collazo, N. Hernandez, T. Perrino et al. 2005. High rates of club drug use and risky sexual practices among Hispanic men who have sex with men in Miami, Florida. *Substance Use and Misuse* 40.9/10:1347–1362.

Fernandez, M. I., T. Perrino, G. S. Bowen, N. Hernandez, S. A. Cardenas, D. Marsh et al. 2005. Club drug use, sexual behavior, and HIV risk among community and internet samples of MSM: Implications for clinicians. *Journal of Social Work Practice in the Addictions* 5.4:81–100.

Fickey, J., and G. Grimm. 1998. Boundary issues in gay and lesbian psychotherapy relationships. In C. J. Alexander, ed., *Working with Gay Men and Lesbians in Private Psychotherapy Practice,* 77–93. New York: Haworth Press.

Fields, A. 2004. *Curriculum-Based Motivation Group: A Five-Session Motivational Interviewing Group Intervention.* Vancouver, WA: Hollifield Associates.

Finnegan, D. G., and E. B. McNally. 2000. Making up for lost time: Chemically dependent lesbians in later midlife. *Journal of Gay and Lesbian Social Services* 11.2/3:105–118.

——. 2002. *Counseling Lesbian, Gay, Bisexual, and Transgender Substance Abusers: Dual Identities.* New York: Haworth Press.

Fisher, D. G., R. Malow, R. Rosenberg, G. L. Reynolds, N. Farrell, and A. Jaffe. 2006. Recreational Viagra use and sexual risk among drug abusing men. *American Journal of Infectous Diseases* 2.2:107–114.

Fisher, L., R. Goldschmidt, R. Hays, and J. Catania. 1993. Families of homosexual men: Their knowledge and support regarding sexual orientation and HIV disease. *Journal of the American Board of Family Practice* 6:25–32.

Fitzpatrick, K. K., S. J. Euton, J. N. Jones, and N. B. Schmidt. 2005. Gender role, sexual orientation, and suicide risk. *Journal of Affective Disorders* 87.1:35–42.

Fortunata, B., and C. S. Kohn. 2003. Demographic, psychosocial, and personality characteristics of lesbian batterers. *Violence and Victims* 18.5:557–568.

Fox, R. C. 1995. Bisexual identities. In A. R. D'Augelli and C. J. Patterson, ed. *Lesbian, Gay, and Bisexual Identities Over the Lifespan: Psychological Perspectives,* 48–86. New York: Oxford University Press.

Frederick, R. J. 2004. The multidimensional challenge of psychotherapy with HIV positive gay men. *Journal of Gay and Lesbian Social Services* 17.2:63–79.

Freeman, D. S. 1992. *Family Therapy with Couples.* Northvale, NJ: Jason Aronson.

Freshman, A. 2004. Assessment and treatment of adolescent substance abusers. In S. L. A. Straussner, ed., *Clinical Work with Substance-Abusing Clients,* 305–329. New York: Guilford Press.

Friedman, E. G., and R. Wilson. 2004. The treatment of opiate addiction. In S. L. A. Straussner, ed., *Clinical Work with Substance-Abusing Clients*, 187–208. New York: Guilford Press.

Futcher, J. 1995. Outlaws and addicts: Lesbians and the recovery movement. In K. Jay, ed., *Dyke Life*, 332–343. New York: Basic Books.

Gabriel, M. A., and G. W. Monaco. 1995. Revisiting the question of self-disclosure: The lesbian therapist's dilemma. In J. M. Glassgold and S. Iasenza, eds., *Lesbians and Psychoanalysis: Revolutions in Theory and Practice*, 161–172. New York: Free Press.

Gainor, K. A. 2000. Including transgender issues in lesbian, gay and bisexual psychology. In B. Greene and G. L. Croom, eds., *Education, Research, and Practice in Lesbian, Gay, Bisexual, and Transgendered Psychology*, 131–160. New York: American Psychological Association.

Gair, S. 1995. The false self, shame, and the challenge of self-cohesion. In J. Glassgold and S. Iasenza, eds., *Lesbians and Psychoanalysis: Revolutions in Theory and Practice*, 107–123. New York: Free Press.

Gant, L. M., and D. P. Strom. 2004. HIV/AIDS and intravenous drug users. In S. L. A. Straussner, ed., *Clinical Work with Substance-Abusing Clients*, 443–471. New York: Guilford Press.

Garofalo, R., J. Deleon, E. Osmer, M. Doll, and G. W. Harper. 2006. Overlooked, misunderstood and at-risk: Exploring the lives and HIV risk of ethnic minority male-to-female transgender youth. *Journal of Adolescent Health* 38:230–236.

Garrett, J., J. Landau, R. Shea, M. D. Stanton, G. Baciewicz, and D. Brinkman-Sull. 1997. The ARISE intervention: Using family and network links to engage addicted persons in treatment. *Journal of Substance Abuse Treatment* 15:333–343.

Gay and Lesbian Medical Association (GLMA). 2001. *Healthy People, 2010: Companion Document for Lesbian, Gay, Bisexual, and Transgender (LGBT) Health*. San Francisco, CA: Author.

——. 2006. *Breaking the Grip: Treating Crystal Methamphetamine Addiction Among Gay and Bisexual Men*. San Francisco, CA: Author.

Gay Demographics. 2003. *Percentage of Households with Children Under Eighteen Years*. Retrieved from http://www.gaydemographics.org.

Gilman, S. E., S. D. Cochran, V. M. Mays, M. Hughes, D. Ostrow, and R. C. Kessler. 2001. Risk of psychiatric disorders among individuals reporting same-sex sexual partners in the national comorbidity survey. *American Journal of Public Health* 91.6: 933–939.

Golden, C. 1987. Diversity and variability in women's sexual identities. In Boston Lesbian Psychologies Collective, ed., *Lesbian Psychologies*, 18–34. Urbana: University of Illinois Press.

Goldstein, E. G. 2004. Substance abusers with borderline disorders. In S. L. A. Straussner, ed., *Clinical Work with Substance-Abusing Clients*, 370–391. New York: Guilford Press.

Gonsiorek, J. C. 1991. The empirical basis for the demise of the illness model of homosexuality. In J. C. Gonsiorek and J. D. Weinrich, eds., *Homosexuality: Research Implications for Public Policy*, 115–136. Newbury Park, CA: Sage Publications.

González, F. J., and O. M. Espín. 1996. Latino men, latina women, and homosexuality. In R. P. Cabaj and T. S. Stein, eds., *Textbook of Sexuality and Mental Health*, 583–601. Washington, DC: American Psychiatric Press.

Gorman, E. M., K. R. Nelson, T. Applegate, and A. Scrol. 2004. Club drug and poly-substance abuse and HIV among gay/bisexual men: Lessons gleaned from a community study. *Journal of Gay and Lesbian Social Services* 16.2:1–17.

Grant, B. F., D. S. Hasin, S. P. Chou, F. S. Stinson, and D. A. Dawson. 2004. Nicotine dependence and psychiatric disorders in the United States: Results from the National Epidemiologic Survey on Alcohol and Related Conditions. *Archives of General Psychiatry* 61:1107–1115.

Gray, M., and S. Gibson. 2004. Relapse Prevention. In S. L. A. Straussner, ed., *Clinical Work with Substance-Abusing Clients*, 146–168. New York: Guilford Press.

Green, K., V. Causby, and D. H. Miller. 1999. The nature and function of fusion in the dynamics of lesbian relationships. *Affilia: Journal of Women and Social Work* 14: 78–97.

Green, R. 1998. Transsexuals' children. *International Journal of Transgenderism* 2.4 (serial online).

Green, R. J. 2000. Lesbians, gay men, and their parents: A critique of La Sala and the prevailing clinical wisdom. *Family Process* 39.2:257–266.

Green, R. J., M. Bettinger, and E. Zacks. 1996. Are lesbian couples fused and gay males disengaged? Questioning gender straightjackets. In J. Laird and R. J. Green, eds., *Lesbians and Gays in Couples and Families: A Handbook for Therapists*, 185–230. San Francisco: Jossey-Bass.

Greene, B. 1994. Lesbian women of color: Triple jeopardy. In L. Comas-Diaz and B. Greene, eds., *Women of Color: Integrating Ethnic and Gender Identities in Psychotherapy*, 389–427. New York: Guilford.

Greenwood, G. L., J. P. Paul, L. M. Pollack, D. Binson, J. A. Catania, J. Chang et al. 2005. Tobacco use and cessation among a household-based sample of US urban men who have sex with men. *American Journal of Public Health* 95.1:145–151.

Grossman, A. H., A. R. D'Augelli, and S. L. Hershberger. 2000. Social support networks of lesbian, gay, and bisexual adults 60 years of age and older. *Journal of Gerontology: Psychological Sciences* 55.3:171–179.

Grossman, A. H., A. R. D'Augelli, T. J. Howell, and S. Hubbard. 2005. Parents' reactions to transgender youths' gender nonconforming expression and identity. *Journal of Gay and Lesbian Social Services* 18.1:3–16.

Grov, C., J. T. Parsons, and D. S. Bimbi. 2008. In the shadows of a prevention campaign: Sexual risk behavior in the absence of crystal methamphetamine. *AIDS Education and Prevention* 20.1:42–55.

Gruskin, E. P. 1999. *Treating Lesbians and Bisexual Women: Challenges and Strategies for Health Professionals*. London: Sage Publications.

Gruskin, E., K. Byrne, S. Kools, and A. Altschuler. 2006. Consequences of frequenting the lesbian bar. *Women and Health* 44.2:103–120.

Gruskin, E. P., and N. Gordon. 2006. Gay/lesbian sexual orientation increases risk for cigarette smoking and heavy drinking among members of a large Northern California health plan. *BMC Public Health* 6:241–246.

Gruskin, E., S. Hart, N. Gordon, and L. Ackerson. 2001. Patterns of cigarette smoking and alcohol use among lesbians and bisexual women enrolled in a large health maintenance organization. *American Journal of Public Health* 91.6:976–979.

Guss, J. R. 2000. Sex like you can't even imagine: "Crystal," crack, and gay men. *Journal of Gay and Lesbian Psychotherapy* 3.3/4:105–122.

Haldeman, D. C. 1994. The practice and ethics of sexual orientation conversion therapy. *Journal of Consulting and Clinical Psychology* 62:221–227.

——. 1996. Spirituality and religion in the lives of lesbians and gay men. In R. P. Cabaj and T. S. Stein, eds., *Textbook of Homosexuality and Mental Health*, 881–896. Washington, DC: American Psychiatric Press.

——. 2001. Therapeutic antidotes: Helping gay and bisexual men recover from conversion. *Journal of Gay and Lesbian Psychotherapy* 5.3/4:117–130.

Halkitis, P. N. 2004. Optimism and HIV treatment advances: The impact on sexual risk-taking among gay men. *Health Psychologist* 21.4:10–14.

Halkitis, P. N., and K. A. Green. 2007. Sildenafil (Viagra) and club drug use in gay and bisexual men: The role of drug combinations and context. *American Journal of Men's Health* 1.2:139–147.

Halkitis, P. N., K. A. Green, and D. J. Carragher. 2006. Methamphetamine use, sexual behavior, and HIV seroconversion. *Journal of Gay and Lesbian Psychotherapy* 10.3/4:95–109.

Halkitis, P. N., K. A. Green, and P. Mourgues. 2005. Longitudinal investigation of methamphetamine use among gay and bisexual men in New York City: Findings from Project BUMPS. *Journal of Urban Health* 82.1:18–25.

Halkitis, P. N., K. A. Green, R. H. Remien, M. J. Stirrat, C. C. Hoff, R. J. Wolitski et al. 2005. Seroconcordent sexual partnering of HIV-seropositive men who have sex with men. *AIDS* 19:77–86.

Halkitis, P. N., and R. C. Jerome. 2008. A comparative analysis of methamphetamine use: Black gay and bisexual men in relation to men of other races. *Addictive Behaviors* 33.1:83–93.

Halkitis, P. N., R. W. Moeller, and L. B. DeRaleau. 2008. Steroid use in gay, bisexual, and nonidentified men-who-have-sex-with men; Relations to masculinity, physical, and mental health. *Psychology of Men and Masculinity* 9.2:106–115.

Halkitis, P. N., R. W. Moeller, D. E. Siconolfi, R. C. Jerome, M. Rogers, and J. Schillinger. 2008. Methamphetamine and poly-substance use among gym-attending men who have sex with men in New York City. *Annals of Behavioral Medicine* 35.1:41–48.

Halkitis, P. N., and J. J. Palamar. 2006. GHB use among gay and bisexual men. *Addiction Behavior* 31.11:2135–2139.

Halkitis, P. N., J. J. Palamar, and P. Pandey Mukherjee. 2007. Poly–club drug use among gay and bisexual men: A longitudinal analysis. *Drug and Alcohol Dependence* 89.2/3:153–160.

Halkitis, P. N., P. Pandey Mukherjee, and J. J. Palamar. 2007. Multi-level modeling to explain methamphetamine use among gay and bisexual men. *Addiction* 102.76–83.

Halkitis, P. N., and J. T. Parsons. 2002. Recreational drug use and HIV-risk sexual behavior among men frequenting gay social venues. *Journal of Gay and Lesbian Social Services* 12.4:19–38.

Halkitis, P. N., and M. T. Shrem. 2006. Psychological differences between binge and chronic methamphetamine using gay and bisexual men. *Addictive Behaviors* 31.3:549–552.

Halkitis, P. N., M. T. Shrem, and F. W. Martin. 2005. Sexual behavior patterns of methamphetamine-using gay and bisexual men. *Substance Use and Misuse* 40.5:703–719.

Halkitis, P. N., L. Wilton, R. J. Wolitski, J. T. Parsons, C. C. Hoff, and D. S. Bimbi. 2005. Barebacking identity among HIV-positive gay and bisexual men: Demographic, psychological, and behavioral correlates. *AIDS* 19:27–35.

Hall, J. M. 1994. The experiences of lesbians in Alcoholics Anonymous. *Western Journal of Nursing Research* 16.5:556–576.

Hamer, D. H., S. Hu, V. L. Magnuson, N. Hu, and A. M. Pattatuci. 1993. A linkage between DNA markers on the X chromosome and male sexual orientation. *Science* 253:1034–1037.

Harding, R., J. Bensley, and N. Corrigan. 2004. Targeting smoking cessation to high prevalence communities: Outcomes from a pilot intervention for gay men. *BMC Public Health* 4:43–47.

Hare, J., and L. Richards. 1993. Children raised by lesbian couples: Does context of birth affect father and partner involvement? *Family Relations* 42:249–255.

Harrison, S. 2007. Coming out. *Intelligence Report* 28:55–57.

Hash, K. M., and S. D. Ceperich. 2006. Workplace issues. In D. F. Morrow and L. Messinger, eds., *Sexual Orientation and Gender Expression in Social Work Practice*, 405–426. New York: Columbia University Press.

Hasin, D., M. Hatzenbuehler, and R. Waxman. 2006. Genetics of substance use disorders. In W. R. Miller and K. M. Carroll, eds., *Rethinking Substance Abuse*, 61–77. New York: Guilford Press.

Hassouneh, D., and N. Glass. 2008. The influence of gender-role stereotyping on women's experiences of female same-sex intimate partner violence. *Violence Against Women* 14.3:310–325.

Hatzenbuehler, M. L.,W. R. Corbin, and K. Fromme. 2008. Trajectories and determinants of alcohol use among LGB young adults and their heterosexual peers: Results from a prospective study. *Developmental Psychology* 44.1:81–90.

Havens, J. R., S. G. Sherman, M. Sapun, and S. A. Strathdee. 2006. Prevalence and correlates of suicidal ideation among young injection vs. noninjection drug users. *Substance Use and Misuse* 41:245–254.

Heckman, T. G., B. D. Heckman, A. Kochman, K. J. Sikkema, J. Suhr, and K. Goodkin. 2002. Psychological symptoms among persons 50 years of age and older living with HIV disease. *Aging and Mental Health* 6.2:121–128.

Hellman, R. E. 1996. Issues in the treatment of lesbian women and gay men with chronic mental illness. *Psychiatric Services* 47:1093–1098.

Henriques, Z., and N. Manatu-Rupert. 2001. Living on the outside: Aftican American women before, during, and after imprisonment. *Prison Journal* 81.1:6–19.

Herek, G. M. 1996. Heterosexism and homophobia. In R. P. Cabaj and T. S. Stein, eds., *Textbook of Homosexuality and Mental Health*, 101–113. Washington, DC: American Psychiatric Press.

Hershberger, S. L., and A. R D'Augelli. 2000. Issues in counseling lesbian, gay, and bisexual adolescents. In R. M. Perez, K. A. De Bord, and K. Bieschke, eds., *Handbook of Counseling and Psychotherapy with Lesbian, Gay, and Bisexual Clients*, 225–248. Washington DC: American Psychological Association.

Hesselbrock, V. M., and M. N. Hesselbrock. 1997. Gender, alcoholism, and psychiatric comorbidity. In R. W. Wilsnack and S. C. Wilsnack, eds., *Gender and Alcohol: Individual and Social Perspectives*, 49–71. New Brunswick, NJ: Rutgers Center of Alcohol Studies.

——. 2006. Developmental perspectives on the risk for developing substance abuse problems. In W. R. Miller and K. M. Carroll, eds., *Rethinking Substance Abuse*, 97–114. New York: Guilford Press.

Hicks, D. 2000. The importance of specialized treatment programs for lesbian and gay patients. *Journal of Gay and Lesbian Psychotherapy* 3:81–94.

Hicks, G. R., and T. Lee. 2006. Public attitudes toward gays and lesbians: Trends and predictions. *Journal of Homosexuality* 51.2:57–77.

Hicks, S., and S. Wise. 2000. Lesbian and gay issues in social work. In M. Davies, ed., *The Blackwell Encyclopaedia of Social Work*, 193–195. Oxford: Blackwell.

Higgins, S. T., and N. M. Petry. 1999. Contingency management: Incentives for sobriety. *Alcohol Research and Health* 23.2:122–127.

Hirshfield, S., M. A. Chiasson, and R. H. Remien. 2006. Crystal methamphetamine use among men who have sex with men: Results from two national online studies. *Journal of Gay and Lesbian Psychotherapy* 10.3/4:85–93.

Hirshfield, S., R. H. Remien, M. Humberstone, I. Walavalkar, and M. A. Chaisson. 2004. Substance use and high-risk sex among men who have sex with men: A national online study in the USA. *AIDS Care* 16.8:1036–1047.

Hoburg, R., J. Konik, M. Williams, and M. Crawford. 2004. Bisexuality among self-identified heterosexual college students. *Journal of Bisexuality* 4.1/2:25–36.

Hofman, M. A., L. J. Gooren, D. F. Swaab, and J. N. Zhou. 1997. A sex difference in the human brain and its relation to transsexuality. *International Journal of Transgenderism*, 1.1 (serial online).

Holder, H. D. 2006. Racial and gender differences in substance abuse. In W. R. Miller and K. M. Carroll, eds., *Rethinking Substance Abuse*, 153–165. New York: Guilford Press.

Holleran, P. R., and A. H. Novak. 1989. Support choices and abstinence in gay/lesbian and heterosexual alcoholics. *Alcoholism Treatment Quarterly* 6:71–83.

Hooker, E. 1957. The adjustment of the male overt homosexual. *Journal of Projective Techniques* 21:18–31.

Horliss, H. L., S. D. Cochran, and V. M. Mays. 2002. Reports of parental maltreatment during childhood in a United States population-based survey of homosexual, bisexual, and heterosexual adults. *Child Abuse and Neglect* 26:1165–1178.

Horowitz, L. C. 2000. Resisting amnesia in the countertransference: A clinical strategy for working with lesbian patients. *Clinical Social Work Journal* 28.1:55–70.

Houston, E., and D. J. McKirnan. 2007. Intimate partner abuse among gay and bisexual men: risk correlates and health outcomes. *Journal of Urban Health* 84.5:681–690.

Hughes, T. L., L. E. Day, R. Marcantonio, and E. Tropy. 1997. Gender differences in alcohol and other drug use in young adults. *Substance Use and Misuse* 32.3:319–344.

Hughes, T. L., and M Eliason. 2002. Substance use and abuse in lesbian, gay, bisexual, and transgender populations. *Journal of Primary Prevention* 22.3:263–298.

Hughes, T. L., A. P. Hass, L. Razzano, R. Cassidy, and R. K. Matthews. 2000. Comparing lesbian and heterosexual women's mental health: Findings from a multi-site study. *Journal of Gay and Lesbian Social Services* 11.1:57–76.

Hughes, T. L., T. P. Johnson, and S. C. Wilsnack. 2001. Sexual assault and alcohol abuse: A comparison of lesbians and heterosexual women. *Journal of Substance Abuse* 13:515–532.

Hughes, T. L., T. P. Johnson, S. C. Wilsnack, and L. A. Szalacha. 2007. Childhood risk factors for alcohol abuse and psychological distress among adult lesbians. *Child Abuse and Neglect* 31.7:769–789.

Hughes, T. L., S. C. Wilsnack, L. A. Szalacha, T. Johnson, W. B. Bostwick, R. Seymour et al. 2006. Age and racial/ethnic differences in drinking and drinking-related problems in a community sample of lesbians. *Journal of the Study of Alcohol* 67:579–590.

Humphreys, K., and E. Gifford. 2006. Religion, spirituality, and the troublesome use of substances. In W. R. Miller and K. M. Carroll, eds., *Rethinking Substance Abuse*, 257–274. New York: Guilford Press.

Hunter, S., and J. C. Hickerson. 2003. *Affirmative Practice: Understanding and Working with Lesbian, Gay, Bisexual, and Transgender Persons*. Washington, DC: NASW Press.

Hutchins, L., and L. Kaahumanu, eds. 1991. *Bi Any Other Name: Bisexual People Speak Out*. Boston: Alyson.

Ibañez, G. E., D. W. Purcell, R. Stall, J. J. Parsons, and C. A. Gómez. 2005. Sexual risk, substance use, and psychological distress in HIV-positive gay and bisexual men who also inject drugs. *AIDS* 19:549–555.

Icard, L. D. 1996. Black gay men and conflicting social identities: Sexual orientation versus racial identity. *Journal of Social Work and Human Sexuality* 4.1/2:83–93.

Ingersoll, K., and C. Wagner. 1997. *Motivational Enhancement Groups for the Virginia Substance Abuse Treatment Outcomes Evaluation (SATOE) Model: Theoretical Background and Clinical Guidelines*. Richmond: Virginia Addiction Technology Transfer Center.

Irvin, J. E., C. A. Bowers, M. E. Dunn, and M. C. Wang. 1999. Efficacy of relapse prevention: A meta-analytic review. *Journal of Consulting and Clinical Psychology* 67.4: 563–571.

Irwin, T. W. 2006. Strategies for the treatment of methamphetamine use disorders among gay and bisexual men. *Journal of Gay and Lesbian Psychotherapy* 10.3/4:131–141.

Irwin, T. W., and J. Morgenstern. 2005. Drug-use patterns among men who have sex with men presenting for alcohol treatment: Differences in ethnic and sexual identity. *Journal of Urban Health* 82.1:127–133.

Israel, G. E., and D. E. Tarver, eds. 1997. *Transgender Care: Recommended Guidelines, Practical Information, and Personal Accounts*. Philadelphia: Temple University Press.

Israel, T., and J. J. Mohr. 2004. Attitudes toward bisexual women and men: Current research, future directions. *Journal of Bisexuality* 4.1/2:117–134.

Jaffe, A., S. Shoptaw, J. A. Stein, C. J. Reback, and E. Rotheram-Fuller. 2007. Depression ratings, reported sexual risk behaviors, and methamphetamine use: Latent growth curve models of positive change among gay and bisexual men in an outpatient treatment program. *Experimental and Clinical Psychopharmacology* 15.3:301–307.

James, S. E., and B. C. Murphy. 1998. Gay and lesbian relationships in a changing social context. In C. J. Patterson and A. R. D'Augelli, eds. *Lesbian, Gay, and Bisexual Identities in Families: Psychological Perspectives*, 99–121. New York: Oxford University Press.

Jeffreys, S. 1997. Transgender activism: A lesbian-feminist perspective. *Journal of Lesbian Studies* 1.3/4:55–74.

Jimenez, A. D. 2003. Triple jeopardy: Targeting older men of color who have sex with men. *Journal of Acquired Immune Deficiency Syndrome* 33:222–225.

Johnson, R. E., M. A. Chutuape, E. C. Strain, S. L. Walsh, M. L. Stitzer, and G. E. Bigelow. 2000. A comparison of leveomethadyl acetate, buprenorphine, and methadone for opioid dependence. *New England Journal of Medicine* 343.18:1290–1297.

Johnson, T. 2000. *Gay Spirituality: The Role of Gay Identity in the Transformation of Human Consciousness*. Los Angeles, CA: Alyson Books.

Johnson, V. 1986. *Intervention: How to Help Someone Who Doesn't Want Help*. Minneapolis, MN: Johnson Institute.

Join Together. 2004. Ten drug and alcohol policies that save lives. Retrieved from http://www.jointogether.org.

Jones, B. E., and M. J. Hill. 1996. African American lesbians, gay men, and bisexuals. In R. P. Cabaj and T. S. Stein, eds., *Textbook of Homosexuality and Mental Health*, 549–561. Washington, DC: American Psychiatric Press.

Jones-Webb, R. 1998. Drinking patterns and problems among African Americans: Recent findings. *Alcohol Health and Research World* 22.4:260–265.

Jordan, K. M. 2000. Substance abuse among gay, lesbian, bisexual, transgender, and questioning adolescents. *School of Psychology Review* 29.2:201–207.

Jorm, A. F., A. E. Korten, B. Rodgers, P. A. Jacomb, and H. Christensen. 2002. Sexual orientation and mental health: Results from a community survey of young and middle-aged adults. *British Journal of Psychiatry* 180:423–427.

Joseph, A. M., M. L. Willenbring,S. M. Nugent, and D. B. Nelson. 2004. A randomized trial of concurrent versus delayed smoking intervention for patients in alcohol dependence treatment. *Journal of Studies on Alcohol* 65:681–691.

Juhnke, B. A., and W. B Hagedorn. 2006. *Counseling Addicted Families*. New York: Routledge.

Kadushin, G. 1996. Gay men with AIDS and their families of origin: An analysis of social support. *Health and Social Work* 21.2:141–150.

Kalichman, S. C. 2000. HIV transmission risk behaviors of men and women living with HIV/AIDS: Prevalence, predictions, and emerging clinical interventions. *Clinical Psychology: Science and Practice* 7.1:32–47.

Kalichman, S. C., C. Gore-Felton, E. Benotsch, M. Cage, and D. Rompa. 2004. Trauma symptoms, sexual behaviors, and substance abuse: Correlates of childhood sexual abuse and HIV risks among men who have sex with men. *Journal of Child Sexual Abuse* 13.1:1–15.

Kalichman, S. C., D. Rompa, M. Cage, K. DiFonzo, D. Simpson, J. Austin et al. 2001. Effectiveness of an intervention to reduce HIV transmission risks in HIV-positive people. *American Journal of Preventative Medicine* 21:84–92.

Kammerer, N., T. Mason, and M. Connors. 1999. Transgender health and social service needs in the context of HIV risk. *The International Journal of Transgenderism* 3.1/2 (serial online).

Kanouse, D. E., R. N. Bluthenthal, L. Bogart, M. Y. Iguchi, S. Perry, K. Sand et al. 2005. Recruiting drug-using men who have sex with men into behavioral interventions: A two-stage approach. *Journal of Urban Health* 82.1:109–119.

Karageorge, K., and G. Wisdom. 2001. *Physically and Sexually Abused Women in Substance Abuse Treatment: Treatment Services and Outcomes*. Rockville, MD: National Evaluation Data Services, Center for Substance Abuse Treatment.

Kasl, C. S. 1992. *Many Roads, One Journey: Moving Beyond the 12 Steps*. New York: Harper Collins.

———. 2002. Special issues in counseling lesbian women for sexual addiction, compulsivity, and sexual codependency. *Sexual Addiction and Compulsivity* 9:191–208.

Kelly, B. C., and J. T. Parsons. 2007. Prescription drug misuse among club drug-using young adults. *American Journal of Drug and Alcohol Abuse* 33.6:875–884.

Kelly, B. C., J. T. Parsons, and B. E. Wells. 2006. Prevalence and predictors of club drug use among club-going young adults in New York City. *Journal of Urban Health* 83.5:884–895.

Kennamer, J. D., J. Honnold, J. Bradford, and M. Hendricks. 2000. Differences in disclosure of sexuality among African American and white gay/bisexual men: Implications for HIV/AIDS prevention. *AIDS Education and Prevention* 12.6:519–531.

Kerby, M., R. Wilson, T. Nicholson, and J. B. White. 2005. Substance use and social identity in the lesbian community. *Journal of Lesbian Studies* 9.3:45–56.

Khantzian, E. 1997. The self-medication hypotheses of substance use disorders: A reconsideration and recent applications. *Harvard Review of Psychiatry* 4:231–244.

Kim, A. A., C. K. Kent, and J. D. Klausner. 2002. Increased risk of HIV and sexually transmitted disease transmission among gay or bisexual men who use Viagra: San Francisco, 2000–2001. *AIDS* 12.10:1425–1428.

Kimberly, J. D., and J. M. Serovich. 1999. The role of family and friend social support in reducing risk behaviors among HIV-positive gay men. *AIDS Education and Prevention* 11:465–475.

Kinsey, A. C., W. B. Pomeroy, and C. E. Martin. 1948. *Sexual Behavior in the Human Male.* Philadelphia: W. B. Saunders.

Kipke, M. D., G. Weiss, M. Ramirez, F. Dorey, A. Ritt-Olson, E. Iverson et al. 2007. Club drug use in Los Angeles among young men who have sex with men. *Substance Use and Misuse* 42.11:1723–1743.

Kipke, M. D., G. Weiss, and C. F. Wong. 2007. Residential status as a risk factor for drug use and HIV risk among young men who have sex with men. *AIDS and Behavior* 11:56–69.

Kirk, S. C., and C. Kulkarni. 2006. The whole person: A paradigm for integrating the mental and physical health of trans clients. In M. D. Shankle, ed., *The Handbook of Lesbian, Gay, Bisexual, and Transgender Public Health*, 145–174. New York: Haworth Press.

Kite, M. E. 1994. When perceptions meet reality: Individual differences in reactions to lesbians and gay men. In B. Greene and G. M. Herek, eds., *Lesbian and Gay Psychology*, 25–53. London: Sage Publications.

Kitzinger, C. 1996. Heteropatriarchial language: The case against "homophobia." In L. Mohin, ed., *An Intimacy of Equals: Lesbian Feminist Ethics*, 34–40. New York: Harrington Park Press.

Klitzman, R. L., J. D. Greenberg, L. M. Pollack, and C. Dolezal. 2002. MDMA ("ecstasy") use, and its association with high risk behaviors, mental health, and other factors among gay/bisexual men in New York City. *Drug and Alcohol Dependence* 66.2: 115–125.

Koblin, B. A., C. Murrill, M. Camacho, G. Xu, K. L. Liu, S. Raj-Singh et al. 2007. Amphetamine use and sexual risk among men who have sex with men: Result from the National HIV Behavioral Surveillance Study—New York City. *Substance Use and Misuse* 42.10:1613–1628.

Koh, A. S., C. A. Gómez, S. Shade, and E. Rowley. 2005. Sexual risk factors among self-identified lesbians, bisexual women, and heterosexual women accessing primary care settings. *Sexually Transmitted Diseases* 32.9:563–569.

Kolodny, A. J. 2006. Psychiatric consequences of methamphetamine use. *Journal of Gay and Lesbian Psychotherapy* 10.3/4:67–72.

Komti, A., F. Judd, P. Grech, A. Mijch, J. Hoy, J. H. Lloyd, and A. Street. 2001. Suicidal behaviors in people with HIV/AIDS: A review. *Australian and New Zealand Journal of Psychiatry* 35.6:747–757.

Korfhage, B. A. 2006. Psychology graduate students' attitudes toward lesbians and gay men. *Journal of Homosexuality* 51.4:145–159.

Koroloff, N., and S. C Anderson. 1989. Alcohol-free living centers: Hope for homeless alcoholics. *Social Work* 34.6:497–504.

Kort, J. 2007. Gay guise: What to do when your client has sex with men, but is straight. *Psychotherapy Networker* (July/August): 65–70.

Krestan, J., and C. S. Bepko. 1980. The problem of fusion in the lesbian relationship. *Family Process* 19:277–289.

Kulik, L. 2004. Transmission of attitudes regarding family life from parents to adolescents in Israel. *Families in Society* 85.3:345–353.

Kuss, R. J. 1988. Alcoholism and non-acceptance of gay self: The critical link. *Journal of Homosexuality* 15.1/2:25–41.

Kuyper, L. M., T. M. Lampinen, K. Chan, M. L. Miller, A. Schilder, and R. S. Hogg. 2005. Similar sexual behaviors with casual partners among gay men with and without a regular partner. *Sexually Transmitted Diseases* 32.3:203–205.

LaBrie, J. W., T. F. Lamb, E. R. Pedersen, and T. Quinlan. 2006. A group motivational interviewing intervention reduces drinking and alcohol-related consequences in adjudicated college students. *Journal of College Student Development* 47.3:267–280.

Laird, J. 1994. Lesbian families: A cultural perspective. In M. P. Mirkin, ed., *Women in Context*, 118–148. New York Guilford Press.

Laird, J., and R. J. Green. 1996. *Lesbians and Gays in Couples and Families: A Handbook for Therapists*. San Francisco: Jossey-Bass.

Landau, J., and J. Garrett. 2008. Neurobiology and addiction: Assisting the family and support system to get resistant loved ones into treatment. *American Family Therapy Academy Monograph Series: Neurobiology*, 29–37. Washington, DC: American Family Therapy Academy.

Landau, J., M. D. Stanton, D. Brinkman-Sull, D. Ikle, D. McCormick, J. Garrett et al. 2004. Outcomes with the ARISE approach to engaging reluctant drug- and alcohol-dependent individuals in treatment. *American Journal of Drug and Alcohol Abuse* 30:711–748.

Larkins, S., C. J. Reback, S. Shoptaw, and R. Veniegas. 2005. Methamphetamine-dependent gay men's disclosure of their HIV status to sexual partners. *AIDS Care* 17.4:521–532.

La Sala, M. C. 2000. Lesbians, gay men, and their parents: Family therapy for the coming-out crisis. *Family Process* 39:67–81.

——. 2001. Monogamous or not: Understanding and counseling gay male couples. *Families in Society* 82.6:605–611.

——. 2005. The importance of partners to lesbians' intergenerational relationships. In F. J. Turner, ed., *Social Work Diagnosis in Contemporary Practice*, 149–157. New York: Oxford Press.

——. 2007. Too many eggs in the wrong basket: A queer critique of the same-sex marriage movement. *Social Work* 52.2:181–183.

Laumann, O., J. H. Gagnon, R. T. Michael, and S. Michael. 1994. *The Social Organization of Sexuality: Sexual Practices in the United States.* Chicago: University of Chicago Press.

Lawrence, A. A., J. D. Shaffer, W. R. Snow, C. Chase, and B. T. Headlam. 1996. Health care needs of transgender patients [Letter to the editor]. *Journal of the American Medical Association* 276:874.

Lee, S. J., M. Galanter, H. Dermatis, and D. McDowell. 2003. Circuit parties and patterns of drug use in a subset of gay men. *Journal of Addictive Diseases* 22.4:47–60.

Lev, A. I. 2004. *Transgender Emergence: Therapeutic Guidelines for Working with Gender-Variant People and Their Families*. New York: Haworth Press.

Lev, A. I., and S. S. Lev. 1999. Sexual assault in the lesbian, gay, bisexual, and transgendered communities. In J. C. McClennen and J. G. Gunther, eds., *A Professional Guide to Understanding Gay and Lesbian Domestic Violence: Understanding Practice Interventions*, 35–62. Lewiston, NY: Edwin Mellen.

LeVay, S. 1991. A difference in hypothalamic structure between heterosexual and homosexual men. *Science* 253:1034–1037.

——. 1994. Evidence for a biological influence in male homosexuality. *Scientific American* 270.5:44.

Levine, A. M. 2002. Evaluation and management of HIV-infected women. *Annals of Internal Medicine* 136:228–242.

Levounis, P., and J. S. Ruggiero. 2006. Outpatient management of crystal methamphetamine dependence among gay and bisexual men: How can it be done? *Primary Psychiatry* 13.2:75–80.

Li, L., J. Ford, and D. Moore. 2000. An exploratory study of violence, substance abuse, disability, and gender. *Social Behavior and Personality* 28.1:61–72.

Lichtenstein, B. 2000. Secret encounters: Black men, bisexuality, and AIDS in Alabama. *Medical Anthropology Quarterly* 14.3:374–393.

Lidderdale, M. A. 2002. Practitioner training for counseling lesbian, gay and bisexual clients. *Journal of Lesbian Studies* 6.3/4:111–120.

Liddle, B. J. 1999. Gay and lesbian clients' ratings of psychiatrists, psychologists, social workers, and counselors. *Journal of Gay and Lesbian Psycotherapy* 3:81–93.

Liddle, H. A., and G. A. Dakof. 1995. Family-based treatment for adolescent drug use: State of the science. NIDA Research Monograph 156:218–254.

Liddle, H. A., G. A. Dakof, K. Parker, G. S. Diamond, K. Barrett, and M. Tejada. 2001. Multidimensional family therapy for adolescent drug abuse: Results of a randomized clinical trial. *American Journal of Drug and Alcohol Abuse* 27.4:651–688.

Logan, T. K., and C. Leukefeld. 2000. HIV risk behavior among bisexual and heterosexual drug users. *Journal of Psychoactive Drugs* 32.3:239–248.

Lombardi, E., and S. M. Davis. 2006. Transgender health issues. In D. F. Morrow and L. Messinger, eds., *Sexual Orientation and Gender Expression in Social Work Practice*, 343–363. New York: Columbia University Press.

Lombardi, E. L., and G. van Servellen. 2000. Building culturally sensitive substance use prevention and treatment programs for transgendered populations. *Journal of Substance Abuse Treatment* 19:291–296.

Lombardi, E. L., R. A. Wilchins, D. Priesing, and D. Malouf. 2001. Gender violence: Transgender experiences with violence and discrimination. *Journal of Homosexuality* 42.1:89–101.

London, E. D., S. L. Simon, S. M. Berman, M. A. Mandelkern, A. M. Lichtman, J. Bramen et al. 2004. Mood disturbances and regional cerebral metabolic abnormalities in recently abstinent methamphetamine abusers. *Archives General Psychiatry* 61.1: 73–84.

MacMaster, S. A. 2004. Harm reduction: A new perspective on substance abuse services. *Social Work* 49.3:356–363.

Makadon, H. J. 2006. Improving health care for the lesbian and gay communities. *New England Journal of Medicine* 354:895–897.

Mansergh, G., G. N. Colfax, G. Marks, M. Rader, R. Guzman, and S. Buchbinder. 2001. The circuit party men's health survey: Findings and implications for gay and bisexual men. *American Journal of Public Health* 91.6:953–958.

Markowitz, R. 2004. Dynamics and treatment issues with children of drug and alcohol abusers. In S. L. A. Straussner, ed., *Clinical Work with Substance-Abusing Clients*, 284–303. New York: Guilford Press.

Maroda, K. J. 2000. On homoeroticism, erotic countertransference, and the postmodern view of life: A commentary on papers by Rosiello, Tholfsen, and Meyers. *Journal of Gay and Lesbian Psychotherapy* 4.2:61–70.

Marsh, J. C., D. Cao, and T. D'Aunno. 2004. Gender differences in the impact of comprehensive services in substance abuse treatment. *Journal of Substance Abuse Treatment* 27:289–300.

Marshall, M. P., M. S. Friedman, R. Stall, K. M. King, J. Miles, M. A. Gold et al. 2008. Sexual orientation and adolescent substance use: A meta-analysis and methodological review. *Addiction* 103.4:546–556.

Martin, A., and E. Hetrick. 1988. The stigmatization of the gay and lesbian adolescent. *Journal of Homosexuality* 15.1/2:163–183.

Mason, G. 2002. *The Spectacle of Violence: Homophobia, Gender, and Knowledge*. London: Routledge.

Mate-Kole, C., M. Freschi, and A. Robin. 1990. A controlled study of psychological and social changes after surgical gender reassignment in selected male transsexuals. *British Journal of Psychiatry* 157:261–264.

Mathy, R. M. 2002. Transgender identity and suicidality in a nonclinical sample: Sexual orientation, psychiatric history, and compulsive behaviors. *Journal of Psychology and Human Sexuality* 14.4:47–65.

Matthews, C. R., and M. M Selvidge. D. 2005. Lesbian, gay, and bisexual clients' experiences in treatment for addiction. *Journal of Lesbian Studies* 9.3:79–90.

Matthews, C. R., P. Lorah, J. Fenton. 2005. Toward a grounded theory of lesbians' recovery from addiction. *Journal of Lesbian Studies* 9.3:57–68.

——. 2006. Treatment experiences of gays and lesbians in recovery from addiction: A qualitative inquiry. *Journal of Mental Health Counseling* 28.2:110–132.

Matthews, A. K., J. Tartaro, and T. L. Hughes. 2003. A comparative study of lesbian and heterosexual women in committed relationships. *Journal of Lesbian Studies* 7.1: 101–114.

Mattson, M., F. Del Boca, K. Carroll, N. Cooney, C. DiClimente, D. Donovan et al. 1998. Patient compliance in Project MATCH: Session attendance predictors and relationship to outcome. *Alcoholism: Clinical and Experimental Research* 22:1328–1339.

Mausbach, B. T., S. J. Semple, S. A. Strathdee, J. Zians, and T. L. Patterson. 2007. Efficacy of a behavioral intervention for increasing safer sex behaviors in HIV-positive MSM methamphetamine users: Results from the EDGE study. *Drug and Alcohol Dependence* 87:249–257.

May, P. A. 1996. Overview of alcohol abuse epidemiology for American Indian populations. In G. D. Sandefur, R. R. Rindfuss and B. Cohen, eds., *Changing Numbers, Changing Needs: American Indian Demography and Public Health*, 235–261. Washington, DC: National Academy Press.

Mayer, K. H. 2006. Speed bumps: Concerns about methamphetamine and other club drug use among men who have sex with men. *Brown University Digest of Addiction Theory and Application* 25.3:8.

Mays, V. M., and S. D. Cochran. 2001. Mental health correlates of perceived discrimination among lesbian, gay, and bisexual adults in the United States. *American Journal of Public Health* 91.11:1869–1876.

McCandlish, B. M. 1982. Therapeutic issues with lesbian couples. *Journal of Homosexuality* 7:71–78.

McCann, B. S., and P. Roy-Byrne. 1998. Attention-deficit/hyperactivity disorder, substance abuse, and posttraumatic stress disorder: A case study with implications for harm reduction. *In Session: Psychotherapy in Practice* 4.1:53–67.

McCarn, S. R., and R. E. Fassinger. 1996. Revisioning sexual minority identity formation: A new model of lesbian identity and its implications for counseling and research. *Counseling Psychologist* 24:508–534.

McCrady, B. S. 2006. Family and other close relationships. In W. R. Miller and K. M. Carroll, eds., *Rethinking Substance Abuse*, 166–181. New York: Guilford Press.

McDaniel, J. S., D. Purcell, A. R. D'Augelli. 2001. The relationship between sexual orientation and risk for suicide: Research findings and future directions for research and prevention. *Suicide and Life-Threatening Behavior* 31:84–105.

McDowell, D. M. 2002. Group therapy for substance abuse with gay men and lesbians. In D. W. Brook and H. I. Spitz, eds., *The Group Therapy of Substance Abuse*, 257–274. New York: Haworth Press.

McGoldrick, M., R. Gerson, and S. Shellenberger. 1999. *Genograms: Assessment and Intervention*. 3rd ed. New York: Norton.

McHenry, S. S., and J. W. Johnson. 1993. Homophobia in the therapist and gay or lesbian client: Conscious and unconscious collusions in self-hate. *Psychotherapy* 30.1:141–151.

McIntyre, J. R. 2004. Family treatment of substance abuse. In S. L. A. Straussner, ed., *Clinical Work with Substance-Abusing Clients*, 237–263. New York: Guilford Press.

McKay, J. R., A. I. Alterman, J. S. Cacciola, M. J. Rutherford, C. P. O'Brien, and J. Koppenhaver. 1997. Group counseling versus individualized relapse prevention aftercare following intensive outpatient treatment for cocaine dependence: Initial results. *Journal of Consulting and Clinical Psychology* 65.5:778–788.

McKirnan, D. J., M. Tolou-Shams, L. Turner, K. Dyslin, and B. Hope. 2006. Elevated risk for tobacco use among men who have sex with men is mediated by demographic and psychosocial variables. *Substance Use and Misuse* 41.8:1197–1208.

McLean, K. 2004. Negotiating (non)monogamy: Bisexuality and intimate relationships. *Journal of Bisexuality* 4.1/2:83–97.

McLellan, A. T. 1991. *Outcome Report*. Eden Prairie, MN: PRIDE Institute.

———. 2002. Is addiction an illness—can it be treated? In M. R. Haack and H. Adger, eds., *Strategic Plan for Interdisciplinary Faculty Development: Arming the Nation's Health Professional Workforce for a New Approach to Substance Use Disorders*, 67–94. Providence, RI: Association for Medical Education and Research in Substance Abuse.

———. 2006. What we need is a system. In W. R. Miller and K. M. Carroll, eds., *Rethinking Substance Abuse*, 275–292. New York: Guilford Press.

McLellan, A. T., G. E. Woody, L. Luborsky, and L. Goehl. 1988. Methamphetamine-dependent gay men's disclosure of their HIV status to sexual partners: Treatment success among four counselors. *Journal of Nervous and Mental Disease* 16:423–430.

McNally, E. B. 1989. "Lesbian Recovering Alcoholics in Alcoholics Anonymous: A Qualitative Study of Identity Transformation." Diss., New York University, New York.

McNeece, A. 2003. After the war on drugs is over: Implications for social work education. *Journal of Social Work Education* 39.2:193–212.

McVinney, L. D. 2006. Harm reduction, crystal methamphetamine, and gay men. *Journal of Gay and Lesbian Psychotherapy* 10.3/4:159–169.

Meeks, A. and Stevens, R. 2004. The latest rage: Methamphetamine abuse. *Resident Staff Physician* 50.9:26–30.

Mee-Lee, D., G. D. Shulman, J. F. Callahan, M. Fishman, D. Gastfriend, R. Hartman et al., eds. 2001. *Patient Placement Criteria for the Treatment of Substance-Related Disorders*. 2nd ed., rev. PPC-2R. Chevy Chase, MD: American Society of Addiction Medicine.

Melchert, T. P., and M. M. Patterson. 1999. Duty to warn and intervention with HIV-positive clients. *Professional Psychology: Research and Practice* 30.2:180–186.

Mencher, J. 1990. *Intimacy in Lesbian Relationships: A Critical Re-Examination of Fusion*. Work in Progress 42. Wellesley, MA: Wellesley College, Stone Center for Developmental Services and Studies.

Messinger, L. 2006a. Social welfare policy and advocacy. In D. F. Morrow and L. Messinger, eds., *Sexual Orientation and Gender Expression in Social Work Practice*, 427–459. New York: Columbia University Press.

——. 2006b. Toward affirmative practice. In D. Morrow and L. Messinger, eds., *Sexual Orientation and Gender Expression in Social Work Practice: Working with Gay, Lesbian, Bisexual, and Transgender People*, 461–470. New York: Columbia University Press.

Mettey, A., R. Crosby, R. J. DiClimente, and D. R. Holtgrave. 2003. Associations between Internet sex-seeking and STI-associated risk behaviors among men who have sex with men. *Sexually Transmitted Infections* 79.6:466–468.

Metzger, D. S., H. Navaline, and G. E. Woody. 1998. Drug abuse treatment as AIDS prevention. *Public Health Report* 113:97–106.

Meyer, I. H., J. Dietrich, and S. Schwartz. 2008. Lifetime prevalence of mental disorders and suicide attempts in diverse lesbian, gay, and bisexual populations. *American Journal of Public Health* 98:6:1004–1006.

Meyer, W., W. Bockting, P. Cohen-Kettenis, E. Coleman, D. Di Ceglie, H. Devor et al. 2001. Harry Benjamin International Gender Dysphoria Association's Standards of Care for Gender Identity Disorders—Sixth Version. *International Journal of Transgenderism* 5.1 (serial online).

Meyers, R. J., W. R. Miller, D. E. Hill, and J. S. Tonigan. 1999. Community reinforcement and family training (CRAFT): Engaging unmotivated drug users in treatment. *Journal of Substance Abuse* 10.3:291–308.

Meyers, R. J., and J. E. Smith. 1995. *Clinical Guide to Alcohol Treatment: The Community Reinforcement Approach*. New York: Guilford Press.

Michaels, S. 1996. The prevalence of homosexuality in the United States. In R. P. Cabaj and T. S. Stein, eds., *Textbook of Homosexuality and Mental Health*, 43–63. Washington, DC: American Psychiatric Association.

Miller, M., M. Serner, and M. Wagner. 2005. Sexual diversity among black men who have sex with men in an inner-city community. *Journal of Urban Health* 82.1:26–34.

Miller, W. R. 2006. Motivational factors in addictive behaviors. In W. R. Miller and K. M. Carroll, eds., *Rethinking Substance Abuse*, 134–150. New York: Guilford Press.

Miller, W. R., and L. M Baca. 1983. Two-year follow-up of bibliotherapy and therapist-directed controlled drinking training for problem drinkers. *Behavior Therapy* 14: 441–448.

Miller, W. R., R. G. Benefield, and J. S Tonigan. 1993. Enhancing motivation for change in problem drinking: A controlled comparison of two therapist styles. *Journal of Consulting and Clinical Psychology* 61:455–461.

Miller, W. R., and K. M. Carroll. 2006. Drawing the science together. In W. R. Miller and K. M. Carroll, eds., *Rethinking Substance Abuse*, 293–311. New York: Guilford Press.

Miller, W., and R. Harris. 2000. A simple scale for Gorski's warning signs for relapse. *Journal of Studies on Alcohol* 61:759–765.

Miller, W. R., R. J. Meyers, and S. Hiller-Sturmhofel. 1999. The community-reinforcement approach. *Alcohol Research and Health* 23.2:116–121.

Miller, W. R., R. J. Meyers, and S. J. Tonigan. 1999. Engaging the unmotivated in treatment for alcohol problems: A comparison of three strategies for intervention through family members. *Journal of Consulting and Clinical Psychology* 67:688–697.

Miller, W. R., and S. Rollnick. 2002. *Motivational Interviewing: Preparing People for Change*. 2nd ed. New York: Guilford Press.

Miller, W. R., A. Zweben, C. DiClemente, and R. Rychtarik. 1995. *Motivational Enhancement Therapy Manual: A Clinical Research Guide for Therapists Treating Individuals with Alcohol Abuse and Dependence*. National Institute on Alcohol Abuse and Alcoholism, Project MATCH Monograph 2, NIH Pub. No. 94-3723. Rockville, MD: U.S. Department of Health and Human Services.

Millett, G. A., J. L. Peterson, R. J. Wolitski, and R. Stall. 2006. Greater risk of HIV infection of black men who have sex with men: A critical literature review. *American Journal of Public Health* 96.6:1007–1019.

Milton, M., A. Coyle, and C. Legg. 2005. Countertransference issues in psychotherapy with lesbian and gay clients. *European Journal of Psychotherapy, Counselling, and Health* 7.3:181–197.

Mimiaga, M. J., A. D. Fair, K. H. Mayer, K. Koenen, S. Gortmaker, A. M. Tetu et al. 2008. Experiences and sexual behaviors of HIV-infected MSM who acquired HIV in the context of crystal methamphetamine use. *AIDS Education and Prevention* 20.1:30–41.

Minton, H. L. S., and G. J. McDonald. 1984. Homosexual identity formation as a developmental process. *Journal of Homosexuality* 9.2/3:91–104.

Mohr, J. J., T. Israel, and W. E. Sedlacek. 2001. Counselors' attitudes regarding bisexuality as predictors of counselors' clinical responses: An analogue study of a female bisexual student. *Journal of Counseling Psychology* 48:212–222.

Moon, M. W., K. Fornili, and A. L. O'Briant. 2007. Risk comparison among youth who report sex with same-sex versus both-sex partners. *Youth and Society* 38.3:267–284.

Moos, R. H. 2006. Social contexts and substance use. In W. R. Miller and K. M. Carroll, eds., *Rethinking Substance Abuse*, 182–200. New York: Guilford Press.

Morbidity and Mortality Weekly Report (MMWR). 2003. Internet use and early syphilis infection among men who have sex with men–San Francisco, California, 1999–2003. *CDC* 52.50:1229–1232.

——. 2005. Trends in HIV/AIDS diagnoses–33 states, 2001–2004. *CDC* 54.45:1149–1153.

Morgenstern, J., T. W. Irwin, M. L. Wainberg, J. T. Parsons, F. Muench, D. A. Bux et al. 2007. A randomized controlled trial of goal choice interventions for alcohol use disorders among men who have sex with men. *Journal of Consulting and Clinical Psychology* 75.1:72–84.

Morin, S. F. 1997. Heterosexual bias in psychological research on lesbianism and male homosexuality. *American Psychologist* 39:247–251.

Morris, J. F., and K. F. Balsam. 2003. Lesbian and bisexual women's experiences of victimization: Mental health, revictimization, and sexual identity development. *Journal of Lesbian Studies* 7:67–85.

Morris, J. F., K. F. Balsam, and E. D. Rothblum. 2002. Lesbian and bisexual mothers and nonmothers: Demographics and the coming out process. *Journal of Family Psychology* 2:144–156.

Morris, J. F., C. R. Waldo, and E. D. Rothblum. 2001. A model of predictors and outcomes of outness among lesbian and bisexual women. *American Journal of Orthopsychiatry* 71:61–71.

Morrow, D. F. 2003. Cast into the wilderness: The impact of institutionalized religion on lesbians. *Journal of Lesbian Studies* 7.4:109–124.

——. 2006. Gay, lesbian, and bisexual identity development. In D. F. Morrow and L. Messinger, eds., *Sexual Orientation and Gender Expression in Social Work Practice*, 81–104. New York: Columbia University Press.

Morrow, D. F., and B. Tyson. 2006. Religion and spirituality. In D. F. Morrow and L. Messinger, eds., *Sexual Orientation and Gender Expression in Social Work Practice*, 384–404. New York: Columbia University Press.

Mosher, W. D., A. Chandra, and J. Jones. 2005. *Sexual Behavior and Selected Health Measures: Men and Women 15–44 Years of Age. United States, 2002.* Advance Data from Vital and Health Statistics 362. Hyattville, MD: National Center for Health Statistics.

Mravcak, S. A. 2006. Primary care for lesbians and bisexual women. *American Family Physician* 74.2:279–286.

Mueser, K. T., R. E. Drake, W. Turner, and M. McGovern. 2006. Comorbid substance use disorders and psychiatric disorders. In W. R. Miller and K. M. Carroll, eds., *Rethinking Substance Abuse*, 115–133. New York: Guilford Press.

Murphy, B. C. 1989. Lesbian couples and their parents: The effects of perceived parental attitudes on the couple. *Journal of Counseling and Development* 68:46–51.

Murphy, T. F. 1992. Redirecting sexual orientation: Techniques and justifications. *Journal of Sex Research* 29.4:501–523.

Mustanski, B. S., M. L. Chivers, and J. M. Bailey. 2002. A critical review of recent biological research on human sexual orientation. *Annual Review of Sex Research* 13:89–140.

Najavits, L. M. 2002. *Seeking Safety: A Treatment Manual for PTSD and Substance Abuse.* New York: Guilford Press.

——. 2007. Seeking safety: An evidence-based model for substance abuse and trauma/PTSD. In K. A. Witkiewitz and G. A. Marlatt, eds., *Therapist's Guide to Evidence-Based Relapse Prevention: Practical Resources for the Mental Health Professional*, 141–167. San Diego: Elsevier.

Nakajima, G. A., Y. H. Chan, K. Lee. 1996. Mental health issues for gay and lesbian Asian Americans. In R. P. Cabaj and T. S. Stein, eds., *Textbook of Homosexuality and Mental Health*, 563–581. Washington, DC: American Psychiatric Press.

Nanin, J. E., and J. T. Parsons. 2006. Club drug use and risky sex among gay and bisexual men in New York City. *Journal of Gay and Lesbian Psychotherapy* 10.3/4:111–122.

Nardi, P. M. 1982. Alcohol treatment and the non-traditional "family" structures of gays and lesbians. *Journal of Alcohol and Drug Education* 27:83–89.

National Association of Social Workers. 1996. *NASW Code of Ethics.* Washington, DC: NASW Press.

——. 2003. *Social Work Speaks: National Association of Social Workers Policy Statements, 2003–2006.* 6th ed. Washington, DC: NASW Press.

National Coalition of Anti-Violence Programs. 2007. *Lesbian, Gay, Transgender, And Bisexual (LGBT) Domestic Violence in 2006.* New York: Author.

National Institute on Alcohol Abuse and Alcoholism (NIAAA). 2002. *Social Work Education for the Prevention and Treatment of Alcohol Use Disorders.* Bethesda, MD: Author.

National Institute on Drug Abuse (NIDA). 2007. *The Science of Addiction.* NIH Pub No. 07-5605. Bethesda, MD: U.S. Department of Health and Human Services.

——. 2008a. *NIDA Info Facts: Club Drugs.* Bethesda, MD: U.S. Department of Health and Human Services.

——. 2008b. *NIDA Info Facts: Heroin.* Bethesda, MD: U.S. Department of Health and Human Services.

National Quality Forum (NQF). 2005. *Evidence-Based Treatment Practices for Substance Use Disorders.* Washington, DC: Author.

Nawyn, S. J., J. A. Richman, K. M. Rospenda, and T. L. Hughes. 2000. Sexual identity and alcohol-related outcomes: Contributions of workplace harassment. *Journal of Substance Abuse* 11.3:289–304.

Nelson, T. S. 1989. Differentiation in clinical and nonclinical women. *Journal of Feminist Family Therapy* 1:49–62.

Nemoto, T., D. Luke, L. Mamo, A. Ching, and J. Patria. 1999. HIV risk behaviors among male-to-female transgenders in comparison with homosexual or bisexual males and heterosexual females. *AIDS Care* 11:297–312.

Nemoto, T., D. Operario, and J. Keatley. 2005. Health and social services for male-to-female transgender persons of color in San Francisco. *International Journal of Transgenderism* 8.2/3:5–19.

Nemoto, T., D. Operario, J. Keatley, L. Han, and T. Soma. 2004. HIV risk behaviors among male-to-female transgender persons of color in San Francisco. *American Journal of Public Health* 94.7:1193–1199.

Nemoto, T., D. Operario, J. Keatley, and D. Villegas. 2004. Social context of HIV risk behaviors among male-to-female transgenders of colour. *AIDS Care* 16.6:724–735.

Nemoto, T., L. A. Sausa,D. Operario, and J. Keatley. 2006. Need for HIV/AIDS education and intervention for MTF transgenders: Responding to the challenge. *Journal of Homosexuality* 51.1:183–202.

Newfield, E., S. Hart, S. Dibble, and L. Kohler. 2006. Female-to-male transgender quality of life. *Quality of Life* 15.9 (serial online).

Nieves-Rosa, L., A. Carballo-Diéguez, and C. Dolezal. 2000. Domestic abuse and HIV-risk behavior in Latin American men who have sex with men in New York City. *Journal of Gay and Lesbian Social Services* 11:77–90.

Noell, J. W., and L. M. Ochs. 2001. Relationship of sexual orientation to substance, suicidal ideation, suicide attempts, and other factors in a population of homeless adolescents. *Journal of Adolescent Health* 29:30–36.

Nosek, M., C. Howland, and M. Young. 1997. Abuse of women with disabilities: Policy implications. *Journal of Disability Policy Studies* 8:157–176.

Oakley, D. A., and D. L. Dennis. 1996. Responding to the needs of homeless people with alcohol, drug, and/or mental disorders. In J. Baumohl, ed., *Homelessness in America*, 179–186. New York: Oryx Press.

Obert, J. L., M. J. McCann, P. Marinelli-Casey, A. Weiner, S. Minsky, P. Brethen et al. 2000. The matrix model of outpatient stimulant abuse treatment: History and description. *Journal of Psychoactive Drugs* 32.2:157–164.

Ockert, D. M., A. R. Baier, and E. E. Coons. 2004. Treatment of stimulant dependence. In S. L. A. Straussner, ed., *Clinical Work with Substance-Abusing Clients*, 209–233. New York: Guilford Press.

O'Connel, A. 1999. Voices from the heart: The developmental impact of a mother's lesbianism on her adolescent children. In J. Laird, ed., *Lesbians and Lesbian Families: Reflections on Theory and Practice*, 261–280. New York: Columbia University Press.

O'Connor, L. E., M. Esherick, and C. Vieten. 2002. Drug and alcohol-abusing women. In S. L. A. Straussner and S. Brown, eds., *The Handbook of Addictions Treatment for Women*, 75–98. San Francisco: Jossey-Bass.

O'Dwyer, P. 2004. Treatment of alcohol problems. In S. L. A. Straussner, ed., *Clinical Work with Substance-Abusing Clients*, 171–186. New York: Guilford Press.

O'Farrell, T. J., and W. Fals-Stewart. 2006. *Behavioral Couples Therapy for Alcoholism and Drug Abuse*. New York: Guilford Press.

Office of Applied Studies. 2006. Results from the 2005 National Survey on Drug Use and Health. Retrieved from http://www.oas.samhsa.gov.

Oggins, J., and J. Eichenbaum. 2002. Engaging transgender substance users in substance use treatment. *International Journal of Transgenderism* 6.2 (serial online).

Olkin, R. 1999. *What Psychotherapists Should Know About Disability*. New York: Guilford Press.

Olson, E. D. 2000. Gay teens and substance use disorders: Assessment and treatment. *Journal of Gay and Lesbian Psychotherapy* 3.3/4:69–80.

O'Malley, S. S., and T. R. Kosten. 2006. Pharmacotherapy of addictive disorders. In W. R. Miller and K. M. Carroll, eds., *Rethinking Substance Abuse*, 240–256. New York: Guilford Press.

Ompad, D. C., S. Galea, C. M. Fuller, D. Phelan, and D. Vlahov. 2004. Club drug use among minority substance users in New York City. *Journal of Psychoactive Drugs* 36.3:397–399.

Operario, D., and T. Nemoto. 2005. Sexual risk behavior and substance use among a sample of Asian Pacific Islander transgendered women. *AIDS Education and Prevention* 17.5:430–443.

Orlin, L., M. O'Neill, and J. Davis. 2004. Assessment and intervention with clients who have coexisting psychiatric and substance-related disorders. In S. L. A. Straussner, ed., *Clinical Work with Substance-Abusing Clients*, 102–124. New York: Guilford Press.

Ostrow, D. G., and R. D. Shelby. 2000. Psychoanalytic and behavioral approaches to drug-related sexual risk taking: A preliminary conceptual and clinical integration. *Journal of Gay and Lesbian Psychotherapy* 3.3/4:123–139.

Oswald, R. F., and L. S. Culton. 2003. Under the rainbow: Rural gay life and its relevance for family providers. *Family Relations* 52:72–81.

O'Toole, C. J., and A. A. Brown. 2003. No reflection in the mirror: Challenges for disabled lesbians accessing mental health services. *Journal of Lesbian Studies* 7.1:35–49.

Page, E. H. 2004. Mental health services experiences of bisexual women and bisexual men: An empirical study. *Journal of Bisexuality* 4.1/2:137–160.

Palamar, J. J., and P. N. Halkitis. 2006. A qualitative analysis of GHB use among gay men: Reasons for use despite potential adverse outcomes. *International Journal of Drug Policy* 17.1:23–28.

Parks, C. A., and T. L. Hughes. 2007. Age differences in lesbian identity development and drinking. *Substance Use and Misuse* 42:361–380.

Parsons, J. T., and P. N. Halkitis. 2002. Sexual drug-using practices of HIV-positive men who frequent public and commercial sex environments. *AIDS Care* 14.6:815–826.

Parsons, J. T., B. C. Kelly, and B. E. Wells. 2006. Differences in club drug use between heterosexual and lesbian/bisexual females. *Addictive Behaviors* 31:2344–2349.

Parsons, J. T., J. Vicioso, A. Kutnick, J. C. Punzalan, P. N. Halkitis, and P. N. Velasquez. 2004. Alcohol use and stigmatized sexual behaviors of HIV seropositive gay and bisexual men. *Addictive Behaviors* 2.5:1045–1051.

Pasick, P., and C. White. 1991. Challenging General Patton: A feminist stance in substance abouse treatment and training. *Journal of Feminist Family Therapy* 3:87–102.

Patheia, P., A. Hajat, J. Schillinger, S. Blank, R. Sell, and F. Mostashari. 2006. Discordance between sexual behavior and self-reported sexual activity: A population-based survey of New York City men. *Annals of Internal Medicine* 145.6:416–425.

Patterson, C. J. 1995. Lesbian mothers, gay fathers, and their children. In A. R. D'Augelli and C. J. Patterson, eds., *Lesbian, Gay, and Bisexual Identities Over the Lifespan*, 262–290. New York: Oxford University Press.

——. 1997. Children of lesbian and gay parents. In T. Ollendick and R. Prinz, eds., *Advances in Clinical Child psychology*, 235–282. New York: Plenum Press.

——. 2000. Family relationships of lesbians and gay men. *Journal of Marriage and the Family* 62.4:1052–1070.

Patterson, T. L., S. J. Semple, J. K. Zians, and S. A. Strathdee. 2005. Methamphetamine-using HIV-positive men who have sex with men: Correlates of polydrug use. *Journal of Urban Health* 82.1:120–126.

Paul, J. P., J. Catania, L. Pollack, and R. Stall. 2001. Understanding childhood sexual abuse as a predictor of sexual risk-taking among men who have sex with men: The urban men's health study. *Child Abuse and Neglect* 25:557–584.

Paz, J. 2002. Culturally competent substance abuse treatment with Latinos. *Journal of Human Behavior in the Social Environment* 5.3/4:123–136.

Paz-Bailey, G., A. Meyers, S. Blank, J. Brown, S. Rubin, J. Braxton et al. 2004. A case-control study of syphilis among men who have sex with men in New York City: Association with HIV infection. *Sexually Transmitted Diseases* 31.10:581–587.

Pearlman, S. F. 1989. Distancing and connectedness: Impact on couple formation in lesbian relationships. *Women and Therapy* 8:77–88.

——. 1996. Lesbian clients/lesbian therapists: Necessary conversations. *Women and Therapy* 18.2:71–80.

Peck, J. A., C. J. Reback, X. Yang, E. Rotheram-Fuller, and S. Shoptaw. 2005a. Sustained reductions in drug use and depression symptoms from treatment for drug abuse in methamphetamine-dependent gay and bisexual men. *Journal of Urban Health* 82:100–108.

Peck, J. A., S. Shoptaw, E. Rotheram-Fuller, C. J. Reback, and B. Bierman. 2005b. HIV-associated medical, behavioral, and psychiatric characteristics of treatment-seeking, methamphetamine-dependent men who have sex with men. *Journal of Addictive Diseases* 24.3:115–132.

Pelucchi, C., S. Gallus, W. Garavello, C. Bosetti, and C. La Vecchia. 2006. Cancer risk associated with alcohol and tobacco use: Focus on upper aero-digestive tract and liver. *Alcohol Research and Health* 29.3:193–198.

Peplau, L. A. 1991. Lesbian and gay relationships. In J. C. Gonsiorek and J. D. Weinrich, eds., *Homosexuality: Research Implications for Public Policy*, 179–196. Newbury Park, CA: Sage.

Peplau, L. A., and S. D. Cochran. 1990. A Relationship Perspective on Homosexuality. In D. P. McWhirter, S. A. Sanders, and J. M. Reinisch, eds., *Homosexuality/Heterosexuality: Concepts of Sexual Orientation*, 321–349. New York: Oxford University Press.

Perdue, T., H. Hagan, H. Thiede, and L. Valleroy. 2003. Depression and HIV risk behavior among Seattle-area injection drug users and young men who have sex with men. *AIDS Education and Prevention* 15.1:81–92.

Peters, R. H., and H. A. Hills. 1997. *Intervention Strategies for Offenders with Co-occurring Disorders: What Works?* Co-Delmar, NY: National GAINS Center.

Pilkington, N. W., and A. R. D'Augelli. 1995. Victimization of lesbian, gay, and bisexual youth in community settings. *Journal of Community Psychology* 23:33–56.

Plankey, M. W., D. G. Ostrow, R. Stall, C. Cox, L. Xiuhong, J. A. Peck et al. 2007. The relationship between methamphetamine and popper use and risk of HIV seroconversion in the Multicenter AIDS Cohort Study. *JAIDS: Journal of Acquired Immune Deficiency Syndrome* 45.1:85–92.

Poppen, P. J., C. A. Reisen, M. C. Zea, F. T. Bianchi, and J. J. Echeverry. 2004. Predictors of unprotected anal intercourse among HIV-positive Latino gay and bisexual men. *AIDS and Behavior* 8.4:379–389.

Poteat, V. P., and D. L. Espelage. 2007. Predicting psychological consequences of homophobic victimization in middle school students. *Journal of Early Adolescence* 27: 175–191.

Prendergast, M., D. Podus, J. Finney, L. Greenwell, and J. Roll. 2006. Contingency management for treatment of substance use disorders: A meta-analysis. *Addiction* 101.11:1546–1560.

Prochaska, J. O., and C. C. DiClemente. 1982. Transtheoretical therapy: Toward a more integrative model of change. *Psychotherapy: Theory, Research, and Practice* 19:276–288.

——. 1992. Stages of change in the modification of problem behaviors. In M. Hersen, R. M. Eisler, and P. M. Miller, eds., *Progress in Behavior Modification*, 184–214. Sycamore, IL: Sycamore Press.

Project MATCH Research Group 1997. Matching alcoholism treatments to client heterogeneity: Project MATCH posttreatment drinking outcomes. *Journal of Studies on Alcohol* 58:7–29.

Purcell, D. W., J. T. Parsons, P. N. Halkitis, Y. Mizano, and W. J. Woods. 2001. Substance use and sexual transmission risk behavior of HIV-positive men who have sex with men, *Journal of Substance Abuse* 13:185–200.

Purcell, D. W., R. J. Wolitski, C. C. Hoff, J. T. Parsons, W. J. Woods, and P. N. Halkitis. 2005. Predictors of the use of Viagra, testosterone, and antidepressants among HIV-seropositive gay and bisexual men. *AIDS* 19:57–66.

Rachlin, K. 2002. Transgender individuals' experiences of psychotherapy. *International Journal of Transgenderism* 6.1 (serial online).

Rahman, Q. 2005. The neurodevelopment of human sexual orientation. *Neuroscience and Biobehavioral Reviews* 29:1057–1066.

Raj, R. 2002. Towards a transpositive therapeutic model: Developing clinical sensitivity and cultural competence in the effective support of transsexual and transgendered clients. *International Journal of Transgenderism* 6.2 (serial online).

Ramirez-Valles, J., D. Garcia, R. T. Campbell, R. M. Diaz, and D. D. Heckathorn. 2008. HIV infection, sexual risk behavior, and substance use among Latino gay and bisexual men and transgender persons. *American Journal of Public Health* 98.6: 1036–1042.

Randolph, W., C. Stroup-Benham, S. Black, and K. Markides. 1998. Alcohol use among Cuban-Americans, Mexican-Americans, and Puerto Ricans. *Alcohol Health and Research World* 22.4:265–270.

Rankow, E. J., K. M. Cambre, and K. Cooper. 1998. Health care-seeking behavior of adult lesbian and bisexual survivors of childhood sexual abuse. *Journal of the Gay and Lesbian Medical Association* 2.2:69–76.

Ratner, E. 1988. Model for the treatment of lesbian and gay alcohol abusers. *Alcoholism Treatment Quarterly* 5.1/2:25–46.

Rawson, R. A., M. J. McCann, F. Flammino, S. Shoptaw, K. Miotto, C. Reiber, and W. Ling. 2006. A comparison of contingency management and cognitive-behavioral approaches for stimulant-dependent individuals. *Addiction* 101:267–274.

Rawson, R. A., P. Marinelli-Casey, M. D. Anglin, A. Dickow, Y. Frazier, C. Gallagher et al. 2004. A multi-site comparison of psychosocial approaches for the treatment of methamphetamine dependence. *Addiction* 99:708–716.

Rawson, R. A., S. J. Shoptaw, J. L. Obert, M. J. McCann, A. L. Hasson, P. J. Marinelli-Casey et al. 1995. An intensive outpatient approach for cocaine abuse treatment: The Matrix model. *Journal of Substance Abuse Treatment* 12.2:117–127.

Ray, N. 2006. *Lesbian, Gay, Bisexual and Transgender Youth: An Epidemic of Homelessness.* New York: National Gay and Lesbian Task Force Policy Institute and the National Coalition for the Homeless.

Razzano, L. A., J. A. Cook, M. M. Hamilton, T. L. Hughes, and A. K. Matthews. 2006. Predictors of mental health services use among lesbian and heterosexual women. *Psychiatric Rehabilitation Journal* 29.4:289–298.

Reading, B., and M. Weegmann. 2004. *Group Psychotherapy and Addiction.* London: Whurr.

Reback, C. J., S. Larkins, and S. Shoptaw. 2004. Changes in the meaning of sexual risk behaviors among gay and bisexual male methamphetamine abusers before and after drug treatment. *AIDS and Behavior* 8.1:87–98.

Reback, C. J., and E. L. Lombardi. 1999. HIV-risk behaviors of male-to-female transgenders in a community-based harm reduction program. *International Journal of Transgenderism* 3.1/2 (serial online).

Reback, C. J., E. L. Lombardi, P. A. Simon, and D. M. Frye. 2005. HIV seroprevalence and risk behaviors among transgendered women who exchange sex in comparison with those who do not. *Journal of Psychology and Human Sexuality* 17.1/2:5–22.

Reece, M. 2003. Sexual compulsivity in HIV serostatus disclosure among men who have sex with men. *Sexual Addiction and Compulsivity* 10:1–11.

Remajedi, G. 2007. Lesbian, gay, bisexual, and transgender youths: Who smokes, and why? *Nicotine and Tobacco Research* 9:65–71.

Reyes, M. 1998. Latina lesbian and alcohol and other drugs: Social work implications. *Alcoholism Treatment Quarterly* 16.1/2:179–192.

Reynolds, A. L., and W. F. Hanjorgiris. 2000. Coming out: Lesbian, gay, and bisexual identity development. In R. M. Perez, K. A. DeBord, and K. J. Bieschke, ed. *Handbook of Counseling and Psychotherapy with Lesbian, Gay, and Bisexual Clients*, 35–55. Washington, DC: American Psychological Association.

Rhodes, R., and A. Johnson. 1997. A feminist approach to treating alcohol and drug-addicted African American women. *Women and Therapy* 20.3:23–37.

Richard, C. A., and A. H Brown. 2006. Configurations of informal social support among older lesbians. *Journal of Women and Aging* 18.4:49–65.

Riddle, D. L., and B. Sang. 1978. Psychotherapy with lesbians. *Journal of Social Issues* 34:84–100.

Ridner, S. L., K. Frost, and A. S. LaJoie. 2006. Health information and risk behaviors among lesbian, gay, and bisexual college students. *Journal of the American Academy of Nurse Practitioners* 18.8:374–378.

Rietmeijer, C. A., S. S. Bull, S. Sheana, M. McFarlane, J. L. Patnick, and J. M. Douglas. 2003. Risks and benefits of the internet for populations at risk for sexually transmitted infections (STIs): Results of an STI clinic survey. *Sexually Transmitted Diseases* 30:15–19.

Roberts, S. J., C. G. Grindel, C. A. Patsdaughter, and R. DeMarco. 2005. Lesbian use and abuse of alcohol: Results of the Boston Lesbian Health Project II. *Substance Abuse* 25.4:1–9.

Roberts, S. J., C. G. Grindel, C. A. Patsdaughter, R. DeMarco, and M. S. Tarmina. 2004a. Lesbian use and abuse of alcohol: Results of the Boston Lesbian Health Project II. *Substance Abuse* 24.4:1–9.

Roberts, S. J., C. G. Grindel, C. A. Patsdaughter, K. Reardon, and M. S. Tarmina. 2004b. Mental health problems and use of services of lesbians: Results of the Boston Lesbian Health Project II. *Journal of Gay and Lesbian Social Services* 17.4:1–16.

Robin, L., N. D. Brener, S. F. Donahue, T. Hack, K. Hale, and C. Goodenow. 2002. Associations between health risk behaviors and opposite-, same-, and both-sex sexual partners in representative samples of Vermont and Massachusetts high school students. *Archives of Pediatric and Adolescent Medicine* 156:349–355.

Robins, A. G., M. A. Dew, L. A. Kingsley, and J. T. Becker. 1997. Do homosexual and bisexual men who place others at potential risk for HIV have unique psychosocial profiles? *AIDS Education and Prevention* 9:239–251.

Rodriguez, E. M., and S. C. Ouellette. 2000. Gay and lesbian Christians: Homosexual and religious identity integration in the members and participants of a gay-positive church. *Journal for the Scientific Study of Religion* 39.3:333–347.

Rollnick, S., and M. Morgan. 1995. Motivational interviewing: Increasing readiness for change. In A. M. Washton, ed., *Psychotherapy and Substance Abuse*, 179–191. New York: Guilford Press.

Romanelli, F., and K. M. Smith. 2004. Recreational use of Sildenafil by HIV-positive and -negative homosexual/bisexual males. *Annals of Pharmacotherapy* 38.6:1024–1030.

Romanelli, F., K. M. Smith, and C. Pomeroy. 2003. Use of club drugs by HIV-seropositive and HIV-seronegative gay and bisexual men. *Topics in HIV Medicine* 11.1:25–32.

Roozen, H. G., J. J. Boulogne, M. W. van Tulder, W. van den Brink, C. A. J. De Jong, and A. J. F. M. Kerkhof. 2004. A systematic review of the effectiveness of the community reinforcement approach in alcohol, cocaine, and opioid addiction. *Drug and Alcohol Dependence* 74.1:1–13.

Rosario, M., J. Hunter, and M. Gwadz. 1997. Exploration of substance use among lesbian, gay, and bisexual youth: Prevalence and correlates. *Journal of Adolescent Research* 12.4:454–476.

Rosenberg, J. 2001. Lesbians are more likely than U.S. women overall to have risk factors for gynecologic and breast cancer. *Family Planning Perspectives* 33.4:183–184.

Rosenblum, A., S. Magura, D. J. Kayman, and C. Fong. 2005. Motivationally enhanced group counseling for substance users in a soup kitchen: A randomized clinical trial. *Drug and Alcohol Dependence* 80.1:91–103.

Ross, M. W., E. J. Essien, M. L. Williams, and M. E. Fernandez-Esquer. 2003. Concordance between sexual behavior and sexual identity in street outreach samples of four racial/ethnic groups. *Sexually Transmitted Diseases* 30:110–113.

Ross, M. W., A. M. Mattison, and D. R. Franklin. 2003. Club drugs and sex on drugs are associated with different motivations for gay circuit party attendance in men. *Substance Use and Misuse* 38.8:1173–1183.

Rotgers, F., M. F. Kern, and R Hoetzel. 2002. *Responsible Drinking: A Moderation Management Approach for Problem Drinkers*. Oakland, CA: New Harbinger Publications.

Rowe, C. L., and H. A. Liddle. 2003. Substance abuse. *Journal of Mental and Family Therapy* 29:97–120.

Russell, S. T. 2003. Sexual minority youth and suicide risk. *American Behavioral Scientist* 46.9:1241–1257.

Russell, S. T., A. K. Driscoll, and N. Truong. 2002. Adolescent same-sex romantic attractions and relationships: Implications for substance use and abuse. *American Journal of Public Health* 92.2:198–202.

Russell, S. T., and K. Joynder. 2001. Adolescent sexual orientation and suicide risk: Evidence from a national study. *American Journal of Public Health* 91.8:1276–1281.

Ryan, C. 1994. Lesbian and gay health concerns. In C. Ryan and R. Bogard. *What Every Lesbian and Gay American Needs to Know About Health Care Reform*. Washington, DC: Human Rights Campaign Foundation.

Ryan, C., and E. Gruskin. 2006. Health concerns for lesbians, gay men, and bisexuals. In D. F. Morrow and L. Messinger, eds., *Sexual Orientation and Gender Expression in Social Work Practice*, 307–342. New York: Columbia University Press.

Ryan, H., P. M. Wortley, A. Easton, L. L. Pederson, G. L. Greenwood. 2001. Smoking among lesbians, gays and bisexuals: A review of the literature. *American Journal of Preventive Medicine* 21:142–149.

Saarela, B. 2005. *Substance Abuse Courses in MSW Programs: An Overview of Offerings Through a Syllabus Analysis*. Unpublished manuscript.

Safren, S. A., and R. G. Heimberg. 1999. Depression, hopelessness, suicidality, and related factors in sexual minority and heterosexual adolescents. *Journal of Consulting and Clinical Psychology* 67:859–866.

Safren, S. A., G. Hollander, T. A. Hart, and R. G. Heimberg. 2001. Cognitive-behavioral therapy with lesbian, gay, and bisexual youth. *Cognitive and Behavioral Practice* 8:215–223.

Samet, J. H., S. Rollnick, and H. Barnes. 1996. Beyond CAGE: A brief clinical approach after detection of substance abuse. *Archives of Internal Medicine* 156.20:22287–22293.

Sanchez, C. 2007. Straight like me. *Intelligence Report* 128:48–57.

Sanders, G. L. 1993. The love that dares to speak its name: From secrecy to openness in gay and lesbian affiliations. In E. Imber-Black, ed., *Secrets in Families and Family Therapy*, 215–242. New York: Norton.

Santa Ana, E. J., E. Wulfert, and P. J. Nietert. 2007. Efficacy of group motivational interviewing (GMI) for psychiatric inpatients with chemical dependence. *Journal of Consulting and Clinical Psychology* 75.5:816–822.

Satre, D. D. 2006. Use and misuse of alcohol and drugs. In D. Kimmel, T. Rose, and S. David, eds., *Lesbian, Gay, Bisexual, and Transgender Aging*, 131–151. New York: Columbia University Press.

Savin-Williams, R. C. 2001. *Mom, Dad, I'm Gay: How Families Negotiate Coming Out.* Washington, DC: American Psychological Association.

Savin-Williams, R. C., and G. L. Ream. 2003. Suicide attempts among sexual-minority male youth. *Journal of Clinical Child and Adolescent Psychology* 32.4:509–522.

Scheer, S., I. Peterson, K. Page-Shafer, V. Delgado, A. Gleghorn, J. Ruiz et al. 2002. Sexual and drug use behavior among women who have sex with both women and men: Results of a population-based survey. *American Journal of Public Health* 92.7:1110–1112.

Scheffler, S. 2004. Substance abuse in homeless persons. In S. L. A. Straussner, ed., *Clinical Work with Substance-Abusing Clients*, 423–442. New York: Guilford Press.

Scheidlinger, S. 2000. The group psychotherapy movement at the millennium: Some historical perspectives. *International Journal of Group Psychotherapy* 50.3:315–339.

Schilit, R., G. Y. Lie, and M. Montagne. 1990. Substance use as a correlate of violence in intimate lesbian relationships. *Journal of Homosexuality* 19.3:51–65.

Schmitz, J. M., L. M. Oswald, S. D. Jacks, T. Rustin, H. M. Rhoades, and J. Grabowski. 1997. Relapse prevention treatment for cocaine dependence: Group vs. individual format. *Addictive Behaviors* 22.3:405–418.

Schope, R. D. 2002. The decision to tell: Factors influencing the disclosure of sexual orientation by gay men. *Journal of Gay and Lesbian Social Services* 14.1:1–22.

Schope, R., and M. Eliason. 2000. Thinking versus acting: Assessing the relationships between heterosexual attitudes and behaviors toward homosexuals. *Journal of Gay and Lesbian Social Services* 11.4:69–92.

Schuck, K. D., and B. J. Liddle. 2001. Religious conflicts experienced by lesbian, gay, and bisexual individuals. *Journal of Gay and Lesbian Psychotherapy* 5.2:63–82.

Schuster, M. A., R. Collins, W. E. Cunningham, S. C. Morton, S. Zierler, M. Wong et al. 2005. Perceived discrimination in clinical care in a nationally representative sample of HIV-infected adults receiving health care. *Journal of General Internal Medicine* 20:807–813.

Schwartz, R. D. 1989. When the therapist is gay: Personal and clinical reflections. *Journal of Gay and Lesbian Psychotherapy* 1.1:41–51.

Seiger, B. H. 2004. The clinical practice of harm reduction. In S. L. A. Straussner, ed., *Clinical Work with Substance-Abusing Clients*, 65–81. New York: Guilford Press.

Seil, D. 2004. The diagnosis and treatment of transgendered patients. *Journal of Gay and Lesbian Psychotherapy* 8.1/2:99–116.

Sember, R., A. Lawrence, and J. Xavier. 2000. Transgender health concerns. *Journal of the Gay and Lesbian Medical Association* 4.3:125–134.

Semple, S. J., T. L. Patterson, and I. Grant. 2002. Motivations associated with methamphetamine use among HIV and men who have sex with men. *Journal of Substance Abuse Treatment* 22:149–156.

———. 2003. Binge use of methamphetamine among HIV-positive men who have sex with men: Pilot data and HIV prevention implications. *AIDS Education and Prevention* 15.2:133–147.

———. 2004. A comparison of injection and non-injection methamphetamine-using HIV positive men who have sex with men. *Drug and Alcohol Dependence* 76:203–212.

Semple, S. J., J. Zians, I. Grant, and T. L. Patterson. 2006a. Methamphetamine use, impulsivity, and sexual risk behavior among HIV-positive men who have sex with men. *Journal of Addictive Diseases* 25.4:105–114.

———. 2006b. Sexual compulsivity in a sample of HIV-positive methamphetamine-using gay and bisexual men. *AIDS Behavior* 10:587–598.

———. 2006c. Sexual risk behavior of HIV-positive methamphetamine-using men who have sex with men: The role of partner serostatus and partner type. *Archives of Sexual Behavior* 35.4:461–471.

Senreich, E., and E. Vairo. 2004. Treatment of gay, lesbian, and bisexual substance abusers. In S. L. A. Straussner, ed., *Clinical Work with Substance-Abusing Clients*, 392–422. New York: Guilford Press.

Serovich, J. M., A. J. Esbensen, T. L. Mason. 2005. HIV disclosure by men who have sex with men to immediate family over time. *AIDS Patient Care and STDs* 19.8:506–517.

Serovich, J. M., D. G. Oliver, S. A. Smith, T. L. Mason. 2005. Methods of HIV disclosure by men who have sex with men to casual sexual partners. *AIDS Patient Care and STDs* 19.12:823–832.

Shankle, M. D., C. A. Maxwell, E. S. Katzman, and S. Landers. 2003. An invisible population: Older lesbian, gay, bisexual, and transgender individuals. *Clinical Research and Regulatory Affairs* 20.2:159–182.

Shedlin, M. G., and S. Deren. 2002. Cultural factors influencing HIV risk behavior among Dominicans in New York City. *Journal of Ethnicity in Substance Abuse* 1.1:71–95.

Sherer, R. A. 2007. Drug abuse hitting middle-aged more than gen-Xers. *Psychiatric Times* 23.4:1–2.

Sherman, E. 2002. Homoerotic countertransference: The love that dare not speak its name? *Psychoanalytic Dialogues* 12.4:649–666.

Shernoff, M. 2001. Steroids and the pursuit of bigness. *Gay and Lesbian Review Worldwide* 8.4:32–33.

———. 2006. Condomless sex: Gay men, barebacking, and harm reduction. *Social Work* 51.2:106–113.

Shoptaw, S., and D. Frosch. 2000. Substance abuse treatment as HIV prevention for men who have sex with men. *AIDS and Behavior* 4.2:193–203.

Shoptaw, S., R. A. Rawson, M. J. McCann, and J. L. Obert. 1994. The matrix model of outpatient stimulant abuse treatment: Evidence of efficacy. *Journal of Addictive Diseases* 13.4:129–141.

Shoptaw, S., and C. J. Reback. 2007. Methamphetamine use and infectious disease-related behaviors in men who have sex with men: Implications for interventions. *Addiction* 102:130–135.

Shoptaw, S., C. J. Reback, T. E. Freese, and R. A. Rawson. 1998. *Behavioral Interventions for Methamphetamine-Abusing Gay and Bisexual Men: A Treatment Manual Combining Relapse Prevention and HIV Risk-Reduction Interventions*. Los Angeles: Friends Research Institute.

Shoptaw, S., C. J. Reback, J. A. Peck, X. Yang, E. Rotheram-Fuller, S. Larkins et al. 2005. Behavioral treatment approaches for methamphetamine dependence and HIV-related sexual risk behaviors among urban gay and bisexual men. *Drug and Alcohol Dependence* 78.2:125–134.

Shoptaw, S., E. Rotheram-Fuller, X. Yang, D. Frosch, D. Nahom, and M. E. Jarvik. 2002. Smoking cessation in methadone maintenance. *Addiction* 97:1317–1328.

Shuster, R. 1987. Sexuality as a continuum: The bisexual identity. In Boston Lesbian Psychologies Collective, ed., *Lesbian Psychologies: Explorations and Challenges*, 56–71. Chicago: University of Illinois Press.

Siegel, K., H. Lune, and I. H. Meyer. 1998. Stigma management among gay/bisexual men with HIV/AIDS. *Qualitative Sociology* 21.1:3–24.

Siegel, K., E. W. Schrimshaw, and D. Karus. 2004. Racial disparities in sexual risk behaviors and drug use among older gay/bisexual and heterosexual men living with HIV/AIDS. *Journal of the National Medical Association* 96.2:215–223.

Silenzio, V. M. B., J. B. Pena, P. R. Duberstein, J. Cerel, and K. L. Knox. 2007. Sexual orientation and risk factors for suicidal ideation and suicide attempts among adolescents and young adults. *American Journal of Public Health* 97.11:2017–2019.

Simmons, T., and O'Connell, M. 2003. *Married-Couple and Unmarried-Partner Households: 2000.* Census 2000 Special Reports. Washington, DC: U.S. Census Bureau.

Simoni, J. M., K. L. Walters, K. F. Balsam, and S. B. Meyers. 2006. Victimization, substance use, and HIV risk behaviors among gay/bisexual/two-spirit and heterosexual American Indian men in New York City. *American Journal of Public Health* 96.12:2240–2245.

Simpson, E. K., and C. A. Helfrich. 2005. Lesbian survivors of intimate partner violence: Provider perspectives on barriers to accessing services. *Journal of Gay and Lesbian Social Services* 18.2:39–59.

Skinner, W. F. 1994. The prevalence and demographic predictors of illicit and licit drug use among lesbians and gay men. *American Journal of Public Health* 84.8:1307–1310.

Slesnick, N., J. L. Prestopnik, R. J. Meyers, and M. Glassman. 2007. Treatment outcome for street-living, homeless youth. *Addictive Behaviors* 32:1237–1251.

Sloven, J. 1991. Codependent or empathetically responsive? Two views of Betty. *Journal of Feminist Family Therapy* 3:195–210.

Smith, A. 1997. Cultural diversity and the coming-out process: Implications for therapy practice. In B. Greene, ed., *Ethnic and Cultural Diversity Among Lesbians and Gay Men*, 279–300. Newbury Park, CA: Sage.

Smith, J. E., R. J. Meyers, and H. D. Delaney. 1998. The community reinforcement approach with homeless alcohol-dependent individuals. *Journal of Consulting and Clinical Psychology* 66.3:541–548.

Smith, J. E., R. J. Meyers, and W. R. Miller. 2001. The community reinforcement approach to the treatment of substance use disorders. *American Journal on Addictions* 10:51–59.

Smolinski, K. M., and Y. Colón. 2006. Silent voices and invisible walls: Exploring end of life care with lesbians and gay men. *Journal of Psychosocial Oncology* 24.1:51–64.

Solomon, S. E., E. D. Rothblum, and K. F Balsam. 2004. Pioneers in partnership: Lesbian and gay male couples in civil unions compared with those not in civil unions, and heterosexual married siblings. *Journal of Family Psychology* 18:275–286.

——. 2005. Money, housework, sex, and conflict: Same-sex couples in civil unions, those not in civil unions, and heterosexual married siblings. *Sex Roles* 52:561–575.

Sperber, J., S. Landers, and S. Lawrence. 2005. Access to health care for transgendered persons: Results of a needs assessment in Boston. *International Journal of Transgenderism* 8.2/3:75–91.

Spiegel, B. R., and C. H. Fewell. 2004. 12-step programs as a treatment modality. In S. L. A. Straussner, ed., *Clinical Work with Substance-Abusing Clients*, 125–145. New York: Guilford Press.

Spindler, H. H., S. Scheer, S. Y. Chen, J. D. Klausner, M. H. Katz, L. A. Valleroy et al. 2007. Viagra, methamphetamine, and HIV risk: Results from a probability sample of MSM, San Francisco. *Sexually Transmitted Diseases* 34.3:1–6.

Stacey, J., and T. Biblarz. 2001. (How) Does the sexual orientation of parents matter? *American Sociological Review* 66:159–183.

Staddon, P. 2005. Labeling out: The personal account of an ex-alcoholic lesbian feminist. *Journal of Lesbian Studies* 9.3:69–78.

Stall, R. D., G. L. Greenwood, M. Acree, J. Paul, and T. J. Coates. 1999. Cigarette smoking among gay and bisexual men. *American Journal of Public Health* 89:1875–1878.

Stall, R., J. P. Paul, G. Greenwood, L. M. Pollack, E. Bein, G. M. Crosby et al. 2001. Alcohol use, drug use, and alcohol-related problems among men who have sex with men: The Urban Men's Health Study. *Addiction* 96:1589–1601.

Stein, T. 1996. Critique of approaches to changing sexual orientation. In R. Cabaj and T. Stein, eds., *Textbook of Homosexuality and Mental Health,* 525–538. Washington, DC: American Psychiatric Press.

Stein, T. S. 1998. Social constructionism and essentialism: Theoretical and clinical considerations relevant to psychotherapy. *Journal of Gay and Lesbian Psychotherapy* 2.4:29–49.

Stoller, R. J. 1972. Etiological factors in female transsexualism: A first approximation. *Archives of Sexual Behavior* 12.1:47–64.

——. 1968. *Sex and Gender*, vol. 1: *The Development of Masculinity and Femininity*. New York: Jason Aronson.

Straussner, S. L. A. 2004. Assessment and treatment of clients with alcohol and other drug abuse problems: An overview. In S. L. A. Straussner, ed., *Clinical Work with Substance-Abusing Clients*, 3–35. New York: Guilford Press.

Strommen, E. 1990. Hidden branches and growing pains: Homosexuality and the family tree. In F. Bozett and M. Sussman, eds., *Homosexuality and Family Relations*, 9–34. New York: Harrington Park Press.

Strona, F. V., J. McCright, H. Hjord, K. Ahrens, S. Tierney, S. Shoptaw et al. 2006. The acceptability and feasibility of the Positive Reinforcement Opportunity Project, a community-based contingency management methamphetamine treatment program for gay and bisexual men in San Francisco. *Journal of Psychoactive Drugs* 3:377–383.

Swigonski, M. E. 2006. Violence, hate crimes, and hate language. In D. F. Morrow and L. Messinger, eds., *Sexual Orientation and Gender Expression in Social Work Practice*, 364–383. New York: Columbia University Press.

Szapocznik, J., and R. A. Williams. 2000. Brief strategic family therapy: Twenty-five years of interplay among theory, research, and practice in adolescent behavior problems and drug abuse. *Clinical Child and Family Psychology Review* 3.2:117–134.

Tallen, B. S. 1990. Twelve step programs: A lesbian feminist critique. *NWSA Journal* 2.3:390–407.

Tang, H., G. L. Greenwood, D. W. Cowling, J. C. Lloyd, A. G. Roeseler, and D. G. Bal. 2004. Cigarette smoking among lesbians, gays and bisexuals: How serious a problem? *Cancer Causes and Control* 15:797–803.

Tatarsky, A. 1998. An integrative approach to harm reduction psychotherapy: A case of problem drinking secondary to depression. *In Session: Psychotherapy in Practice* 4.1:9–24.

——. 2002. *Harm Reduction Psychotherapy: A New Treatment for Drug and Alcohol Problems.* Northvale, NJ: Jason Aronson.

Tesar, C. M., and S. L. D. Rovi. 1998. Survey of curriculum on homosexuality/bisexuality in departments of family medicine. *Family Medicine* 30:283–287.

Tharinger, D., and G. Wells. 2000. An attachment perspective on the developmental challenges for gay and lesbian adolescents: The need for continuity of caregiving from family and schools. *School Psychology Review* 29.2:158–173.

Tievsky, D. L. 1988. Homosexual clients and homophobic social workers. *Journal of Independent Social Work* 2:51–62.

Tikkanen, R., and M. W. Ross. 2000. Looking for sexual compatability: Experiences among Swedish men in visiting Internet gay chatrooms. *Cyberpsychology and Behavior* 3:605–616.

Toro, P. A., S. M. Wolfe, C. W. Bellavia, D. M. Thomas, L. L. Rowland, C. V. Daeschler et al. 1999. Obtaining representative samples of homeless persons: A two-city study. *Journal of Community Psychology* 27.2:157–178.

Toro-Alfonso, J., and S. Rodriguez-Madera. 2004. Domestic violence in Puerto Rican gay male couples: Perceived prevalence, intergenerational violence, addictive behaviors, and conflict resolution skills. *Journal of Interpersonal Violence* 19.6:639–654.

Tozer, E. E., and M. K. McClanahan. 1999. Treating the purple menace: Ethical considerations of conversion therapy and affirmative alternatives. *Counseling Psychologist* 27.5:722–742.

Transgender Law and Policy Institute. 2006. Non-Discrimination Laws That Include Gender Identity and Expression. Retrieved from http://www.transgenderlaw.org/ndlaws/index.htm.

Transgender Substance Abuse Treatment Policy Group of the San Francisco Lesbian, Gay, Bisexual, and Transgender Substance Abuse Task Force. 1995. *Transgender Protocol: Treatment Services Guidelines for Substance Abuse Treatment Providers.* San Francisco: Author.

Trocki, K. F., L. Drabble, and L. Midanik. 2005. Use of heavier drinking contexts among heterosexuals, homosexuals, and bisexuals: Results from a National Household Probability Survey. *Journal of the Study of Alcohol* 66.1:105–110.

Troiden, R. R. 1979. Becoming homosexual: A model of gay identity acquisition. *Psychiatry* 42:362–373.

Tunnell, G., and D. E. Greenan. 2004. Clinical issues with gay male couples. *Journal of Couple and Relationship Therapy* 3.2/3:13–26.

Turell, S. C., and L. Cornell-Swanson. 2005. Not all alike: Within-group differences in seeking help for same-sex relationship abuses. *Journal of Gay and Lesbian Social Services* 18.1:71–88.

Valanis, B. G., D. J. Bowen, T. Bassford, E. Whitlock, P. Charney, and R. A. Carter. 2000. Sexual orientation and health: Comparisons in the women's health initiative sample. *Archives of Family Medicine* 9.9:843–853.

Vanable, P. A., M. P. Carey, D. C. Blair, and R. A Littlewood. 2006. Impact of HIV-related stigma on health behaviors and psychological adjustment among HIV-positive men and women. *AIDS and Behavior* 10.5:473–482.

Van Beneden, C. A., K. O'Brien, S. Modesitt, S. Yusem, A. Ross, and D. Fleming. 2002. Sexual behaviors in an urban bathhouse fifteen years into the HIV epidemic. *Journal of Acquired Immune Deficiency Syndromes* 30.5:522–526.

Van Kesteren, P. J. M., H. Asscheman, J. A. J. Megens, L. J. G. Gooren. 1977. Mortality and morbidity in transsexual subjects treated with cross-sex hormones. *Clinical Endocrinology* 47:337–342.

Van Voorhis, R., and M. Wagner. 2002. Among the missing: Content on lesbian and gay people in social work journals. *Social Work* 47.4:345–354.

van Wormer, K. 2004. *Confronting Oppression, Restoring Justice: From Policy Analysis to Social Action.* Alexandria, VA: Counsel on Social Work Education.

van Wormer, K., and D. R. Davis. 2003. *Addiction Treatment: A Strengths Perspective.* Pacific Grove, CA: Brooks/Cole.

Velasquez, M. M., G. G. Maurer, C. Crouch, and C. C. DiClemente. 2001. *Group Treatment for Substance Misuse: A Stages of Change Manual.* New York: Guilford Press.

Wainberg, M. L., A. J. Kolodny, and J. Drescher. 2006. Introduction: A look inside the "crystal" ball. *Journal of Gay and Lesbian Psychotherapy* 10.3/4:1–7.

Wainwright, J. L., S. T. Russell, and C. J. Patterson. 2004. Psychosocial adjustment, school outcomes, and romantic relationships of adolescents with same-sex parents. *Child Development* 75.6:1886–1898.

Waldo, C. R., W. McFarland, M. H. Katz, D. MacKellar, and L. A. Valleroy. 2000. Very young gay and bisexual men are at risk for HIV infection: The San Francisco Bay Area Men's Survey II. *Journal of Acquired Immune Deficiency Syndromes* 24.2:168–174.

Waldron, H. B. 1997. Adolescent substance abuse and family therapy outcome: A review of randomized trials. *Advances in Clinical Child Psychology* 19:199–234.

Waldron, H. B., and N. Slesnick. 1998. Treating the family. In W. Miller and N. Heather, eds., *Treating Addictive Behaviors,* 259–270. New York: Plenum Press.

Walls, N. E., S. Freedenthal, and H. Wisneski. 2008. Suicidal ideation and attempts among sexual minority youths receiving social services. *Social Work* 53.1:21–29.

Walsh, F., and M. Scheinkman. 1989. (Fe)male: The hidden gender dimension in models of family therapy. In M. McGoldrick, C. M. Anderson, and F. Walsh, eds., *Women in Families: A Framework for Family Therapy,* 16–41. New York: Norton.

Walters, G. D. 2000. Behavioral self-control training for problem drinkers: A meta-analysis of randomized control studies. *Behavioral Therapy* 31:135–149.

Walters, S. T., L. Bennett, and J. E. Miller. 2000. Reducing alcohol use in college students: A controlled trial of two brief interventions. *Journal of Drug Education* 30: 361–372.

Watkins, K. E., A. Burman, F.-Y. Kung, and S. Paddock. 2001. A national survey of care for persons with co-occurring mental and substance use disorders. *Psychiatric Services* 52.8:1062–1068.

Weber, G. N. 2008. Using to numb the pain: Substance use and abuse among lesbian, gay, and bisexual individuals. *Journal of Mental Health Counseling* 30.1:31–48.

Weinberg, G. 1972. *Society and the Healthy Homosexual.* New York: Anchor.

Weinberg, M., S. Williams, and D. Pryor. 1994. *Dual Attraction: Understanding Bisexuality.* New York: Oxford University Press.

Weinberg, T. S. 1994. *Gay Men, Drinking, and Alcoholism*. Carbondale: Southern Illinois University Press.

Weingardt, K. R., and G. A. Marlatt. 1999. Sustaining change: Helping those who are still using. In W. R. Miller and N. Heather, eds., *Treating Addictive Behaviors*, 2nd ed., 337–351. New York: Plenum Press.

Weinstein, D. L. 1992. Application of family therapy concepts in the treatment of lesbians and gay men, *Journal of Chemical Dependency and Treatment* 5.1:141–155.

Wetchler, J. L., E. E. McCollum, T. S. Nelson, T. C. Trepper, and R. A. Lewis. 1993. Systemic couples therapy for alcohol-abusing women. In T. J. O'Farrell, ed., *Treating Alcohol Problems*, 236–260. New York: Guilford Press.

Whetten, K., S. S. Reif, S. Napravnik, M. S. Swartz, N. M. Thielman, J. J. Eron et al. 2005. Substance abuse and symptoms of mental illness among HIV-positive persons in the Southeast. *Southern Medical Journal* 98.1:9–14.

Whitbeck, L. B., X. Chen, D. R. Hoyt, K. A. Tyler, and K. D. Johnson. 2004. Mental disorder, subsistence strategies, and victimization among gay, lesbian, and bisexual homeless and runaway adolescents. *Journal of Sex Research* 41.4:329–342.

White, T., and R. Ettner. 2004. Disclosure, risks, and protective factors for children whose parents are undergoing a gender transition. *Journal of Gay and Lesbian Psychotherapy* 8.1/2:129–145.

Willenbring, M., and W. D. Spring. 1988. Evaluating alcohol use in elders. *Generations* 12.4:27–31.

Wills, G., and C. Crawford. 2000. Attitudes toward homosexuality in Shreveport-Bossier City, Louisiana. *Journal of Homosexuality* 38.97–115.

Wilsnack, S. C. 1996. Patterns and trends in women's drinking: Recent findings and some implications for prevention. In *Women and Alcohol: Prevention Throughout the Lifespan*, 19–63. National Institute on Alcohol Abuse and Alcoholism (NIAAA): Research Monograph Series. Department of Health and Human Services. Washington, DC: U.S. Government Printing Office.

Wilsnack, S. C., R. W. Wilsnack, and S. Hiller-Sturmhofel. 1994. How women drink: Epidemiology of women's drinking and problem drinking. *Alcohol Health and Research World* 18.3:173–184.

Winslow, B. T., K. I. Voorhees, and K. A. Pehl. 2007. Methamphetamine abuse. *American Family Physician* 76.8:1169–1174.

Wolfe, B. L., and R. J. Meyers. 1999. Cost-effective alcohol treatment: The community reinforcement approach. *Cognitive and Behavioral Practice* 6:105–109.

Woodman, N., and H. Lenna. 1980. *Counseling with Gay Men and Women*. New York: Jossey-Bass.

Woods, I. 1998. Bringing harm reduction to the Black community. In G. Marlatt, ed., *Harm Reduction: Pragmatic Strategies for Managing High-Risk Behaviors*, 301–326. New York: Guilford Press.

Wright, E. R., and B. L. Perry. 2006. Sexual identity distress, social support, and the health of gay, lesbian, and bisexual youth. *Journal of Homosexuality* 51.1:81–110.

Wynn, G. H., K. L. Cozza, M. J. Zapor, G. W. Wortmann, and S. C. Armstrong. 2005. Antiretrovirals, Part III: Antiretrovirals and drugs of abuse. *Psychosomatics* 46.1:79–87.

Xavier, J. M. 2000. *The Washington, DC Transgender Needs Assessment Survey: Final Report for Phase Two*. Washington, DC: Administration for HIV/AIDS, Department of Health of the District of Columbia Government.

Xavier, J. M., M. Bobbin, B. Singer, and E. Budd. 2005. A needs assessment of transgendered people of color living in Washington, DC. *International Journal of Transgenderism* 8.2/3:31–47.

Yarhouse, M. A. 2003. Working with families affected by HIV/AIDS. *American Journal of Family Therapy* 31:125–137.

Young, R. M., S. R. Friedman, P. Case, M. A. Asencio, and M. Clatts. 2000. Women injection drug users who have sex with women exhibit increased HIV infection and risk behaviors. *Journal of Drug Issues* 30:499–524.

Zacks, E., R. J. Green, and J. Marrow. 1988. Comparing lesbian and heterosexual couples on the Circumplex model: An initial investigation. *Family Process* 27:471–484.

Zelvin, E. 2004. Treating the partners of substance abusers. In S. L. A. Straussner, ed., *Clinical Work with Substance-Abusing Clients,* 264–283. New York: Guilford Press.

Zelvin, E., and D. R. Davis. 2001. Harm reduction and abstinence-based recovery: A dialogue. *Journal of Social Work Practice in the Addictions* 1.1:121–133.

Zickler, P. 2000. NIDA-funded researchers identify compound that inhibits nicotine metabolism, decreases urge to smoke. *NIDA Notes* 15.5:1–3.

Ziyadeh, N. J., L. A. Prokop, L. B. Fisher, M. Rosario, A. E. Field, C. A. Camargo et al. 2007. Sexual orientation, gender, and alcohol use in a cohort study of U.S. adolescent girls and boys. *Drug and Alcohol Dependence* 87.2/3:119–130.

Zweben, A., and S. Pearlman. 1983. Evaluating the effectiveness of conjoint treatment of alcohol-complicated marriages: Clinical and methodological issues. *Journal of Marital and Family Therapy* 9:61–72.

Index

GPSR Authorized Representative: Easy Access System Europe, Mustamäe tee 50, 10621 Tallinn, Estonia, gpsr.requests@easproject.com

www.ingramcontent.com/pod-product-compliance
Lightning Source LLC
Chambersburg PA
CBHW032118020426
42334CB00016B/999